Nonprofit Asset Management

Nonprofit Asset Management

Effective Investment Strategies and Oversight

MATTHEW R. RICE
ROBERT A. DiMEO
MATTHEW P. PORTER

WILEY

John Wiley & Sons, Inc.

Published by John Wiley & Sons, Inc., Hoboken, New Jersey.
Published simultaneously in Canada.

For general information on our other products and services or for technical support, please contact
our Customer Care Department within the United States at (800) 762-2974, outside the United States
at (317) 572-3993, or fax (317) 572-4002.

Wiley also publishes its books in a variety of electronic formats. Some content that appears in print
may not be available in electronic books. For more information about Wiley products, visit our web
site at www.wiley.com.

Library of Congress Cataloging-in-Publication Data:

Rice, Matthew, 1974-
    Nonprofit asset management : effective investment strategies and oversight / Matthew Rice,
Robert A. DiMeo, Matthew Porter.
        p. cm. – (Wiley nonprofit authority ; 3)
    Includes index.
    ISBN 978-1-118-00452-4 (cloth); ISBN 978-1-118-19919-0 (ebk);
    ISBN 978-1-118-19917-6 (ebk); ISBN 978-1-118-19914-5 (ebk)
    1. Nonprofit organizations–Finance. 2. Nonprofit organizations–Management. I. DiMeo,
Robert A. II. Porter, Matthew, 1971- III. Title.
    HG4027.65.R53 2012
    658.15'2–dc23
                                                                            2011035474

Printed in the United States of America

10 9 8 7 6 5 4 3 2 1

Contents

Preface   xi

Acknowledgments   xv

CHAPTER 1   The Three Levers and the Investment Policy   1

    The Three Levers   1
    Investment Policy Statement   5
    Statement of Purpose   6
    Statement of Objectives   6
    Liquidity Constraints   8
    Unique Constraints or Priorities   10
    Investment Strategy   11
    Duties and Responsibilities   14
    Investment Manager Evaluation   15
    Conclusion   16

CHAPTER 2   Asset Allocation   17

    Modern Portfolio Theory   17
    Capital Market Assumptions: The Building Blocks of
       Portfolio Construction   20
    Shortcomings of Modern Portfolio Theory   20
    Probabilistic Optimization Models—The Frontier Engineer^{TM} 24
    In the Long Run . . .   26
    Strategic, Tactical, and Integrated Asset Allocation
       Steering Mechanisms   27
    The Low Volatility Tailwind   29
    Tail Risk Hedging   31
    Counterparty Risk   33
    Portfolio Rebalancing   34
    Conclusion   38
    Notes   38

CHAPTER 3   Traditional Global Financial Asset Classes   39

    Global Fixed-Income Asset Classes   39
    Global Equity Asset Classes   55

Conclusion   59
Notes   59

CHAPTER 4 Traditional Asset Class Manager Selection   61

Manager Search and Selection   61
Investment Vehicles   67
Active versus Passive Management   68
When to Terminate a Manager   70
Conclusion   72

CHAPTER 5 Hedge Funds   73

The Evolution of Hedge Funds   73
Modern Hedge Fund Strategies   74
Why Invest in Hedge Funds?   78
Alpha-Beta Framework, Hedge Funds, and Fees   85
Hedge Fund Indices and Benchmarks   87
Hedge Fund Terms and Structures   88
Fund of Hedge Funds versus Direct Investment   89
Hedge Fund Investment Due Diligence   90
Hedge Fund Operational Due Diligence   92
Hedge Funds in the Post-2008 World   93
Conclusion   94
Notes   94

CHAPTER 6 Private Equity   95

Private Equity Investment Strategies   95
Why Invest in Private Equity?   98
Structure and Terms   99
Private Equity Risks   100
Direct Private Equity versus Private Equity Fund of Funds   101
Selecting Private Equity Managers   102
Benchmarks   102
Conclusion   103
Notes   103

CHAPTER 7 Real Assets   105

Commodities   106
Equity Real Estate Investment Trusts and Private Real Estate   108
Farmland   109
Energy Infrastructure Master Limited Partnerships   111
Broad Infrastructure Investing   112
Timberland   113
Gold   115
Other Investible Real Asset Categories   116

	Conclusion	117
	Note	117
CHAPTER 8	Performance Measurement and Evaluation	119
	Why Monitor Performance?	119
	Performance Calculations	119
	Benchmarks	120
	Market Index Basics	120
	Investment Style	121
	Major Market Indices	123
	Determining the Right Index	124
	Peer Group Universes	124
	Modern Portfolio Theory Performance Metrics	126
	Style Analysis	127
	Portfolio Analysis	128
	Performance Reporting	128
	Conclusion	129
CHAPTER 9	Structuring an Effective Investment Committee	131
	Procedures	131
	Committee Structure	132
	Committee Makeup	133
	When an Investment Committee Needs Outside Help	134
	Effective Use of the Consultant	135
	Conclusion	136
CHAPTER 10	Outsourced Chief Investment Officer Services	137
	Overview	137
	Why Outsource?	138
	Outsourced Services	139
	What Is Done in Conjunction with the Committee?	139
	Potential Benefits	139
	Finding a Firm	140
	Characteristics	140
	The RFP	141
	Interviewing Finalists	141
	Fees	142
	The Contract	142
	Reporting	143
	Conclusion	143
CHAPTER 11	Environmental, Social, and Corporate Governance-Focused Investing	145
	History and Evolution	145
	Negative Screening	146

Positive Screening   146
Shareholder Advocacy   146
Community Investing   147
Strategy Considerations   148
Investment Selection   149
Separate Accounts   149
Mutual Funds   149
Commingled Funds   149
Exchange-Traded Funds   150
Alternative Investments   150
Performance Impact of ESG   151
Incorporating ESG into Investment Policy   151
Conclusion   152
Notes   152

CHAPTER 12   Selecting Vendors   153

Custodians   153
Record Keepers and Administrators   156
Broker/Dealers   157
Transition Managers   158
Conclusion   160

CHAPTER 13   Hiring an Investment Consultant   161

The Investment Consultant   162
Identifying a Qualified Investment Consultant   162
Effective Use of a Consultant   168
Conclusion   168

CHAPTER 14   Behavioral Finance   169

Trying to Break Even   170
Snake Bitten   170
Biased Expectations and Overconfidence   170
Herd Mentality   171
Asset Segregation or Mental Accounting   171
Cognitive Dissonance   171
Anchors   172
Fear of Regret and Seeking Pride   172
Representativeness   172
Familiarity   173
Investor Personality Types   173
Risk-Seeking Behavior   173
Naturally Occurring Ponzi Schemes and Market Bubbles   174
Conclusion   175
Note   175

CHAPTER 15   Legal Aspects of Investing Charitable Endowment, Restricted, and
Other Donor Funds   177

Nature of Endowment or Restricted Funds   177
Endowments Created by the Board   178
Donor-Created Endowment Funds   178
Donor-Created Restricted Gifts or Funds   179
GAAP Accounting Treatment   179
General Statement about Investing Endowment   179
Context: The Historical Prudent Man Rule   180
Trusts: The Prudent Investor Act   180
Uniform Prudent Management of Institutional Funds Act   181
Private Foundation Rules   184
Conclusion   185

Final Thoughts   187

Takeaways   188
Conclusions   188

Appendix: Case Study: Developing Capital Market Assumptions   189

About the Authors   209

About the Contributing Authors   211

Index   215

Preface

"May you live in interesting times!" The ancient Chinese curse has never seemed more apropos. There are some positives for this tired old world, but no shortage of challenges!

On the one hand, scientific advances have increased life expectancies, enhanced global food production, and hold the promise of eradicating diseases that have plagued mankind for thousands of years. The fall of Communism promised to usher in an era of greater peace and stability. Increased computing power and new industrial production methods have led to a geometric increase in productivity. New forms of energy production such as wind and solar power are just beginning to have an impact.

On the other hand, there are more threats than ever before. First of all, global demographics work against us. While our technology has enabled food production to stay ahead of population growth, we may be approaching a tipping point. We can almost feed seven billion people if we could only solve the distribution problems. But how will we feed the nine billion expected before the middle of the century? What will be the impact on other resources or on the planet itself?

Secondly, there is a plethora of other problems. Worldwide religious intolerance is increasing. Fanatical terrorists welcome the chance to die if it means that they can simultaneously kill their perceived enemy (mostly innocent men, women, and children).

Disasters, natural and otherwise, somehow seem more numerous. From the devastation of Hurricane Katrina to unprecedented numbers of earthquakes, to massive oil spills, there seems to be no shortage of crises. New diseases, from AIDS to antibiotic-resistant strains of old scourges like tuberculosis, threaten to overwhelm the medical advances mentioned above.

Trade globalization is a double-edged sword. As a society we enjoy cheaper goods and services, but some workers find their jobs outsourced. Likewise, the Internet gives us instant connectivity and facilitates the flow of information around the planet but it also allows cyber-criminals to steal identities from half a world away. The 30-year war on drugs has been a monumental failure. Despite uncounted billions of dollars, and prisons filled to overflowing, a high school student in any town in the United States can buy pot by firing off a text message to one of his classmates.

If one were to count a dollar a second, working day and night with no breaks or days off, it would take 31 years to count out a billion dollars. Yet, our elected "servants" spend *thousands* of billions, seemingly with no other goal than rewarding their supporters and punishing their opponents. It's no surprise that the country has become more polarized than at any time in recent memory.

In short, there is a crying need for all of the services provided by nonprofit organizations.

Money Is Tight

Whatever the mission, there is undoubtedly more need than money. So far the twenty-first century has been a difficult financial environment. The 2000 to 2002 bear market was just a warm-up for the financial meltdown of 2007 to 2009. Fiduciaries for nonprofit funds have understandably become gun-shy. Many threw in the towel in early 2009 and abandoned equities for fixed income only to kick themselves for missing the run up of the next two years.

Persistently high unemployment is a near-term deflationary force that has politicians and central bankers running scared. No one wants a repeat of the Great Depression and its misbegotten offspring, World War II!

Unprecedented government spending (part "stimulus" and part social engineering) and our entitlement system have resulted in unsustainable budget deficits. There are only four possible solutions: default; raise taxes dramatically; severely cut discretionary spending and entitlement programs; or monetize the debt (e.g., let inflation reduce the real value of the debt). History provides no comfort, given that a current dollar is only worth four cents compared to a 1913 dollar (the year the Fed was created).

To add to the litany of woes, donating is down. Appreciated securities are in short supply. Tax and financial uncertainty may make even the wealthy clutch their purse strings a little tighter.

Topics

While we cannot solve the world's ills, we can help fiduciaries become better stewards for their funds. We will explore wide-ranging challenges for nonprofit funds of all kinds and provide the reader with practical solutions.

We will outline a systematic approach to fund oversight that includes determining the fund's *Three Levers* (inflows, outflows, and required returns) and the corresponding *Ability and Willingness to Tolerate Risk*. We will show how these important inputs are reflected in well-written *Investment Policy Statements* for nonprofit funds with varied objectives and risk constraints.

We will share our best ideas for optimizing *Asset Allocation Strategy*, which is the single most important step in the investment process. This includes a review of *Traditional Global Financial Asset Classes* and *Alternative Asset Classes* like *Hedge Funds, Real Assets,* and *Private Equity,* and the role each plays in well-diversified portfolios.

We will outline a systematic multi-step approach to improve success when *Selecting Traditional and Alternative Investment Managers*. We will also share a framework for evaluating the fund's investment managers on an ongoing basis and how to make the critical *Manager Retention and Termination Decisions*. We will also identify where *Active and Passive* management makes the most sense in a portfolio.

We will show investment committee members how they can identify and avoid traps set by our human *Behavioral Finance* quirks, and how they can save a non-profit fund millions of dollars in opportunity costs.

We will also discuss *Fiduciary and Legal Issues* for nonprofits and provide a framework for evaluating and selecting *Investment Consultants, Brokers, Vendors, Record Keepers, and Other Resources* for the fund.

How to Use This Book

One can read it cover to cover. Alternately, each chapter is modular, and can be used as a how-to guide for a specific project or task. Wherever practical, this book includes charts, graphs, and case studies designed to make explanations as straightforward as possible.

Who Should Use This Book?

The primary audience for this book is fund fiduciaries. Included in this group are *investment committee members,* trustees, *officers, board members,* and *internal staff* should find it a helpful resource. Advisors to nonprofits should also find it useful. This group includes *accountants, auditors, consultants, and attorneys* who advise the fund. Vendors to nonprofit funds may also find it useful. This group includes *money managers, brokers, custodians,* and others who provide services for a fee. Finally, legislators, teachers, students, reporters, and any other interested parties may find useful information in this book.

Acknowledgments

In addition to our many terrific contributing authors, we want to thank all of the other talented individuals at DiMeo Schneider & Associates, L.L.C., whose valuable contributions to our firm and this book are far too numerous to count. We would also like to thank Richard Gallagher, who authored Chapter 15.

We also want to thank our wonderful clients who have given us the honor of making us trusted partners. We are grateful for your trust and friendship.

CHAPTER 1

The Three Levers and the Investment Policy

The *investment policy statement* (IPS) articulates the nonprofit fund's purpose, objectives, and constraints. It also articulates the time horizon(s) and the fund's ability and willingness to assume risk. A well-designed IPS also acts as an investment committee's guide for procedures, principles, and strategies.

The Three Levers

A well-written IPS is an invaluable resource for an investment committee. However, in order to be effective, it must be written and periodically revised to accommodate the fund's *three levers*. The three levers are *inflows, outflows,* and *required investment returns.* The balance among these three components is unique to each investor. Whether the fund's purpose is to finance a perpetual spending need, a project over a finite period, act as a reserve for a "rainy day," or for any other purpose, its *three levers* will determine the appropriate objective (see Exhibit 1.1.).

The three levers exercise is arguably a nonprofit investment committee's most important task when developing investment policy. If this crucial step is skipped, or done in haste, it is just a matter of time before painful symptoms emerge. Symptoms may include investment losses greater than the institution can afford during a bear market, or insufficient long-term investment earnings to fund spending needs. One needs to understand the size, volatility, and rigidity (or flexibility) of each lever, as well as how each interacts with the others in order to make effective investment objective, risk budgeting, and asset allocation strategy decisions.

You need to start by asking the right questions. Investment committees and non-profit boards typically consist of smart people accustomed to making decisions, but they do not always focus on the right questions. Answers to the following questions should be instructive:

Inflows

- What is the expected size of annual inflows relative to portfolio assets?
- How predictable or volatile are these inflows?

EXHIBIT 1.1 The Three Levers

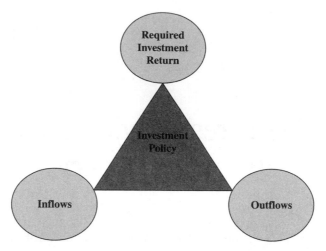

- What control, if any, does the institution have over the size of inflows?
- Do any anticipated changes to the size or rate of inflows loom on the horizon?
- What factors have driven the historical variability of inflows?

Outflows

- What is the spending policy?
- Is there a formula that drives spending?
- What is the expected size of annual outflows as a percentage of assets?
- How predictable or volatile are the outflows (or spending needs)?
- What control, if any, does the institution have over the size of outflows?
- To what extent can outflows (or spending) be reduced or delayed in a crisis without jeopardizing the sustainability of the organization's basic mission?
- What factors have driven the historical variability of outflows?

Required Return

- What are expected annual *net* cash flows as a percentage of portfolio assets?
- What minimum rate of return (above inflation) is required to sustain the fund's long-term mission?

Desired Return versus the *Willingness* and *Ability* to Assume Risk

- Can the organization meet its basic long-term *spending needs* by investing solely in a laddered U.S. Treasury or Treasury Inflation-Protected Securities (TIPS) portfolio? If not, what incremental return is required?
- At what size loss do loan covenants, agency ratings, or other balance-sheet considerations become critical to the organization's health or survival?
- What rate of return above the minimum *required* rate of return would allow the fund to finance the "the next step" toward enhancing its mission?
- Are limitations on the fund's ability to assume risk compatible with its long-term spending objectives? If not, how will long-term *spending* and *risk* budgeting conflicts be reconciled?

Why invest in stocks, hedge funds, commodities, and other risky assets if objectives can be met without them? If an investment committee determines its fund can finance objectives by investing solely in U.S. Treasuries or TIPS, it should vote to do so, call it a day, and adjourn. Most funds cannot meet their objectives that way, but quantifying the expected shortfall of a Treasury-only investment creates a baseline to establish a minimum required rate of return.

A terrific asset allocation strategy implemented by excellent investment managers is insufficient to assure success unless the portfolio's investment policy objectives and strategy compliment the fund's three levers. Many institutional investors discovered the painful mismatch between their funds' three levers and their investment policies during the severe 2007 to 2009 bear market (see Exhibit 1.2).

When the three levers exercise is skipped or given insufficient thought, the investment objective (and strategy) can end up being too aggressive. Policies set during periods of strong market performance often lead to overly aggressive portfolios. "Good times" also frequently lead to looser spending policies as boards begin to extrapolate recent performance indefinitely into the future.

During the 2007 to 2009 bear market, all investors who sought even a modicum of capital appreciation suffered losses, but those who invested more aggressively than necessary suffered *needlessly*. For example, perhaps a fund needs a 6.0 percent long-term annual return to fund its mission. If it instead was positioned to target an 8.0 percent annual return, the added risk proved to be significant. From October 2007 to February 2009, the global stock market declined about 55 percent. A well-diversified portfolio with an expected 8.0 percent long-term return declined about 40 percent peak to trough. But a well-diversified portfolio designed to earn a 6.0 percent return declined only about half as much (or 20 percent). See Chapter 2 for more information about capital market assumptions and asset allocation strategy.

EXHIBIT 1.2 Hierarchy of Importance

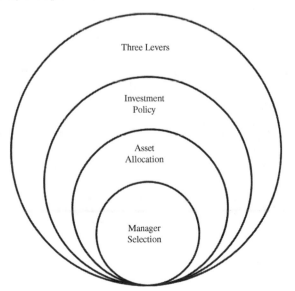

EXHIBIT 1.3 Target Long-Term Hurdle Returns versus the 2007 to 2009 Bear Market

In Exhibit 1.3, a 100 percent TIPS portfolio represents the 3.0 percent target-return mix. This laddered TIPS portfolio illustrates a theoretical risk-free portfolio over an investment horizon, assuming a 2.5 percent inflation rate. At the other end of the spectrum, the highest expected return portfolio allocates 100 percent to global stocks (with a 9.3 percent expected return). All portfolios between these two mixes are broadly diversified among bonds, stocks, and alternative investments. For reference, the portfolio targeting a 6.0 percent return allocates 58 percent to fixed income, 22 percent to global equity, and 18 percent to alternative investments; the portfolio targeting an 8 percent return allocates 26 percent to fixed income, 50 percent to global equity, and 24 percent to alternative investments. An investment committee that cannot articulate a rationale for the portfolio's heavy allocation to stocks or alternative investments is more prone to make reactive (and destructive) decisions during difficult markets.

Rational investors allocate to risk-free assets if objectives can be met by doing so. Wise investors take only as much risk as they must to meet objectives. Unfortunately, most spending ambitions require taking investment risk. For example, a 5 percent spending policy may need to generate a real return of 5 percent above the inflation rate. If the inflation assumption is 3 percent, the endowment may need to target an 8 percent (or greater) return. As previously illustrated in Exhibit 1.3, an 8 percent return target requires significant investment risk. See Chapter 2 for more about capital market assumptions.

Investment committees with high spending hurdles have few choices:

■ Slash the budget (and spending) and invest in Treasuries or TIPS.
■ Invest in an equity and/or alternative investment-heavy portfolio that seeks to meet the long-term hurdle, while assuming considerable investment risk.
■ Build a thoughtful and well-diversified portfolio that balances risk-aversion and disciplined spending targets.

EXHIBIT 1.4 $100MM Endowment with Various Spending Targets

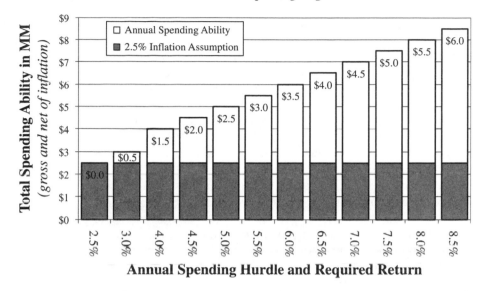

Committee members must "connect all the dots" in order to determine whether an investment strategy can achieve the fund's objectives. It is wonderful when the investment pool is large enough to avoid taking risk. However, even large sums of money can generate small amounts of spendable investment return if invested too conservatively. Exhibit 1.4 shows how funds available for spending shrink considerably with lower investment returns.

Determining the appropriate level of risk is a complex chore for investment committees. Signing up for too little risk can adversely impact the organization's mission. A hospital may have to cut beds; a school may have to cut scholarships; or a community may have to cut projects and services. The decision to avoid risk must not be made in a vacuum. The organization's mission, objectives, and priorities are at the heart of the *three levers* exercise.

Investment Policy Statement

Only after the investment committee has a handle on the three levers should it draft or revise the IPS. As previously stated, the investment policy outlines the portfolio's purpose, objectives, risk tolerance, liquidity needs, and constraints. A well-written IPS is also clear and concise in outlining procedures and principles to govern future investment decisions.

The IPS is critical to the ongoing oversight of your investment process. It memorializes your vision. It sets the parameters by which you will monitor responsibilities and track the progress of associated parties. It also outlines your procedures for fund oversight and continuity of that oversight. It's not uncommon for committee members to serve limited terms, sometimes as short as one or two years. A well-written IPS is indispensable if your fund has a constant rotation of members.

New committee members want to make their marks. Unfamiliar with the initial three levers exercise, they may question the fund's objectives or investment strategy. They may have preconceived notions about the use of certain asset classes or overall asset allocation strategy. They may even have a basic misunderstanding of investment or diversification principles. A well-written investment policy helps educate new members. It acts as a manual to provide new and existing members with a clear, concise description of the fund's objectives and strategy.

Organization is the key to drafting a policy. The IPS should provide a clear road map for committee members. Specifically, it must provide policy direction and procedural guidelines. It is important to customize the document to address the organization's specific needs, but the following are elements that should be included in an IPS.

The following are summaries of various segments of an IPS, including examples for three fictional nonprofit investors:

- The Great State University Endowment Fund
- The Community Foundation of Bedford Falls
- The General Hospital Reserves Fund III

Statement of Purpose

The purpose section of the IPS summarizes why the fund or organization exists. Avoid the temptation to be long winded. A concise summary can be more effective. A simpler statement makes it easier for the "main thing" to remain at the forefront of investment committee members' thinking.

The following are examples of purpose statements for our three nonprofit funds:

- The *Great State University Endowment Fund's* mission is to promote, encourage, and advance education and to improve degree and non-degree educational functions by establishing scholarships, professorships, fellowships, academic chairs, and other academic endeavors as determined by Great State University's board of directors.
- The *Community Foundation of Bedford Falls'* mission is to bridge community needs with timely giving. The purpose is to improve the lives of Bedford Falls' residents by awarding grants to nonprofit organizations that improve the community.
- The *General Hospital Reserves Fund III* exists as a capital reserves fund that may be used to close unanticipated short-term budget gaps or for other purposes as determined by the board of directors.

Statement of Objectives

The *statement of objectives* articulates the definition of success. "Objective" and "strategy" are often incorrectly used interchangeably in investment policies. The *objective* is an expression of goals; the *strategy* is implemented by the investment committee to pursue that objective. Objectives vary significantly among different types of nonprofit investors. Even nonprofit funds that seem similar may have vastly different objectives. Objectives span a wide spectrum, ranging from "short-term capital preservation" to "multi-generational growth." The statement of objectives should include return targets, risk constraints, and time horizons.

The statement of objectives must be reasonable and attainable and accommodate the fund's three levers. An example of an *unreasonable* objective is, "The endowment's primary goals are to generate a 7 percent real (after inflation) long-term return to increase real spending power AND to minimize short-term capital losses." When an investment committee is faced with an impossible objective like this, it has no reasonable principle to guide investment strategy. Should they target an after-inflation return of 7 percent, or should they seek to minimize short-term losses? They certainly can't do both! A 7 percent long-term after-inflation return target is already a very ambitious goal without any risk constraints. This is the type of "objective" that should be weeded out during the three levers exercise.

You must also avoid the "say nothing" objective. An example of such an objective is, "The fund seeks a reasonable rate of return with reasonable risk." An investment committee has very little basis to build an investment strategy that fits such a poorly defined objective. In this case, the term "reasonable" is never defined and investment committee members can have dramatically different interpretations of what it means. This type of objective sets the committee up for unnecessary conflicts, as well as a portfolio risk budget that can swing wildly and arbitrarily, depending on an evolving definition of "reasonable." This is another type of objective that should get weeded out during the three levers exercise.

The best-written statements of objectives are straightforward. They can be understood by an investment committee with rotating membership (and varying world views). In 1999, *irrationally exuberant* investment committee members wanted heavy allocations to Internet stocks; in early 2009, nervous Nellies wanted to buy and store gold bullion in the basement. Some committee members even oscillate between *irrational exuberance* and *nervousness* from one quarter to the next. An effective statement of objectives helps rein them in. Inevitably, all investment committees face market turmoil as well as periods of excessive optimism. During such times, the investment policy's statement of objective anchors the committee to the "main thing."

The following are well-written statements of objectives for our three nonprofit funds:

- The primary objective of the *Great State University Endowment Fund* is to preserve the purchasing power of the endowment after spending. This means that *Great State University Endowment* must achieve, on average, an annual total rate of return equal to inflation plus actual spending. This purchasing-power preservation objective emphasizes the need for a long-term perspective in formulating spending and investment policies.
- The primary objective of the *Community Foundation of Bedford Falls* is to earn 10-year annual rolling returns that preserve purchasing power of foundation

assets, assuming a 3 percent minimum annual spending rate. Therefore, the primary objective is to earn 10-year total (rolling) returns that meet or exceed a total return of 3 percent (for spending) plus the annual inflation rate. Additional gifts to the foundation may be used to supplement spending, but current policies limit spending to 5 percent annually (3 percent of assets plus 2 percent gifts) of total assets. The secondary objective is to moderate short- and intermediate-term capital losses so the 3 percent annual spending policy can be preserved (without excessive spending of principal) over rolling five-year periods, regardless of market performance.

■ The primary objective of the *General Hospital Reserves Fund III* is to preserve capital. The maximum one-in-ten-year annual expected (nominal) calendar-year loss should not exceed 5 percent (modeled on reasonable return, standard deviation, and correlation assumptions). The secondary objective is to maximize total nominal expected returns within risk constraints.

Liquidity Constraints

The three levers exercise and the statement of objectives help the investment committee to determine liquidity needs and develop liquidity constraints. However, one must consider institution-specific information before crafting liquidity constraints.

Many nonprofits found they had underestimated liquidity needs during and after the 2008 financial crisis. As stock markets collapsed, liquidity dried up in some bond market segments and hedge funds threw up gates, yet private equity capital calls still came in. Many nonprofits with heavy (illiquid) real estate, timberland, and/or private equity allocations faced a dilemma: Should they indiscriminately sell *all* available liquid assets just to meet short-term liquidity needs? Many of those liquid assets (e.g., publicly traded global stocks, high-yield bonds, etc.) were also trading at depressed levels.

2008 taught many investors painful lessons about managing liquidity needs. When investors need liquidity the most in order to either rebalance or meet spending obligations (in the context of a shrinking asset base), liquidity can be at its driest. As investors were forced to spend down liquid assets, the remaining *illiquid* assets became a larger and larger percentage of the portfolio. Some high profile endowment funds had to resort to dumping private partnerships onto the secondary market (at steep discounts) just to meet short-term liquidity needs. If there was a silver lining to the 2008 crisis, it created opportunities for investors to opportunistically allocate to distressed (and illiquid) investments. Unfortunately, many investors already had too much allocated to illiquid investments and were unable to capitalize on the opportunities.

In 2006, the Financial Accounting Standards Board (FASB) issued SFAS 157 (currently called Revised FASB ASC 820), a pronouncement that defined fair value measurement and created ground rules for financial statement footnote disclosures. The pronouncement defined fair value as the amount that would be received to sell an asset or paid to transfer a liability in an orderly transaction between market participants at the financial statement measurement date.

SFAS 157 established a three-level hierarchy that categorized valuation inputs. It also created new accounting and auditing challenges for nonprofits. The levels of fair value are defined as follows:

- *Level 1*—Unadjusted quoted prices in active markets that are accessible at the measurement date for identical, unrestricted assets or liabilities.
- *Level 2*—Quoted prices for instruments that are identical or similar in markets that are not active and model derived valuations for which all significant inputs are observable, either directly or indirectly in active markets.
- *Level 3*—Prices or valuations that require inputs that are both significant to the fair value measurement and are unobservable.

The hierarchy requires observable data when available, and investments are classified in their entirety based on the lowest level of input that is significant to fair value measurement.

The SFAS 157 framework provides one way for nonprofits to classify assets based on relative liquidity. For example, assets that can be valued with *Level 1 inputs* have price quotes in active markets. These are typically the most liquid assets. Some asset classes that are (usually) compatible with *Level 1 inputs* include the following:

- Cash/Treasury-Bills
- TIPS
- Investment-grade U.S. bonds [treasury, agency, corporate, mortgage-backed securities (MBS), asset-backed securities (ABS), etc.]
- Foreign publicly traded bonds (sovereign and corporate)
- High-yield bonds
- U.S. publicly traded stocks
- Foreign-developed publicly traded stocks
- Emerging-markets publicly traded stocks
- Publicly traded real estate investment trusts (REITs)
- Commodity futures contracts
- Publicly traded energy infrastructure master limited partnerships (MLPs)
- 1940 Act mutual funds
- Exchange-traded funds (ETFs)
- Closed-end funds

Level 2 inputs are not from directly quoted prices like *Level 1 inputs*, but are from price quotes for similar assets in active (or inactive) markets. *Level 2* assets are usually less liquid than *Level 1*. Some of the asset classes or investment strategies that are compatible with a *Level 2 input* include:

- Less liquid fixed income market segments (or securities) such as convertible bonds.
- Some very liquid hedge fund strategies
- Swaps and other OTC derivatives

Level 3 inputs are unobservable. There is little, if any, market activity for the asset at the measurement date. Level 3 assets are usually the least liquid. Some of the asset classes or investment strategies that are compatible with *Level 3* inputs include:

- Hedge funds
- Fund of hedge funds
- Private equity
- Timberland
- Private infrastructure investments

Deciding whether an asset should be classified as a Level 1, 2, or 3 is a complex task and requires analysis of each underlying investment by accountants with SFAS 157 expertise. All investors are advised to seek advice from legal and accounting experts; the above examples are for illustrative purposes only.

Some liquidity constraints are necessary to maintain the integrity of investment strategy and rebalancing policies and to ensure that spending obligations can be met. Other constraints may be needed in order for some nonprofits to meet bond covenants or ratings requirements. For example, bond covenants may require non-profits to maintain a minimum collateral allocation to *Level 1 assets*.

Each of our three nonprofit investors has different liquidity needs and constraints:

- The *Great State University Endowment Fund* will limit investments with less than annual liquidity to no more than 30 percent of total portfolio assets. Total daily liquid assets must exceed 50 percent of portfolio assets (at the time of investment).
- The *Community Foundation of Bedford Falls* will limit investments with less than annual liquidity to no more than 20 percent of total portfolio assets. Daily liquid assets must exceed 70 percent of portfolio assets at the time of investment. If market action drives daily liquid investments below 65 percent of total assets, the committee will return liquid assets to at least the 70 percent level over a reasonable period of time (so as to not dispose of illiquid assets at distressed levels).
- The *General Hospital Reserves Fund III* will limit investments with less-than-annual liquidity to a maximum of 10 percent of portfolio assets. However, a minimum of 80 percent of total assets must be compatible with Level 1 (SFAS 157) inputs. Assets consistent with Level 3 (SFAS 157) inputs must be capped at 5 percent of assets at the time of investment. If Level 3 assets rise above 8 percent, the committee will use reasonable means over a reasonable period of time so as to not dispose of illiquid assets at distressed levels to reduce Level 3 assets below 5 percent.

Unique Constraints or Priorities

Other portfolio constraints may also include anything that is unique or specific to a nonprofit institution's mission. For example, it is common for nonprofits to practice *Environmental, Social, and Corporate Governance Focused (ESG) Investing* (see Chapter 11). Another constraint example might be a cap on the fixed-income portfolio's allocation to below-investment-grade securities. ESG and any other unique constraints (or priorities) must be reflected in the broad investment policy and in any manager-specific investment guidelines. Each of our three nonprofit investors has different priorities and constraints:

- The *Great State University Endowment Fund's* emerging markets stock investment manager must refrain from purchasing securities of companies that have been identified as doing business in Sudan or with the government of Sudan when the same investment goals can be achieved through the purchase of another security.
- The *Community Foundation of Bedford Falls* will support the local community by allocating up to 3 percent of total portfolio assets to local community investments. Community investments will flow through local community banks, credit unions, community loan funds, and microenterprise development funds.
- The *General Hospital Reserves Fund III* will cap "high-yield" corporate securities to no greater than 5 percent of total assets (at the time of investment). High-yield corporate securities are fixed income securities that have long term credit ratings below Ba1 (Moody's) or BB+ (S&P and Fitch). If any *single* rating agency lists a security below investment grade, it will be considered a high yield security. Furthermore, the *General Hospital Reserves Fund III* will limit total non-U.S. denominated fixed income assets to no greater than 5 percent of the total fixed income portfolio allocation (at the time of investment). If foreign denominated or high-yield fixed income securities rise above these caps at the end of a quarterly measurement period, timely action will be taken to reduce these securities back to their constrained levels over a reasonable period of time.

Investment Strategy

The investment committee must develop an *investment strategy* to pursue the portfolio's objectives as articulated in the *statement of objectives*. The investment strategy must also accommodate all liquidity and other unique constraints outlined in the investment policy.

The investment strategy is usually reflected in a target asset allocation (or ranges among assets) to various asset classes or investment strategies. Since portfolio rebalancing is a critical component of any investment action, the investment strategy should also include rebalancing procedures (see Chapter 2).

There are typically two ways to reflect the investment and asset allocation strategy within an IPS. The first is to establish specific targets for each underlying asset class (e.g., 25 percent large cap stocks, 10 percent small caps, 14 percent hedge funds, etc.). The second method is to establish ranges for asset classes (e.g., 15 to 40 percent U.S. stocks, 5 to 20 percent hedge funds, etc.). This second method allows the investment committee to evolve the explicit target asset allocation without revising the IPS. Depending on internal processes both methods have merit.

If the investment committee plans to revisit the target asset allocation on an annual basis and draft explicit targets, the nonprofit needs a mechanism for timely revisions to the IPS. This either requires the board to delegate that authority to the investment committee, or for the board to be able to make timely responses to the investment committee's investment policy recommendations.

The *Great State University Endowment Fund's* investment strategy (shown below) is *broad enough* that it does not require revision if the asset allocation strategy changes modestly. It gives significant latitude to the investment committee to design and implement investment and rebalancing strategy. This approach puts a premium on establishing a very clear *statement of objectives*. It also requires trust and effective communication between the board and investment committee.

The Great State University Endowment Fund's investment strategy will be reviewed and updated by the investment committee on at least an annual basis to ensure it remains consistent with investment objectives. In addition to meeting investment objectives, the goal is to outperform (on a risk-adjusted basis) a custom benchmark of underlying indices that reflect its evolving asset class allocation over full market cycles. The investment committee will be charged with rebalancing the portfolio to make sure the portfolio allocation remains consistent with investment objectives. The investment committee will establish explicit target asset allocations within the following broad guidelines:

	Min	*Max*
Global Fixed Income (cash, TIPS, U.S. bonds, foreign bonds, high-yield bonds)	*10%**	*25%*
*Global Public Equity (domestic, developed foreign & emerging markets***)*	*50%*	*80%*
Real Assets (real estate, infrastructure, commodities, MLPs, timberland, etc.)	*10%*	*25%*
Absolute Return Strategies (hedge funds)	*5%*	*25%*
Private Equity (buyout, venture capital, etc.)	*3%*	*15%*

High-yield bonds must be excluded when calculating the minimum fixed-income requirement.
**Emerging markets allocation must reflect ESG constraints.*

At the opposite end of the spectrum, the *Community Foundation of Bedford Falls'* investment strategy (shown below) is very *specific* and requires revision whenever the explicit asset allocation targets are revised. Therefore, there should be a *timely* IPS revision process by the board and investment committee.

The Community Foundation of Bedford Falls investment strategy will be reviewed annually by the investment committee to ensure it remains consistent with objectives. The portfolio will be rebalanced back to its target allocation whenever any broad asset class (i.e., fixed-income, equities, or alternatives) are 3 percent above or below target allocations at the end of any evaluation period. The current investment strategy's target asset allocation is designed to achieve a

7.2 percent total (nominal) annualized return over the next 10 years with the lowest possible volatility:

Asset Classification	Target Allocation
Total Fixed Income:	*40%*
Cash	*0%*
TIPS	*10%*
U.S. Investment-Grade Bonds	*14%*
Foreign Bonds	*6%*
High yield Bonds	*10%*
Total Equity:	*32%*
U.S.	*17%*
International Developed	*10%*
Emerging Markets	*5%*
Total Alternative Assets:	*28%*
Commodity Futures	*7%*
Real Estate	*6%*
Hedge Funds Portfolio	*10%*
Energy Infrastructure MLPs	*5%*

The *General Hospital Reserves Fund III's* investment strategy (shown below) is highly *constrained* and *restrictive*. Presumably, the board is in a better position than investment committee members to understand and anticipate liquidity needs or evolving objectives. This warrants still tighter reins.

The General Hospital Reserves Fund III's investment strategy will be reviewed on a periodic basis. Any revision to the investment strategy must first be approved by the General Hospital's board of directors. The current allocation is:

Asset Class	Min	Target	Max
Cash	*50%*	*55%*	*60%*
TIPS	*1%*	*3%*	*5%*
U.S. Bonds	*17%*	*21%*	*25%*
International Bonds	*1%*	*3%*	*5%*
High-yield Bonds	*0%*	*2%*	*5%*
U.S. Equity	*2%*	*4%*	*6%*
REITs	*0%*	*1%*	*3%*
International Equity	*1%*	*2%*	*4%*
Emerging Markets	*0%*	*1%*	*3%*
Commodity Futures	*0%*	*1%*	*3%*
Hedge Funds Portfolio	*0%*	*5%*	*7%*
Energy Infrastructure MLPs	*0%*	*2%*	*4%*

Our three fictional nonprofit investors have very different investment strategies. The investment strategies require three different levels of board and investment committee interaction. Take into account the structure of the board and investment committee when drafting the investment strategy section in your investment policy. Make sure the procedures for revising the IPS are workable.

Duties and Responsibilities

The IPS should include a summary of duties and responsibilities of all parties involved in overseeing fund assets. There can be some natural overlap among parties. In particular, board and investment committee duties and responsibilities should be clearly delineated. Nonprofit investors should customize the list based on their structures, but the following is an example of how duties might be divided:

Board of Directors/Trustees

- Select qualified members to serve on the investment committee.
- Review investment committee's proposed changes to investment policy statement.
- Ratify investment committee's proposed changes to the IPS before any changes are implemented.
- Periodically request a performance summary from the investment committee.
- Avoid prohibited transactions and conflicts of interest.

Investment Committee

- Oversee the management of assets.
- Act solely in the best interest of the fund and its mission.
- Determine investment objectives, develop investment (and asset allocation) strategies, and create performance guidelines.
- Set and revise the investment policies and receive board approval before IPS implementation.
- Select investment consultants, investment managers, custodians, and any other vendors required to administer and manage the fund.
- Periodically review all fund-related expenses to ensure they are competitive and appropriate. Take action if they are not.
- Review and evaluate investment results and make changes as needed.
- Provide periodic performance reports to the board.
- Avoid prohibited transactions and conflicts of interest.

Investment Consultant

- Assist in the development and periodic review of the investment policy.
- Proactively recommend changes to enhance the effectiveness of the investment policy, investment strategy, or asset allocation.
- Make proactive investment manager hire and fire recommendations.
- Monitor aggregate and manager-level performance to ensure compliance with stated objectives.

- Provide the investment committee with quarterly performance and attribution updates.
- On a timely basis, notify the investment committee if there are pertinent developments with any of the fund's investment managers.

Investment Managers

- Manage assets in accordance with the guidelines and objectives outlined in prospectuses (mutual funds), investment agreements (commingled funds, private partnerships, etc.), or manager-specific investment policies (separate accounts).
- Exercise investment discretion to buy, manage, and sell assets held in the portfolios.
- Promptly vote proxies and related actions in a manner consistent with the long-term interest of investors.
- Communicate all organizational changes, including but not limited to ownership, organizational structure, financial condition, and professional staff.
- Seek "best price and execution" for all transactions. Both explicit and implicit transactions costs should be considered.
- Use the same care, skill, prudence, and due diligence under the circumstances then prevailing that experienced investment professionals acting in a like capacity and fully familiar with such matters would use in like activities for like portfolios with like aims in accordance and compliance with Uniform Prudent Management of Institutional Funds Act (UPMIFA) and all applicable laws, rules, and regulations.

Custodian(s)

- Safeguard portfolio assets.
- Accurately value portfolio holdings.
- Collect all income and dividends owed to the Portfolio.
- Settle all transactions (buy-sell orders) initiated by separate account investment managers.
- Provide monthly reports that detail transactions, cash flows, securities values, and changes in the value of each security and the overall portfolio since the previous report.
- Provide all requested portfolio information to investment consultant and investment committee in a timely manner.

Investment Manager Evaluation

Investment manager benchmarks guide the committee's review. We recommend a multidimensional approach that compares managers to *appropriate market indices*, style-specific *peer groups*, and *risk-adjusted* performance benchmarks over multiple time periods. In Chapter 8, we discuss performance benchmarks, performance evaluation, and instituting an effective oversight process.

In Chapter 4, we discuss the process for hiring and terminating investment managers. The procedures to select and terminate managers should be outlined in the

investment policy. As we discuss in Chapter 4, virtually all quality investment managers will experience stretches of underperformance. Similarly, investment managers
who deviate from their processes and investment styles may undergo periods of outperformance, but that should not make them immune from termination. Therefore,
be careful to use language that doesn't *arbitrarily* force the committee's hand, and
allows it to use its collective talent and insight when making manager hiring and
termination decisions. (Firing a good manager at his or her performance nadir is a
classic rookie mistake.)

Conclusion

The IPS states the fund's objectives and outlines processes. Once finalized and approved, it serves as the blueprint for governing the investment program, so it requires careful thought and must be "executable." Generic template language such as
what was included in this chapter may be a helpful place to start, but the most effective investment policies are customized to fit the fund's specific three levers, objectives, and constraints. Rarely are any two nonprofit funds identical. Your investment
committee will face questions and even criticism from time to time. An effective IPS is
the anchor to windward during turbulent times.

CHAPTER 2

Asset Allocation

As discussed in Chapter 1, the *three levers* exercise arms nonprofit investment committees with a blueprint to develop investment objectives, the investment policy, and ultimately the asset allocation strategy. Assuming that one properly defines investment objectives, the asset allocation strategy will be the key to success or failure.

Asset allocation, or the diversification of a portfolio among asset classes, is the key determinant of both risk and return. In 1991, Brinson, Singer, and Beebower evaluated quarterly returns for 82 pension funds between 1977 and 1987 to measure the R-squared (or coefficient of determination) between each plan's investment policy benchmarks and each plan's actual quarterly returns.[1] This average R-squared was 91.5 percent, meaning that 91.5 percent of the typical pension fund's return variance could be explained by its asset allocation policy. The remaining 8.5 percent was explained by other factors including market timing and security selection (see Exhibit 2.1).

Since this 1991 study was published, several papers have quibbled over the relevance of the R-squared metric since a high R-squared between two portfolios doesn't necessarily equate to similar return levels. For example, it's possible for two portfolios to have a high R-squared value, with one returning 12 percent and the other 3 percent over a 10-year period. Nonetheless, virtually all robust academic studies agreed that asset allocation is of prime importance.

Modern Portfolio Theory

Dr. Harry Markowitz's seminal paper, "Portfolio Selection: The Efficient Diversification of Investments," was published by *The Journal of Finance* in 1952. Markowitz postulated an efficient frontier, a curve that plots the highest expected-returning portfolio at each risk level. His Nobel Prize-winning research later formed the foundation of Modern Portfolio Theory (MPT). MPT has since gained near-universal adoption by the investment industry. MPT provided a mathematical basis for understanding the interaction of systematic risk and reward and has profoundly shaped portfolio management. Because asset class returns were approximately normally distributed, Markowitz was able to apply statistical techniques to *optimize* portfolios, minimizing volatility at every possible level of return. Today, virtually all

EXHIBIT 2.1 Components Explaining Investment Returns

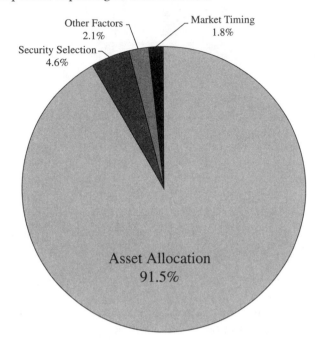

Other Factors
2.1%

Market Timing
1.8%

Security Selection
4.6%

Asset Allocation
91.5%

Fiduciaries rely on MPT, at least to some extent, when overseeing the investment of institutional assets.

MPT's efficient frontier optimization process requires three inputs: The *expected return* for each asset class; the *expected standard deviation (or volatility)* of the returns of each asset class; and the *expected correlation* among all asset class returns. The following is a description of these assumptions:

- Annual Return Forecast: The forecast represents the expected return for an asset class over a specified time horizon.
- Annual Standard Deviation Forecast: The standard deviation expresses the expected (normally distributed) variability of annual returns about the mean over a specified time horizon. The higher the standard deviation, the more uncertain is the outcome.
- Forecasted Correlations among All Asset Classes: The correlation coefficient quantifies the degree to which two assets are expected to move together. The correlation coefficient can range from -1 (perfect negative correlation) to +1 (perfect positive correlation). A correlation of zero means there is no relationship.

The Markowitz model relies on an optimization algorithm using the input assumptions to create the *efficient frontier*. The efficient frontier output provides investors with unambiguous direction. For example, if one's portfolio consisted of Mix A in Exhibit 2.2, he would no doubt prefer either Mix B (equal risk but higher

EXHIBIT 2.2 Efficient Frontier

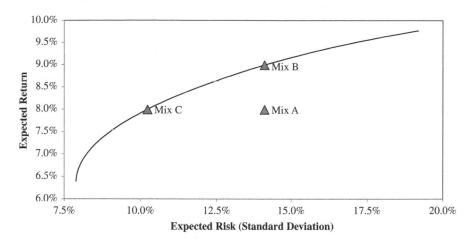

expected returns) or Mix C (equal expected return but lower risk); Mixes B and C are on the efficient frontier; Mix A is inefficient because it is not on the efficient frontier.

Adoption of MPT has benefited the investment processes over the past 60 years. Its main tenet is that investments should not be judged solely on their individual risk-reward profile (in a vacuum), but rather by how the investment impacts the risk and return of the *entire* portfolio. MPT showed that adding risky investments with low correlation can actually reduce the volatility of the entire portfolio. Exhibit 2.3 demonstrates that introducing a 13 percent allocation to a riskier asset class (stocks) to a U.S. government bond portfolio actually reduced the volatility of the entire portfolio between January 1926 and September 2010. Returns also increased. The driver of the risk reduction was the relatively low correlation coefficient (i.e., 0.12) between stocks and bonds. Stocks often "zigged" when bonds "zagged." Although stocks had significantly higher volatility than bonds, the offsetting fluctuations *decreased* overall

EXHIBIT 2.3 S&P 500 & U.S. Government Bond Efficient Frontier

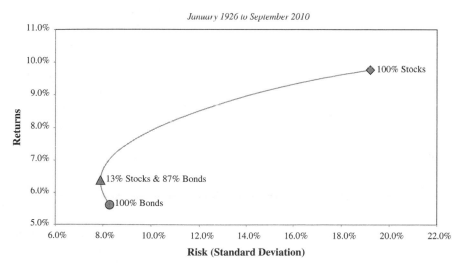

portfolio volatility. The expected return of a two-asset portfolio is simply the weighted average expected (arithmetic) return of the two assets. However, when two assets are less than perfectly correlated, the standard deviation of the portfolio is less than the weighted average standard deviations of the asset classes. The more low correlating assets added to a portfolio, the greater this diversification effect and the farther up (return) and to the left (risk) the efficient frontier moves. This diversification benefit is one of the few quantifiable free lunches the financial markets afford.

Capital Market Assumptions: The Building Blocks of Portfolio Construction

The problem with capital market assumptions is that they are forecasts, and as Yogi Berra once said, "Forecasting is tough, especially if it involves the future." These return, risk, and correlation forecasts should be forward-looking and reflect current times, including interest rates, inflation rates, economic environment, and observable estimated risk premiums. It is not enough to take historical averages for these three inputs.

The case study in this book's appendix illustrates the approach used by DiMeo Schneider & Associates, LLC to create its 10-year capital market forecast assumptions (from 2011 to 2020). (Every year, these capital market assumptions are updated to reflect changes in interest rates, inflation rates, the economic environment, and observable risk premiums.) Skewness and kurtosis forecasts, or the non-normal components of return distributions, are not required for traditional MPT, but their use and application will be discussed later in the chapter.

Shortcomings of Modern Portfolio Theory

While MPT was a great step up from the old "seat of the pants"/"prudent man" framework, it also has some significant shortcomings. For example, MPT has several implicit assumptions:

- *Normally distributed variability*—Risk can be explained by normal (bell-shaped) distributions.
- *Markets follow a random walk pattern*—There is no serial correlation; today's return has no bearing on tomorrow's return.
- *Diversification can be properly quantified by correlation*—Correlation is a mathematical measure of diversification that is based on normal (bell-shaped) distribution assumptions, and is assumed to be relatively static regardless of the environment.

The problem is that all three assumptions are false. Empirical observation shows that capital market returns are prone to extreme events (*fat left tails*), which are inadequately explained by MPT's normal bell-shaped distribution requirements. For example, the high-yield bond market was a particularly egregious fat left tail offender over the 11.25-year period between January 1998 and March 2009 as shown in Exhibit 2.4. High-yield bonds bored investors with steady month-to-month returns until the thunderstorm arrived in late 2008. When it rained, it poured! The October

EXHIBIT 2.4 Fat Tails

Fat Left Tails: January 1998 to March 2009 monthly returns

Metric	TIPS	U.S. Bonds	Int'l Bonds	HY Bonds	U.S. Stocks	REITs	Foreign Developed Equity	Em. Mkts. Equity	Commodity Futures	Fund of Hedge Funds	MLPs
Mean monthly return	0.6%	0.5%	0.5%	0.3%	0.1%	0.3%	0.2%	0.8%	0.7%	0.4%	1.0%
Monthly standard deviation	1.8%	1.1%	1.5%	2.8%	4.7%	6.4%	5.0%	7.6%	5.9%	1.9%	4.8%
100-year monthly loss (normal)	−5.1%	−2.9%	−4.2%	−8.4%	−14.8%	−19.8%	−15.4%	−23.0%	−17.8%	−5.6%	−14.0%
Skewness	−0.9	−0.3	0.3	−2.0	−0.7	−1.9	−1.0	−1.0	−1.1	−0.8	−0.6
Kurtosis*	5.4	1.3	0.1	10.2	1.0	7.0	1.8	1.9	4.6	4.1	2.4
Worst 7 out of 135 months (or ~ worst 5% of returns)											
1st worst month	−8.5%	−3.4%	−2.9%	−16.3%	−16.8%	−32.7%	−20.2%	−28.9%	−29.9%	−7.5%	−17.2%
2nd worst month	−4.8%	−2.6%	−2.7%	−8.4%	−14.5%	−24.7%	−14.4%	−27.4%	−15.5%	−6.5%	−17.1%
3rd worst month	−4.6%	−2.4%	−2.3%	−8.3%	−10.9%	−21.7%	−12.4%	−17.5%	−12.6%	−6.2%	−9.1%
4th worst month	−3.8%	−1.8%	−2.0%	−7.1%	−10.6%	−18.2%	−10.7%	−15.5%	−9.0%	−3.4%	−8.3%
Years between extreme monthly losses based on normal distribution assumptions											
1st worst month	310,893	428	8	71,649,687	464	633,762	4,265	1,891	918,716	4,148	1,162
2nd worst month	57	37	5	97	79	1,742	53	820	29	564	1,091
3rd worst month	35	19	3	88	8	285	15	10	7	299	5
4th worst month	11	4	2	22	7	42	6	5	2	3	3

*Excess Kurtosis

2008 high-yield bond market loss of 16.3 percent was 6.0 standard deviations from the mean. Such an extreme monthly loss should only occur every 72 million years based on normal distribution assumptions. By comparison, the S&P 500 Index's 16.8 percent loss in October 2008 was a mere 1-in-464-year event. While not represented in the 11.25-year sample period shown in Exhibit 2.4, the S&P 500's 21.8 percent monthly loss in October 1987 would have been a 1-in-33,958-year event.

In fact, eight of the eleven asset classes shown in Exhibit 2.4 had 1-in-1,000-plus-year monthly loss events between January 1998 and March 2009 based on MPT's normal bell-shaped distribution assumptions. Clearly, standard deviation and the normal distribution framework is, at best, an incomplete measure of risk.

With the exception of foreign bonds, every asset class represented in Exhibit 2.5 had at least a modest negative *skew*, or a bias toward loss rather than a gain, during the sample period. Exhibit 2.5 illustrates how asset classes performed relative to normal bell-shaped distributions between January 1998 and March 2009. High-yield bonds and real estate investment trusts (REITs) had the fattest left tails versus normal distribution assumptions, or the worst combination of extreme events in the left tail. MPT treats all standard deviations equally, and it ignores the fat tails that cannot be explained by the normal distribution framework.

Contrary to MPT's random walk requirement, capital markets exhibit serial correlation. Serial correlation means that the return of an asset in one period is correlated to the return in a prior period. Exhibit 2.6 illustrates one of the most extreme examples, serial correlation in high-yield bond returns. October 2008's 16.25 percent loss (a 1-in-72 million-year event) is sandwiched between September 2008 (−8.3 percent) and November 2008 (−8.4 percent). Those two months were each approximately 1-in-100-year events based on normal distribution assumptions. Serial correlation in a time series has the effect of dramatically understating an asset's true annual period (or longer-term period) variability of returns. This MPT shortcoming must be fixed by the practitioner.

EXHIBIT 2.5 Fat Left Tails: All Asset Classes

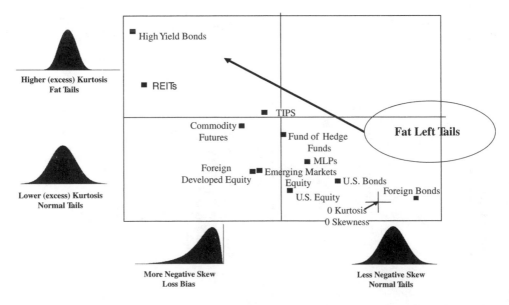

EXHIBIT 2.6 High-Yield Bond Serial Correlation

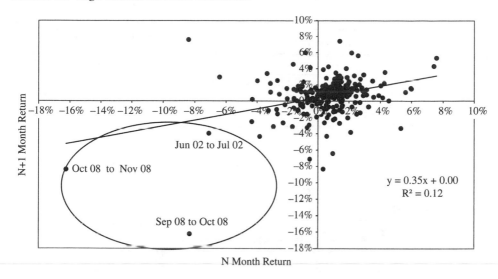

Contrary to MPT assumptions, capital markets are also subject to unstable correlations. For example, Exhibit 2.7 illustrates the 39¼-year relationship between the S&P 500 Index (U.S. stocks) and the MSCI EAFE Index (foreign stocks) between January 1970 and March 2009. The *beta* (linear slope coefficient) of foreign stocks relative to U.S. stocks was 0.65. Therefore, MPT predicts that a 10 percent (monthly) return for U.S. stocks leads to an expected 6.5 percent return for foreign stocks, and a −10 percent return for U.S. stocks leads to an expected −6.5 percent return for foreign stocks. Unfortunately, the facts contradict the theory. Diversification benefits

EXHIBIT 2.7 Nonlinear Beta: S&P 500 vs. MSCI EAFE

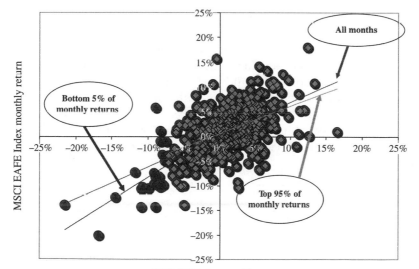

EXHIBIT 2.8 Correlations Before and After 2008

Correlations from January 1988 to October 2007

	U.S. Bonds	HY Bond	Large Cap U.S.	REITs	Int'l Equity	Em. Mkts. Equity	Commodity Futures	Hedge Fund
U.S. Bonds	1.00	0.28	0.18	0.13	0.06	−0.05	0.20	0.14
HY Bond		1.00	0.49	0.41	0.36	0.42	0.01	0.32
Large Cap U.S.			1.00	0.41	0.62	0.58	−0.02	0.43
REITs				1.00	0.28	0.34	−0.02	0.19
Int'l Equity					1.00	0.58	0.05	0.31
Em. Mkts. Equity						1.00	0.11	0.48
Commodity Futures							1.00	0.18
Hedge Fund								1.00

Correlations from November 2007 to February 2009

	U.S. Bonds	HY Bond	Large Cap U.S.	REITs	Int'l Equity	Em. Mkts. Equity	Commodity Futures	Hedge Fund
U.S. Bonds	1.00	0.37	0.38	0.34	0.52	0.40	0.42	0.12
HY Bond		1.00	0.73	0.68	0.76	0.80	0.61	0.71
Large Cap U.S.			1.00	0.83	0.91	0.79	0.47	0.53
REITs				1.00	0.72	0.60	0.39	0.20
Int'l Equity					1.00	0.94	0.61	0.66
Em. Mkts. Equity						1.00	0.66	0.80
Commodity Futures							1.00	0.72
Hedge Fund								1.00

often evaporated when needed the most. For example, during the worst 5 percent of monthly returns (worst 23 out of 471 months), the beta of foreign stocks relative to U.S. stocks was 0.93. A 0.93 beta means that a −10 percent monthly return for U.S. stocks leads to an expected −9.3 percent monthly return for foreign stocks. So, correlations and betas tended to be much lower in the "good times" and much higher in the "bad times."

Exhibit 2.8 compares correlation coefficients of asset classes between January 1988 and October 2007 and between November 2007 and February 2009. November 2007 to February 2009 represents a16-month stretch during which the S&P 500 Index declined 51 percent from peak-to-trough. The correlation coefficients between large cap U.S. stocks and other asset classes are highlighted. As Exhibit 2.8 shows, correlation coefficients rose for virtually all risky assets during the market decline. A jump in correlation, simultaneous with a rise in volatility, leads to rising betas between asset classes.

Asset class correlations and volatilities tend to be relatively low during good times when diversification benefits are less critical. Unfortunately, MPT's cruel joke is that asset class volatilities and correlations have often risen in bad times when diversification benefits are needed the most. While this dynamic was clearly illustrated during the 2008 financial crisis, it was also very evident during prior periods of stress, including the 1998 Long-Term Capital Management crisis and stock market crash of 1987, among others. Again, an asset allocator must account for this dynamic.

Probabilistic Optimization Models—The Frontier Engineer™

So how does one fix MPT's asset allocation problems? For the better part of the past decade, we have advocated breaking free of the traditional efficient frontier framework. DiMeo Schneider and Associates, LLC has developed the proprietary *Frontier Engineer*™. Rather than "betting the farm" on mean returns, volatilities, and correlations, the Frontier Engineer™ relegates "mean expected outcomes" to their (proper) role as an academic exercise. Our model elevates the importance (frequency and magnitude) of "tail outcomes" around median expectations.

The Frontier Engineer™ replaces the academic MPT concept of "mean expectations" with "*median* expectations" for returns, standard deviations, and correlations (among assets), then simulates thousands of possible outcomes for each asset class, factoring in the dynamic relationships among return, volatility, and (non-linear) correlations. It simulates *Fat Tails, Serial Correlations,* and *Unstable Correlations* and accounts for them in the portfolio optimization process.

The Frontier Engineer™ algorithm accounts for diversification benefits among risky assets in "typical" times, but balances this diversification euphoria with the stark reality that low correlations among risky asset classes can be fleeting at the extremes. The correlation coefficients of some low risk/low return assets (i.e., T-bills, Treasury Inflation-Protected Securities [TIPS], nominal U.S. Treasuries, etc.) are more persistent and given greater relative assumed stability than correlation coefficients between risky assets (i.e., U.S. stocks and foreign stocks). Fleeting low betas lead Frontier Engineer™ portfolios, along the entire risk spectrum, to typically have a more barbell (vs. bullet) structure compared to MPT optimized portfolios, which assume stable correlations among moderate and high-risk/return assets across all financial or economic environments. Exhibit 2.9 compares the barbell and bullet structures.

EXHIBIT 2.9 Barbell versus Bullet Investment Structure

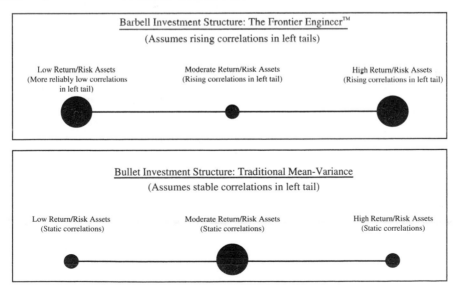

In the Long Run . . .

Another problem with the MPT framework is that it requires the practitioner to make precise but highly dubious forecasts over finite time horizons. For example, "stocks outperform bonds over the long run," right? So what defines "the long run?" Is the long run 10, 20, or 30-plus years? Even if the definition is 30 years, the old adage has not always held. For example, long-term U.S. government bonds had a higher total return than the S&P 500 Index (i.e., 10.56 percent versus 10.46 percent annualized returns) during the 30-year period between September 1, 1980, and August 30, 2010. Not only are stocks not pre-ordained to outperform over periods often classified as the "long run," but, in fact, they sometimes have not! For example, during the 898 rolling 10-year periods between January 1926 and September 2010, bonds outperformed stocks during 15.1 percent of them. Bonds also outperformed stocks during 4.6 percent of all 20-year periods (see Exhibit 2.10).

Probabilistic asset allocation models, including the Frontier Engineer™, capture the "horse race" dynamic among asset classes. While one asset class may be a 10-to-1 favorite to outperform for the next 10 years, it is not assured. While a nonprofit fund may have an infinite investment time horizon, the members of your investment committee probably don't have infinite patience to delay spending waiting for mean-reversion. Therefore, your investment horizon should not be defined as "perpetuity," but rather should be the length of time that the committee will stick with a strategy that does not appear to be working.

The Frontier Engineer™ and other probabilistic optimization models are evolutionary improvements to the Markowitz portfolio optimization framework. Just as 10 tosses of a coin won't always yield five heads and five tails, probabilistic models account for estimation error over finite periods of time. For example, it accounts for the fact that your capital market forecasts (i.e., expected return, expected risk, and correlation) have approximately a 50-50 chance of being too high or too low. So while your median expectation may be for stocks to beat bonds, or emerging markets stocks to beat developed market stocks, the probabilistic framework doesn't "bet the ranch" on it.

EXHIBIT 2.10 Stocks versus Bonds: 1926 to September 2010

	Rolling Periods Between January 1926 and September 2010							
Period Length (in years)	1 Year	3 Years	5 Years	10 Years	15 Years	20 Years	25 Years	30 Years[1]
Period Length (in months)	12	36	60	120	180	240	300	360
Total number of periods	1,006	982	961	898	838	778	718	658
Periods where bonds beat stocks	375	319	276	136	84	36	11	1
% of periods where bonds beat stocks	37.3%	32.5%	28.7%	15.1%	10.0%	4.6%	1.5%	0.2%

[1]September 1980 to August 2010

Probabilistic optimization models run *Monte Carlo* simulations to generate many possible outcomes. These multiple outcomes are generated by simulating many "what if" scenarios based on the annual expected return and standard deviation of asset classes. That is, large-cap stocks may return positive 20 percent in one period, then negative 5 percent and another and so on. It is unlikely that any single simulation will precisely match an asset class forecast, but the important thing is that the median of all the simulations does match. These multiple possible outcomes are then optimized and combined to produce an "all weather" efficient frontier.

Unlike many probabilistic models, The Frontier Engineer™ also accounts for non-normal return distributions (i.e., skewness and kurtosis). Many asset classes have a demonstrable historical track record of losing far more in down markets than their standard deviations suggest they should. For example, as previously discussed, high-yield bonds and REITs are among the worst left tail offenders because they have often lost significantly more than expected. While asset classes that are prone to fat tails shouldn't necessarily be left out of a portfolio, the model should size them appropriately to accommodate their non-normality.

The traditional mean-variance efficient frontier model requires three input assumptions: expected risk, expected return, and expected correlation among asset classes. Probabilistic models add a fourth element, an uncertainty adjustment. The ability of probabilistic models to accommodate non-normal returns and uncertainty creates a much more robust portfolio optimization framework.

Strategic, Tactical, and Integrated Asset Allocation Steering Mechanisms

The asset allocation optimization process creates a roadmap for getting to a desired destination. However, there also needs to be a mechanism to steer the vehicle and correct course. Nonprofit investment committees can use several different types of steering mechanisms at the aggregate portfolio level. The two most common steering mechanisms are *strategic* and *tactical* asset allocation strategies, and both of these strategies can take on several different nuanced forms. However, the following are generalized definitions.

Strategic Allocation

The *strategic asset allocation* strategy sets static asset allocation targets based on very long-term capital market forecasts, and then periodically rebalances the portfolio back to those targets as capital market fluctuations move the portfolio off the original targets. Strategic allocation is often described as a "buy-and-hold" strategy. The strategic asset allocation targets may evolve over time, but that evolution is driven by changes in the investor's objectives or constraints rather than views about the relative attractiveness of underlying asset classes within the portfolio.

Tactical Allocation

With a *tactical asset allocation* strategy, asset allocation targets are also usually established, but broad flexible ranges are applied around those targets. For example, a 60 percent target to stocks might be established, but the investment committee retains the flexibility to raise the equity allocation to 65 percent or lower it to 55 percent depending on a near-term outlook. Tactical allocation is a form of *market timing* since the investment committee retains the flexibility to move equities to the higher and lower ends of a range. In other words, they opportunistically ratchet portfolio risk up or down.

In our experience, the traditional *tactical* model creates a plethora of practical problems. Most nonprofit investment committees, especially those with more than a handful of members, find such a framework untenable. First of all, trying to get committee buy-in for a tactical allocation move requires negotiation. The process eats up valuable time that could be better spent on more productive endeavors. It can end up being a time-sucking activity trap with relatively little potential for improving long-term risk-adjusted performance.

Secondly, tactical allocation involves opportunistically changing the risk budget to move up or down the efficient frontier based on a (usually dubious) market timing call. Even seasoned investment professionals have great difficulty predicting market moves. The odds that part-time committee members will guess correctly are slim to none. A more productive way to improve the risk-reward tradeoff might be to vet additional asset classes that more efficiently spend a "static" risk budget.

Tactically moving the target equity allocation up or down by 5 or 10 percent may seem potentially productive, but the fact is most investment committees are not well-equipped to handle such a framework. There are practical impediments: large investment committees, turnover among committee members, and the time constraints of quarterly review meetings. Even if such modest allocation moves can be done well, they will likely have only a limited impact on the overall portfolio performance compared to other activities.

In order for tactical allocation to have any chance of success, the reason for the tactical move should be proactive rather than reactive, and the time frame of the tactical move must be established at the outset. (Of course, the actual thesis for the tactical call also needs to prove correct—no small task). The success or failure of the tactical move must be pre-defined, as well as the timeframe for unwinding the tactical move. In reality, tactical moves are rarely proactive and pre-defined parameters are either rarely made or rarely followed. Usually committees decide to get out of markets after they've already gone down or to increase allocations to assets that have already gone up . . . hardly a recipe for success.

The extreme form of *strategic* asset allocation is equally problematic. Simply establishing a portfolio target (for example, 60 percent to equity and 40 percent to fixed) based on an expectation for asset class returns and risk from now until eternity, without ever revisiting the underlying allocation, is naïve. Such a strategic framework often leads to excessive time and energy spent nitpicking details, while too little time and energy is spent on more major objectives.

Integrated Allocation

If traditional *strategic* and *tactical* asset allocation frameworks are both fatally flawed, what is left? Our preferred *integrated* asset allocation framework incorporates elements of both strategies, but seeks to avoid the pitfalls of each. Integrated asset allocation allows one to update capital market expectations while considering the overall risk budget when establishing or updating the asset mix.

A portfolio's risk budget should be relatively static because it is determined by the *three levers* exercise discussed in Chapter 1. If the portfolio's overall risk budget is not aligned with objectives and constraints, it is only a matter of time before the allocation becomes untenable.

However, simply setting and forgetting a *strategic* allocation makes little sense in a dynamic world. From an allocation perspective, there are unlimited ways to spend a risk budget. For example, a heavier allocation to a more volatile asset class like emerging market equities may require a heavier allocation to a lower volatility (and correlation) asset class like TIPS to offset the added risk within the aggregate risk budget. There is a broad array of asset classes and strategies in the tool box, and the *integrated* framework allows you to use it.

In an *integrated* asset allocation approach, view asset classes within a uniform window of time. A 10-year window provides ample time for the fundamental valuation of asset classes to mean-revert, blocking out the excessive noise of shorter-term volatility. On at least an annual basis, re-optimize the portfolio, while maintaining risk budget constraints. Every year that passes, one year falls off the 10-year outlook and another year is added at the back end. In some years, the *integrated* asset allocation process may lead to modest changes; changes may be more significant other years.

For example, the 10-year return outlook for REITs in 2007 appeared modest given extreme valuation levels. The run-up in REIT valuations between 2005 and 2007 led to lower expected return forecasts for the 2007 to 2016 period. The reduction in the 10-year return expectation for REITs, coupled with static standard deviation estimates, led to significant reductions for REITs along the entire frontier of portfolios. Competing asset classes including TIPS, energy infrastructure MLPs, emerging market stocks, and others picked up the slack. However, the overall risk budget remained constant at the aggregate portfolio level.

Similarly, the highly distressed valuation levels of high yield bonds at the beginning of 2009 necessitated a significant increase in expected 10-year returns for the 2009 to 2018 forecast period, and ultimately greater allocations all along the frontier. Other competing asset classes were reduced to free capacity for high yield, but again the risk budget at the aggregate portfolio level stayed constant.

The importance of following a practical, systematic, and disciplined asset allocation process cannot be overstated; integrated asset allocation meets this test. Once per year, the investment committee does a deep dive with the assistance of their advisors to determine appropriate changes in allocation using the static risk budget. Unless the risk budget warrants change through a *three levers* exercise, a new optimal allocation mix with the same risk budget is executed.

The Low Volatility Tailwind

Diversification is obviously meant to reduce risk, but, counter intuitively, lowering a portfolio's expected volatility can also *increase* a portfolio's expected long-term return. Reducing a portfolio's volatility by adding a low-correlating investment can increase a portfolio's expected long-term return . . . even if this new low-correlating investment does not have a higher return than the investment it replaced.

To understand the *Low Volatility Tailwind* one needs to differentiate between *arithmetic* and *geometric* investment returns. A simple example is a $100 portfolio that loses 50 percent in one year, and then gains 50 percent in the next year. The average *arithmetic* return is 0 percent, calculated simply by averaging −50 percent and +50 percent. However, losing 50 percent in year 1 takes the $100 portfolio down to $50, and gaining 50 percent in year 2 brings it up from $50 to $75. So, the $100 turned into $75 over the two-year period. So while the average arithmetic return was 0 percent, the portfolio lost $25 (or −13.4 percent compounded per year). The annual *geometric* return is −13.4 percent.

The *arithmetic* and *geometric* returns are only equal when a portfolio has the same return every year (or zero volatility). Otherwise, the geometric return for any time period is less than the arithmetic return. The higher the volatility, the greater the difference between a portfolio's *arithmetic* and *geometric* annual returns. Simply put, investment losses drain a portfolio's long-term return more than investment gains of the same percentage boost it.

The *geometric* return of a portfolio can be estimated by subtracting the portfolio's standard deviation squared, divided by two from the *arithmetic* return. For example, if U.S. stocks are expected to generate a 10 percent annual arithmetic return with a 17 percent annual standard deviation, the annual geometric return is expected to be 8.6 percent (10 percent - $0.17^2/2$). Therefore, any diversifying action that reduces a portfolio's volatility, but maintains the same expected arithmetic return, will increase a portfolio's geometric returns. We spend geometric not arithmetic dollars!

Exhibit 2.11 examines the relationship among arithmetic returns, geometric returns, and volatility (or standard deviation). Exhibit 2.11 makes the assumption that a portfolio has a 10 percent arithmetic return. It also illustrates the relationship

EXHIBIT 2.11 Arithmetic versus Geometric Returns

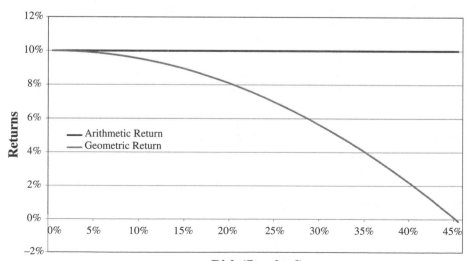

Risk (Standard)

EXHIBIT 2.12 The Low Volatility Tailwind

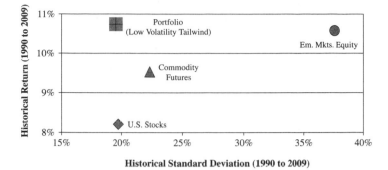

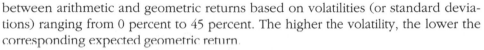

between arithmetic and geometric returns based on volatilities (or standard deviations) ranging from 0 percent to 45 percent. The higher the volatility, the lower the corresponding expected geometric return.

Exhibit 2.12 compares 20-year return-and-risk statistics (1990 to 2009) of large-cap U.S. stocks, commodity futures, and emerging-markets stocks. The diversified Portfolio (Low Volatility Tailwind) reflects return and risk metrics for a portfolio that is allocated 40 percent to large-cap U.S. stocks, 30 percent to commodity futures, and 30 percent to emerging markets (and rebalanced annually).

U.S. stocks, commodity futures, and emerging markets had relatively low correlation to each other during the 20-year sample period, so the diversified portfolio had lower volatility than any of the individual asset classes. The diversified portfolio, rebalanced annually, generated a 10.7 percent annualized geometric return. Meanwhile, the weighted average geometric return of the three asset classes was 9.3 percent based on the total return of U.S. stocks (8.2 percent), commodity futures (9.5 percent), and emerging markets (10.6 percent) during the sample period. Therefore, the diversified mix would have generated 1.4 percent more return per year than the weighted average return of the underlying asset classes. In effect, the diversified portfolio generated a greater return than the sum of its parts. Since the diversification of the three asset classes tightened the band between high and low returns, the volatility (standard deviation) declined. The lower the volatility, the less "damage" is done to the geometric return in down markets. Or said another way, the lower the volatility, the closer the arithmetic and geometric returns become. The *Low Volatility Tailwind* example demonstrates how broad diversification among many low correlating assets is essential to not only control risk, but to maximize long-term returns.

Tail Risk Hedging

In addition to the MPT diversification framework, *tail risk hedging* is another way to mitigate risk at the aggregate portfolio level. Tail risk is often defined as those rare, extreme-loss events that can severely and potentially permanently impair an asset pool's ability to fund a spending need. While a specific nonprofit institution may be able to absorb a one-year 20 percent loss, it may be unable endure a loss of 30 or

40 percent. Tail risk hedging seeks to moderate these disastrous events so that the nonprofit institution can "live to fight another day."

As an example, one possible way to implement a strategic tail risk hedge would be to purchase 12-month 10 percent out-of-the-money puts each year. To keep the example simple, assume that your portfolio is allocated 100 percent to an S&P 500 index fund. Therefore, you buy the S&P 500 index and insure your return stream against a 10 percent (or greater) calendar-year decline. If the S&P 500 declines 30 percent in a calendar year, the S&P 500 Index put option expires 20 percent in the money. In this particular example, you only lose 10 percent at the aggregate portfolio level, assuming the put option had zero cost

At first glance, strategic tail risk hedging sounds like a no-brainer. However, the expense of such a static hedging strategy can be cost-prohibitive. Exhibit 2.13 shows the annual cost of historical 12-month put options. The costs of the 12-month 10 percent out-of-the-money puts have ranged from 1.6 percent to 9.9 percent of the notional hedged value amount between 1994 and 2010. On average, the cost of the hedge was 3.9 percent per year. So if you expected S&P 500 index's forward-looking annual return to be 7.9 percent, you need to apply an approximate 3.9 percent haircut to your expected return, bringing expected return closer to 4 percent. Given the cost, one would be better off just allocating more to lower-risk and lower-return investments like high-quality bonds.

While strategic tail risk hedging may not be practical on a cost-adjusted basis, there are dynamic tail risk-hedging strategies that can potentially be cost-effective. However, these strategies rely on the skill of the tail risk manager to actively manage the hedge to offset the cost of put options (by also writing call options). They also

EXHIBIT 2.13 Cost of 12-Month Put Options

Year	Quoted Put Price Date	Cost of 12-Month 10% Out-of-the-Money S&P 500 Index Puts	Cost of 12-Month 20% Out-of-the-Money S&P 500 Index Puts
1994	01/03/94	1.8%	0.6%
1995	01/03/95	1.9%	0.8%
1996	01/02/96	1.6%	0.6%
1997	12/30/96	2.7%	1.2%
1998	12/29/97	4.3%	2.1%
1999	01/04/99	5.4%	3.4%
2000	12/31/99	3.9%	2.2%
2001	01/12/01	4.1%	2.1%
2002	12/27/01	4.6%	2.2%
2003	01/03/03	6.0%	3.2%
2004	12/26/03	3.0%	1.4%
2005	12/31/04	2.3%	1.1%
2006	12/30/05	2.0%	0.8%
2007	12/29/06	1.8%	0.7%
2008	12/28/07	4.5%	2.5%
2009	01/02/09	9.9%	6.6%
2010	12/31/09	6.0%	3.5%
	Average	3.9%	2.1%

Data Source: The Clifton Group

require bets on the part of the tail risk manager about how much insurance to purchase at various times based on market expectations. Complicating matters further is that the cost of tail-risk hedging is positively correlated to the volatility of markets. When market volatility spikes, the cost of tail-risk insurance becomes significantly more expensive. As shown in Exhibit 2.13, the highest cost year to buy a tail hedge was 2009, coming out of the 2008 financial crisis. In other words, flood insurance becomes extremely expensive if you wait for the river to get to your front door before buying it.

Counterparty Risk

Nonprofit investors often spend significant time and resources analyzing and evaluating market risks embedded in their asset allocation strategies. However, a defaulting counterparty can deliver a surprising and catastrophic blow to an otherwise well-diversified portfolio. The proliferation of derivatives and exotic investment products in recent years has raised the awareness of counterparty risk for alert investors. However, it took the 2008 financial crisis to wake up others who had long been asleep at the switch.

Counterparty risk arises whenever one party is dependent upon another to complete a financial transaction. Examples include relying on a broker to deliver shares after a stock purchase, or relying on an investment bank to deliver the proceeds from a credit default swap. Minimal counterparty risk exists in equity trades due to the existence of independent clearinghouses (or exchanges) between the broker and custodian. However, counterparty risk is more prevalent in over-the-counter (OTC) derivative instruments such as swaps, forwards, or other contracts. As an off-exchange contract approaches maturity, the party that has an unrealized gain faces counterparty risk as it relies upon the losing party to deliver the obligation at expiration. Unlike traditional investments, derivative contracts are a zero-sum game; the profitable party only realizes gains if the losing party does not default.

To help identify and minimize sources of risk in derivatives, *the International Swaps and Derivatives Association (ISDA)* was created in 1985. The Association has created standardized agreements and practices that member firms use to create a more efficient OTC marketplace. However, ISDA does not eliminate counterparty risk, therefore operational diligence must also factor into each investment decision.

There are several ways to manage counterparty risk. The simplest method is to engage only with the most highly rated entities and diversify exposure to any single counterparty. However, the 2008 financial crisis illustrated that even highly rated financial institutions can deteriorate very quickly. Another method to limit counterparty risk is to require collateral to ensure that at least some of the obligation can be paid if a party defaults.

A *netting agreement* allows two parties to combine several contracts at settlement into one net payment from the loser to the winner. This is especially beneficial if the counterparty goes bankrupt à la Lehman Brothers. Consider a scenario where several contracts expire and you owe a counterparty $10 million and the counterparty owes you $9 million. Without a master netting agreement, the bankrupt counterparty collects $10 million while you join their long line of creditors in hopes of one day claiming the $9 million. With a netting agreement you would simply owe the bankrupt firm $1 million, saving a significant initial outlay. A final method entails *marking the positions to market* by calculating the contract's market value at agreed-upon intervals throughout its life. The change in market value during each period is then transferred from the losing party to winning party in order to keep the un-realized gain/loss at a manageable level. Marking to market is required for exchange-traded derivatives, but needs a counterparty agreement for private and OTC contracts. One of the main challenges of marking to market is that it can be difficult to value illiquid securities. This often results in the reliance on models to calculate market values; such models can be inaccurate and costly to maintain.

It is crucial to understand and proactively manage counterparty risk to mitigate potential losses resulting from financial institution or other counterparty failures. While making thoughtful decisions about asset class and investment strategy expo-sures is critical to success, failing to properly understand and manage counterparty risks can lead to dire and unexpected blow ups, especially for any investment prod-uct that relies on the backing of a highly leveraged financial institution.

Portfolio Rebalancing

Asset allocation is the single most important determinant of investment performance, so investment committees rightfully dedicate substantial time, resources, and effort to determining their risk tolerance and optimal asset allocation mix. Then capital mar-ket fluctuations knock the portfolio off its target. Stocks go down, bonds go up, and suddenly your fund is overweight fixed income. So when and how do you reba-lance? Countless tools have been developed to help determine an optimal allocation, yet committees too often "fly by the seat of their pants" when it comes to the reba-lancing decision.

Traditional Rebalancing Methods

Institutional investors have relied on a handful of rebalancing techniques. Each has its own benefits and drawbacks. These methods include the following:

1. *Arbitrary:* Rebalancing based on gut feeling or emotion. The investment com-mittee sits around a table and asks each other, "Well, do you think it's time to reallocate back into stocks?" Of course, it is human nature to want to wait until all information is known. However, by then, markets have already reacted.
2. *Tactical:* Rebalancing based on short-term fundamental or technical considerations.
3. *Time-dependent:* Rebalancing every month, quarter, or year.
4. *Percentage bands:* (The favored methodology for most consulting firms):
   - *Fixed percentage band:* For example, rebalance if asset class is plus or mi-nus 5 percent from target allocation. (The fixed income target is 20 percent, so you rebalance at 15 percent or 25 percent.)
   - *Percentage change relative to target allocation:* For example, rebalance if the asset class is 10 percent different from the target. If your fixed income

target is 20 percent, you rebalance at plus or minus 10 percent (of 20 percent). So you rebalance when the allocation falls outside an 18 to 22 percent band.

- **Standard deviation:** Rebalance as a function of a *multiplier* times the asset class expected standard deviation. The larger the multiplier, the less frequently you rebalance.

Rebalancing Considerations

The *arbitrary* method has severe drawbacks. Humans seem to be "hard-wired" to lose money when investing based on gut reaction. (See Chapter 14 on Behavioral Finance.) There is no evidence that investment committees are more immune to greed and fear than individuals.

Tactical rebalancing might be effective if the decision makers are armed with superior information and employ a thoughtful and contrarian strategy. Unfortunately, tactical rebalancing often turns out to be indistinguishable from the arbitrary method. For one thing, fear and greed typically govern short-term investment decision making. Second, frequent and costly trading is required to make tactical bets; excessive trading is the enemy of long-term portfolio return. Third, most investment committee structures require some degree of consensus among committee members. Consensus building takes time and can lead to a "worst of all possible worlds" outcome. In other words, the tactical rebalancing strategy that results from a compromise may be worse than that of either party. Remember the old saw "A camel is a horse built by committee!"

The *time-dependent and percentage band* methods are at least disciplined rebalancing strategies. As such, they are generally superior to arbitrary and tactical rebalancing methodologies. But, they don't factor in the interaction among the various asset classes. Of the three percentage-band rebalancing strategies, the *standard deviation method* makes the most sense. At least it factors the volatility of the assets into the rebalancing decision. However, none of these methods account for the correlations among the assets.

An effective rebalancing strategy should seek to minimize rebalancing frequency and transaction costs, while keeping expected return and risk objectives constant. In other words, only rebalance when you must. And you must rebalance only when the risk and return profile of the entire portfolio changes.

There is a tradeoff between maintaining the portfolio's risk and return objectives and minimizing trading expenses. If rebalancing is infrequent, transaction fees will be lower, which is a good thing. On the other hand, the lower the rebalancing frequency, the farther the portfolio drifts away from the investment policy's stated objectives. Therefore, a compromise is required; rebalance only frequently enough to make sure the portfolio doesn't drift too far.

A "Better Rebalancing Mousetrap"

Portfolio decisions should be made to maximize return while minimizing risk and expenses. Frequent rebalancing can dampen returns by pulling money away from strong trending asset classes too soon; it also often pushes money toward downward-trending assets before they've started bottoming. The *Portfolio Engineer*^{TM}, a proprietary DiMeo Schneider & Associates, LLC overlay, seeks to generate optimal rebalancing trigger points. The goals are to maximize return, hold risk constant, and minimize implicit and explicit transaction expenses.

As discussed earlier, the efficient frontier is generated based on three input assumptions: *risk, return,* and *correlation* among asset classes. Since those three forecasts are always uncertain, one should be skeptical about the apparent precision of the target asset allocation. Mixes that may appear to be slightly off the efficient frontier may, in fact, be efficient. You should not rebalance unless you are certain that the portfolio has really moved from the target; in other words, until the risk and return characteristics becomes statistically meaningful. Think of a band of uncertainty around the target asset allocation. As long as the portfolio stays within the band one has no way of knowing whether the risk and return characteristics have really changed. Therefore, you don't rebalance.

Unlike traditional rebalancing methods, the model's rebalancing trigger is based on the risk/return parameters of the target portfolio mix compared to the current portfolio mix rather than to the weightings of underlying individual asset classes. The Portfolio Engineer™ looks at how far from the target the current portfolio has drifted on a two-dimensional expected risk and return graph. If the current portfolio strays from the target portfolio by the critical distance, you rebalance back to your targets (see Exhibit 2.14). One of the benefits of such a systematic approach is that committee members don't have to second guess their timing or reasoning when making the rebalancing decision.

In Exhibit 2.14, the black dot represents the expected return and risk of the target allocation. The small rectangles represent monthly historical return/risk snapshots as the asset allocation has fluctuated around the target (between January 1988 and September 2010). The circle represents the *band of uncertainty* around the target allocation. Only if the portfolio drifts outside the circle has the risk and return become statistically different from the target allocation. This constraint circle is set with a radius (or R) of 0.50 percent from the center (or target portfolio). The 0.50 percent R was chosen for this portfolio based on historical and resampling analysis.

EXHIBIT 2.14 Portfolio Engineer™ Rebalancing Methodology

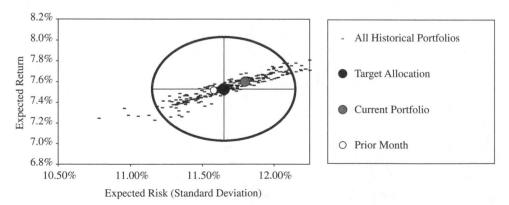

EXHIBIT 2.15 Portfolio Engineer™: Historical Risk

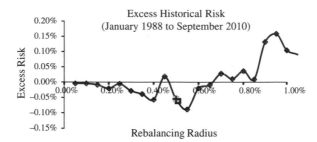

Exhibit 2.15 shows results for that period (January 1988 to September 2010). The vertical axis is risk. The horizontal axis represents "degree of portfolio drift prior to rebalancing." Think of the left side as "constant rebalancing" and the right side as "never rebalancing." The graph illustrates the impact of waiting to rebalance until the portfolio touched the R constraint (the gray square). Up until that point, risk stayed constant (actually there was a statistically insignificant decline in volatility). Once the portfolio drifted beyond R equal to 0.65 percent, volatility began a more permanent trend up.

Exhibit 2.16 shows that by waiting to rebalance until the R constraint was reached, there was an increase in return as well. Not only would the fund have saved on implicit and explicit transaction expenses by rebalancing less frequently than most other disciplined rebalancing methods, but it could have also generated excess return. By rebalancing when R reached 0.50 percent, the fund would have added 0.38 percent of return per year compared to the index benchmark (which is rebalanced monthly). It is worth noting that one did not have to pinpoint a single specific R for the constraint circle to add value. As you can see from the positive slope of the chart in Exhibit 2.16, you could have rebalanced at any point between R equals 0 percent and 0.85 percent, and still increased portfolio return. Of course, when R was greater than 0.65 percent, risk increased and when R was less than 0.20 percent, the portfolio was rebalanced very frequently resulting in unnecessary transaction fees. The upward sloping line when R is between 0 percent and 0.50 percent has been fairly predictable and consistent over a variety of portfolio mixes, market environments, and time intervals.[2]

EXHIBIT 2.16 Portfolio Engineer™: Historical Return

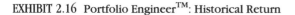

Why not simply establish equity and fixed income allocation constraints (i.e., plus or minus 5 percent from targets), and use those for the rebalancing decision? The answer is that not all stocks and bonds are created equal. Emerging market equities being overweight relative to their target allocation pushed the portfolio toward higher risk (and higher expected returns) more than large cap domestic equities being overweight. On the other hand, being overweight investment-grade intermediate bonds pulls the risk/return characteristics of the portfolio down more than if high yield bonds are overweight. If emerging markets and investment grade bonds are overweight at the same time, you have a netting effect on risk and return. In summary, the key ingredients missing in a simple equity and fixed income rebalancing constraint are the volatility differences among various sub asset classes (e.g., U.S. equity and emerging markets) as well as the correlation between asset classes (e.g., TIPS and foreign developed equities).

Conclusion

Unless one owns an infallible crystal ball, no asset allocation framework or strategy is ever perfect. However, it is absolutely critical for nonprofits to develop and follow effective and disciplined asset allocation frameworks. Making effective asset allocation decisions affords you some latitude to overcome shortcomings elsewhere in the portfolio-construction process. On the other hand, near-perfect execution of more ancillary portfolio construction elements like manager selection cannot overcome poor asset allocation decisions. Whatever asset allocation and portfolio-rebalancing process a fiduciary follows, it should be disciplined, robust, and practical to implement.

Notes

1. Brinson, Singer, and Beebower, *Financial Analysts Journal*, 1991.

2. The results described for the Portfolio Engineer™ rebalancing methodology are from a back test. While the logic is intuitively compelling and non-back test results have been encouraging, past performance does not guarantee future results.

CHAPTER 3

Traditional Global Financial Asset Classes

Nonprofit investors must develop effective asset allocation strategies as discussed in Chapter 2. While many nonprofits also invest in alternative asset classes such as hedge funds, private equity, and real assets (see Chapters 5 through 7), traditional financial asset classes like publicly traded stocks and bonds remain the core of well-diversified portfolios.

We discuss the following asset classes and the role each fills within a broadly diversified portfolio:

Global Fixed Income Asset Classes

- Cash
- Treasury Inflation-Protected Securities (TIPS)
- Investment-Grade U.S. Nominal Bonds
- Foreign Bonds
- High-Yield Bonds

Global Equities

- U.S. Equities (large, mid, and small cap)
- Foreign-Developed Equities
- Emerging-Market Equities

Global Fixed-Income Asset Classes

Fixed-income securities finance borrowing by governments, businesses, other institutions and consumers. The fixed-income markets are massive (estimated at $91 trillion[1] as of 2009). Each segment within the global fixed-income market has unique performance drivers and risks. From *cash* to *high-yield bonds*, fixed-income investments span the range of stability, liquidity, and diversification functions within diversified portfolios.

Cash

Money market funds are the primary cash vehicle, but separate accounts can be used for larger pools. Money market vehicles invest in short-term instruments with maturities of less than 90 days. These instruments include U.S. Treasury bills, agencies, commercial paper, certificates of deposit (CDs), repurchase agreements (repos), bankers' acceptances, and municipals. While the securities are typically liquid and have short maturities, there is still some default risk. Since the money market industry's birth in the early 1970s, two money market funds have "broken the buck,"[2] meaning they lost principal.

In September 2008 during the financial crisis, all money market funds were forced to comply with Rule 2a-7 of the Securities and Exchange Commission (SEC). The rule mandates that money market funds must maintain an average dollar-weighted maturity of 60 days or less and also mandated certain minimum credit quality and liquidity standards.

Nonprofit investors typically invest in cash for short-term liquidity needs or to manage overall portfolio volatility. Cash can preserve (nominal) value during periods of rising inflation. Rising inflation often accompanies rising interest rates and falling bond prices. For example, during the inflationary 1970 to 1979 decade, cash outperformed bonds (and stocks) because rising interest rates could not overcome falling bond prices. On the other hand, in deflationary or disinflationary environments, cash can yield virtually zero as illustrated by the 2009 to early 2011 period.

Treasury Inflation-Protected Securities

Global government issuance of inflation-linked securities exceeds $1.5 trillion. The U.S. Treasury began issuing TIPS in 1997. As of early 2011, U.S. TIPS issuance exceeded $550 billion, representing nearly 8 percent of the U.S. Treasury's marketable securities. Issuance as a percentage of outstanding U.S. debt is likely to grow because TIPS are in high demand, especially by foreign governments that finance much of the United States' ongoing federal budget deficit. TIPS are obligations of the U.S. Treasury and are similar to traditional (nominal) Treasury bonds. The difference is that the principal amount of TIPS adjusts to reflect changes in inflation as measured by the *Consumer Price Index for All Urban Consumers*. Since the *coupon* or stated interest rate for TIPS is applied to the principal amount, the semiannual coupon payment varies as the principal amount fluctuates in response to inflation or deflation. So the TIPS' stated rate is a *real* (after inflation) interest rate. The final principal amount repaid to the TIPS owner at maturity equals the greater of the original principal amount or the inflation-adjusted principal. Therefore, while coupon payments can decline because of deflation, the principal is shielded from deflation.

As an example, assume the U.S. Treasury issues a $100 10-year maturity traditional bond and a 10-year TIPS. This 10-year maturity TIPS has a 1.0 percent real yield, while the traditional nominal U.S. Treasury bond has a higher, but fixed, nominal 3.3 percent annual yield. The 2.3 percent difference should approximate 10-year inflation expectations for bond investors. For a traditional nominal U.S. Treasury bond, the par value and annual interest payment remains constant at $100 and $3.30, respectively, during the entire 10-year life of the bond. However, the par value and interest payments for the TIPS adjust based on changes in the inflation rate. So, if CPI rises 5 percent during the first year, the TIPS par value would rise from $100 to $105, and the annual real yield (1.0 percent of par) would rise from $1.00 to $1.05.

TIPS protect investors from unanticipated inflation and can protect nonprofits with spending needs that rise with inflation. U.S. Treasury debt investors can theoretically lose in two ways over the full life of investment. The first way is if the U.S. Treasury explicitly defaults and debt holders are not repaid. The second way to lose is if inflation wipes out the real value of the bond. Nominal U.S. Treasuries are subject to both risks because inflation can decay the par value of the bond in real terms. On the other hand, TIPS are only subject to the risk of explicit sovereign default. TIPS investors are protected from skyrocketing inflation because the bond's par value keeps pace with inflation.

The Barclays Capital U.S. TIPS Index includes bonds with fixed-rate coupon payments that adjust for inflation as measured by the Consumer Price Index for All Urban Consumers (CPI-U). Each bond included must have a minimum amount outstanding of $5 billion. See Exhibit 3.1 for more information about the index's holdings and construction.

The Barclays Capital U.S. TIPS Index has returned an annualized 6.6 percent with an annualized standard deviation of 6.0 percent between March 1997 and December 2010. The low correlation of 0.03 to U.S. equities made these bonds attractive for diversification purposes (see Exhibit 3.2).

There are also some unique risks and challenges with TIPS. First, TIPS are relatively new securities, and the historical track record is relatively short. So, while it is reasonable to surmise they would have performed well during inflationary periods (like the 1970s), there is no historical TIPS return stream to verify, although inflation-linked securities in non-U.S markets did perform as expected during inflationary periods elsewhere.

Secondly, if *real* yields in the markets rise, TIPS prices fall. Since their stated interest rate is lower than nominal Treasuries and the payoff amount is more back-end loaded (as par value rises with inflation), the prices can be very sensitive to real interest rate fluctuations. Third, TIPS are more *thinly traded* than nominal Treasuries. TIPS sold off in 2008, particularly in the fourth quarter as the credit crisis worsened. While the 2008 financial crisis brought deflationary forces that negatively impacted TIPS, investors also

EXHIBIT 3.1 Barclays Capital U.S. TIPS Index (as of December 31, 2010)

Number of Issues	31
Avg. Maturity	8.9 years
Market Value	$605 billion
Avg. Real Yield to Maturity	1.1%
Avg. Coupon (at issuance)	2.0%
Maturity Spectrum	
1-3 years	16%
3-5 years	22%
5-7 years	13%
7-10 years	19%
> 10 years	30%

EXHIBIT 3.2 Historical Fixed Income Performance and Correlation Statistics (March 31, 1997 to December 31, 2010)

Asset Class	Index	Return	Volatility
Cash	Citigroup 3-month T-bill	3.1%	0.6%
TIPS	Barclays Capital U.S. TIPS	6.6%	6.0%
U.S. Nominal Bonds	Barclays Capital U.S. Aggregate	6.3%	3.7%
Foreign Bonds	Citigroup Non-U.S. WGBI (50/50 Hedged and Unhedged)	6.0%	8.8%
High Yield Bonds	B of A Merrill Lynch High Yield Master	7.1%	9.8%

Correlation Matrix[1]

	Cash	TIPS	U.S. Bond	Non-U.S. Bond Hedged	Non-U.S. Bond Unhedged	High Yield	U.S. Equity	Non-U.S. Equity	EM Equity
Cash	1.00								
TIPS	−0.02	1.00							
U.S. Bond	0.06	0.74	1.00						
Non-U.S. Bond Hedged	0.19	0.44	0.71	1.00					
Non-U.S. Bond Unhedged	−0.09	0.49	0.52	0.42	1.00				
High Yield	−0.16	0.25	0.17	−0.12	0.11	1.00			
U.S. Equity	0.01	0.03	−0.01	−0.18	0.10	0.61	1.00		
Non-U.S. Equity	−0.04	0.08	0.02	−0.19	0.30	0.64	0.85	1.00	
EM Equity	−0.12	0.10	−0.04	−0.22	0.14	0.64	0.76	0.84	1.00

[1]Period 3/1/1997 - 12/31/2010. Cash (Citigroup 3-month T-bill), TIPS (Barclays Capital U.S. TIPS Index), U.S. Bonds (Barclays Capital U.S. Aggregate Bond Index), Non-U.S. Bonds Hedged (Citigroup Non-U.S. WGBI, currency-hedged), Non-U.S. Bonds Unhedged (Citigroup Non-U.S. WGBI), High Yield (Citigroup High-Yield Market), U.S. Equity (S&P 500 index), Non-U.S. Equity (MSCI EAFE Index), EM Equity (MSCI Emerging Markets Free Index).

preferred the more liquid nominal U.S. Treasuries. Flights to safety by investors usually include a flight to the more liquid instrument regardless of quality.

Nonprofit funds typically face ongoing *real* spending needs and must increase nominal spending to keep pace with inflation. TIPS can be a valuable tool to help trustees combat this challenge.

Investment-Grade U.S. Nominal Bonds

Before the 1980s, the U.S. bond market was pretty simple. Borrowers issued bonds at fixed rates, and investors generally held them to maturity. The major risks were defaults, rating downgrades, and the inflationary drag on purchasing power of coupon payments and principal. Over the past 30 years, bonds have become structurally more complex, and investors tend to trade them prior to maturity. The U.S. bond market evolution is displayed in Exhibit 3.3.

Investment-grade nominal bonds are securities that have a credit rating of BBB or higher as ranked by rating agencies such as Moody's or Standard and Poor's. U.S. Treasuries and corporate bonds issued by high-grade issuers are considered investment grade. Bonds are issued with a variety of maturities: *short bonds* are issues with

EXHIBIT 3.3 Composition of the Barclays Aggregate U.S. Bond Index (1986 to 2010)

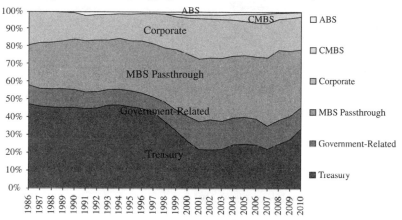

Source: Barclays Capital, as of December 31, 2010.

less than one year remaining to maturity, *intermediate bonds* between 1- and 10-year maturities, and *long bonds* have maturities greater than 10 years. Historically, the greatest issuance volume has been in the intermediate part of the curve.

As of December 31, 2010, the U.S. investment-grade bond market value was $15.1 trillion. The *Barclays Capital U.S. Aggregate Bond Index* represents investment-grade, U.S. dollar-denominated, fixed-rate, taxable bonds that have a maturity greater than one year. Exhibit 3.4 shows details of the Index.

EXHIBIT 3.4 Barclays Capital U.S. Aggregate Bond Index Metrics (December 31, 2010)

Index Data	
Number of Issues	7,999
Avg. Maturity	7.1 years
Market Value	$15.1 trillion
Avg. Yield to Maturity	3.0%
Avg. Coupon	4.2%
Avg. Duration	5.0 years
Maturity Spectrum	
< 1 year	1%
1-3 years	24%
3-5 years	31%
5-10 years	33%
10-20 years	4%
>20 years	7%
Credit Quality	
AAA	78%
AA	4%
A	10%
BBB	8%

EXHIBIT 3.5   Barclays Capital U.S. Aggregate Bond Index Sector Weights

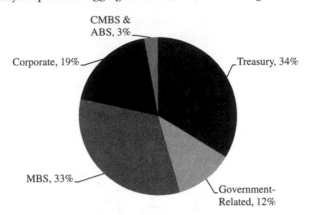

Source: Barclays Capital, as of December 31, 2010.

Exposure to MBS in the index comes mostly from securities issued by *Fannie Mae* (originally called the Federal National Mortgage Association) and *Freddie Mac* (the Federal Home Loan Mortgage Corp). Fannie and Freddie are considered *Government Sponsored Entities* (GSEs). Since the U.S. Treasury placed these two mortgage giants into conservatorship in 2008, about 80 percent of the Index comprises direct and indirect U.S. federal government-related obligations. Nonprofit investors who invest in bond index funds tracking the Barclays Capital U.S. Aggregate Bond Index must be aware that the index grows more government-heavy by the day. Exhibit 3.5 displays the various sectors within the Index.

U.S. Treasuries (historically 20 to 40 percent of the Barclays Aggregate) include zero coupon and coupon-paying bonds issued by the U.S. Treasury, backed by the full faith and credit of the U.S. Government. Treasuries are issued on a monthly basis with the most recently issued securities being referred to as "on-the-run." Historically, market participants have viewed these securities as having zero default risk and generally treat them as a proxy for the (credit) risk-free rate. Treasuries are also used by bond managers to adjust portfolio *duration*. Duration measures the weighted average length of the present value of a bond's cash flows, including principal repayment. The longer the duration, the more sensitive a bond's price is to changes in the market interest rate. By having the ability to allocate capital to various maturities on the curve, managers can dial duration up or down depending on their views of future interest rate movements.

U.S. Government Agency (historically 10 to 15 percent of the Barclays Aggregate) includes Federal agencies—direct arms of the U.S. Government, and GSEs that are privately owned but publically chartered. While the bonds are not guaranteed by the full faith and credit of the U.S. Government, the market generally believes that the Government would intervene to support the agencies in financial distress. In 2008, that assumption was validated when the U.S. government put Fannie Mae and Freddie Mac into conservatorship to protect the debt holders of the financial institutions.

Historically 15 to 25 percent of the Barclays Aggregate Index is comprised of bonds issued by *corporations* rated as investment grade. Companies may issue debt to finance expansion or just to upgrade their capital structures. Unlike the federal government, companies often borrow from banks. However, many companies instead choose to borrow in the deep U.S bond market. This practice typically results in lower borrowing costs. Bond investors have a senior claim on company assets in the event of bankruptcy. They are repaid first before any capital is returned to equity owners.

Corporate securities are called *spread products,* and are priced at a *yield spread* over Treasuries. In periods of economic stress, corporate bond yields tend to increase as the perceived risk of default rises. Bonds that were issued at lower yields decline in price until the resulting increase in yield compensates owners for risk. On the other hand, yield spreads tend to compress during economic recoveries.

Mortgage-backed securities (MBS) have historically been 30 to 40 percent of the Barclays Aggregate. They are a type of *structured credit* that holds a basket of residential mortgages as collateral. As mortgage payments are made each month, interest and principal are distributed to investors through the MBS. An underlying pool of mortgages is typically the source for multiple bonds. Unlike bonds with a stated maturity, the underlying homeowners can sell or refinance their homes at any time. This creates uncertainty over the timing of prepayments. Some investors may be willing to take *prepayment risk* if they can earn a higher yield while others desire a bond without much prepayment risk. Therefore, issuers have sometimes created multiple *tranches* from the same pool. Typically the first tranche has a lower yield but is first in line to receive prepayments. If enough prepayments come in, Tranche A is retired, and the next prepayment is applied to Tranche B, and so forth.

MBS also have *extension risk*, the opposite of prepayment risk. If interest rates rise, homeowners won't refinance their homes or prepay their mortgages as expected, causing the maturity of the security to elongate. Extension risk can also be caused when homeowners lack sufficient home equity to refinance. This was a common problem following the housing bust. A related risk is that the underlying mortgage borrowers fall behind on payments or default on their mortgages. In such a case, tranches are exposed to varying levels of default risk. Exhibit 3.6 details the cash flow structure of a MBS.

Commercial Mortgage-Backed Securities (CMBS) and *Asset-Backed Securities* (ABS) make up the last small slice of the U.S. investment-grade debt market. Both of these sectors have a structure similar to residential MBS. CMBS are backed by commercial mortgages on properties such as office or industrial buildings. ABS are generally backed by auto and student loans, credit card receivables, and loans that are guaranteed by the Small Business Administration (SBA). A key characteristic of ABS is that most collateral is unsecured. Therefore investors prefer some type of credit enhancement or insurance to protect against default.

Investors hold high-grade U.S. bonds to offset volatility elsewhere in a portfolio. Low correlation with other riskier asset classes (see Exhibit 3.7) and a relatively stable return profile are hallmarks of this asset class. Investment-grade bonds also act as a hedge against disinflation and outright *deflation*. While the likelihood of defaults can rise during deflationary environments brought on by recession, coupon payments become more valuable. (Nominal bonds are more likely to outperform TIPS in unanticipated deflationary environments.)

EXHIBIT 3.6   Structure of Mortgage-Backed Securities

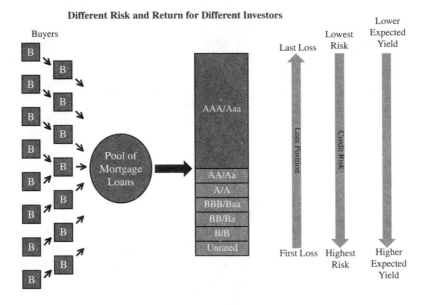

EXHIBIT 3.7   Correlation Matrix: Investment-Grade Bonds

Correlation Matrix[1]									
	Cash	TIPS	U.S. Bond	Non-U.S. Bond Hedged	Non-U.S. Bond Unhedged	High Yield	U.S. Equity	Non-U.S. Equity	EM Equity
Cash	1.00								
TIPS	−0.02	1.00							
U.S. Bond	0.06	0.74	1.00						
Non-U.S. Bond Hedged	0.19	0.44	0.71	1.00					
Non-U.S. Bond Unhedged	−0.09	0.49	0.52	0.42	1.00				
High Yield	−0.16	0.25	0.17	−0.12	0.11	1.00			
U.S. Equity	0.01	0.03	−0.01	−0.18	0.10	0.61	1.00		
Non-U.S. Equity	−0.04	0.08	0.02	−0.19	0.30	0.64	0.85	1.00	
EM Equity	−0.12	0.10	−0.04	−0.22	0.14	0.64	0.76	0.84	1.00

[1]Period 3/1/1997 to 12/31/2010. Cash (Citigroup 3-month T-bill), TIPS, Barclays Capital U.S. TIPS Index), U.S. Bonds (Barclays Capital U.S. Aggregate Bond Index), Non-U.S. Bonds Hedged (Citigroup Non-U.S. WGBI, currency-hedged), Non-U.S. Bonds Unhedged (Citigroup Non-U.S. WGBI), High Yield (Citigroup High-Yield Market), U.S. Equity (S&P 500 Index), Non-U.S. Equity (MSCI EAFE index), EM Equity (MSCI Emerging Markets Free Index).

As mentioned, effective duration is used to measure a bond's interest rate risk. A bond with a five-year duration will decrease or increase in price by about 5 percent for every 1 percent change in interest rates. Therefore, all else being equal, a bond with a shorter duration has less sensitivity to *parallel shifts* in interest rates. However, shorter-term bonds can lose more than longer-duration bonds in a certain kind of rising interest rate environment. If short-term rates are near zero and the yield curve is steep, a flattening of the curve (where short-term rates rise closer to longer-term rates), can lead short-term bonds to lose more value than longer-duration bonds. This is called a *non-parallel rising interest rate environment*. As of early 2011, the yield curve was steep with shorter maturity bonds having yields significantly below longer maturity bonds. If the yield curve flattens, shorter term bonds are susceptible to this type of risk.

Foreign Bonds

A primary purpose for holding bonds in a diversified portfolio is to buffer volatility. In the United States, interest rates have been generally falling since 1982. As bond yields fall, prices rise. The end of this long bull market in domestic bonds may be at hand. While domestic bonds provide some benefit, foreign bonds can further diversify a portfolio's total risk. Foreign bonds offer a broader opportunity set and can take advantage of alternative interest rate environments around the world.

Nearly 60 percent of all bonds are issued outside the United States. *Sovereign bonds* (debts issued by foreign governments) currently make up the lion's share. Governments in developed markets in Europe, the United Kingdom, Japan, Australia, and New Zealand all issue traditional fixed-income securities. These bonds are supported by the full faith and credit of their respective governments.

The Citigroup Non-U.S. Dollar *World Government Bond Index* (WGBI) measures the performance of fixed-rate government bonds issued in developed countries around the world. All bonds that are included must have at least $25 million outstanding. The Index currently comprises only government-issued bonds (see Exhibit 3.8).

As illustrated in Exhibit 3.9, the Index has grown dramatically over the last 10 years due to the increased issuance by developed market countries to finance deficits. Japan is a major issuer of debt, comprising more than 40 percent of the index.

Corporate debt represents a growing sector in the non-U.S. fixed-income market. Foreign corporations have historically used bank borrowing and equity capital to finance growth. However, they have increasingly turned to bond markets as a source of funds. As in the United States, non-government fixed-income securities carry added credit risk, but investors are rewarded with higher yields.

Emerging-market bonds are a growing sub-sector of the foreign debt market. Governments and businesses in Latin America, Eastern Europe, and Asia (excluding Japan) and others issue debt to finance infrastructure projects and business growth. Currently accounting for less than 5 percent of the world's bond issuance, emerging-market countries are growing faster than the developed world. Their capital markets are also increasing in size. While emerging-market debt may have greater political risks, the countries' lower debt levels, lower trade deficits (often surpluses), higher savings rates, and younger population arguably put them in better fiscal positions

EXHIBIT 3.8 Citigroup Non-U.S. Dollar WGBI (December 31, 2010)

Index Data	
Number of Issues	655
Avg. Maturity	8.7 years
Market Value	$13.1 trillion
Avg. Yield to Maturity	2.1%
Avg. Coupon	3.0%
Avg. Duration	6.8 years
Maturity Spectrum	
< 1 year	2%
1-3 years	24%
3-5 years	20%
5-10 years	28%
10-20 years	16%
>20 years	10%

than many of their developed-market counterparts, especially following the 2008 financial crisis.

In the 1980s and early 1990s, the tradable market for emerging-market fixed income was largely external and denominated in U.S. dollars. Bonds denominated in the local currency began to take hold in the 1990s. The total market's size was estimated to be $600 billion by the mid 2000s.[3] The market continued to expand rapidly, comprising approximately $2.1 trillion by the end of 2010.[4]

Emerging market fixed income encompasses three components—*external debt, local currency debt,* and *corporate debt.* External debt is issued in currencies such as the U.S. dollar or euro; the yield of these bonds includes a risk premium based on the

EXHIBIT 3.9 Growth in Citigroup Non-U.S. Dollar WGBI (1985 to 2010)

Citigroup Non-U.S. Dollar WGBI Market Value ($ trillions)

issuing government's creditworthiness. The largest risk to external emerging-market debt is a default or stresses caused by currency fluctuations. For example, if the U.S. dollar appreciates against the Brazilian reál, Brazil's U.S. dollar-denominated interest expense rises imposing a greater financial burden on the Brazilian government. In contrast, local currency debt is issued in the country's home currency. This adds currency risk for U.S.-based investors.

Volatility in local economies, along with political instability, are significant risks. For example, Russia's 1998 default pushed the entire emerging fixed income market into crisis. However, higher risks are generally accompanied by higher yields. As of early 2011, more than 70 percent of the securities in the *J.P. Morgan Emerging Markets Bond Index—Global* were rated as investment grade.

A main benefit of non-U.S. fixed income is its low correlation with domestic fixed-income and global equities. Despite globalization, foreign economies are seldom on the exact same path as the United States. As economies strengthen or weaken, local central banks raise or lower rates in order to slow or speed economic growth. For example, following the financial crisis of 2008, the U.S. Federal Reserve kept key interest rates low. On the other hand, Australia aggressively tightened (raised interest rates) as their economy recovered and experienced rapid expansion. Exhibit 3.10 shows how both hedged and unhedged foreign bonds correlate with other major asset classes.

Non-U.S. bonds have also presented an attractive return-distribution profile. Since their inception, they have exhibited a *positively skewed, platykurtic distribution*. In other words, better upside and thin left tails (see Exhibit 3.11).

Currency fluctuations can have the greatest impact on a foreign bond portfolio's return. Assume a U.S. investor buys a German government bund (denominated in

EXHIBIT 3.10 Correlation for Hedged and Unhedged Foreign Bonds

				Correlation Matrix[1]					
	Cash	TIPS	U.S. Bond	Non-U.S. Bond Hedged	Non-U.S. Bond Unhedged	High Yield	U.S. Equity	Non-U.S. Equity	EM Equity
Cash	1.00								
TIPS	−0.02	1.00							
U.S. Bond	0.06	0.74	1.00						
Non-U.S. Bond Hedged	0.19	0.44	0.71	1.00					
Non-U.S. Bond Unhedged	−0.09	0.49	0.52	0.42	1.00				
High Yield	−0.16	0.25	0.17	−0.12	0.11	1.00			
U.S. Equity	0.01	0.03	−0.01	−0.18	0.10	0.61	1.00		
Non-U.S. Equity	−0.04	0.08	0.02	−0.19	0.30	0.64	0.85	1.00	
EM Equity	−0.12	0.10	−0.04	−0.22	0.14	0.64	0.76	0.84	1.00

[1]Period 3/1/1997 - 12/31/2010. Cash (Citigroup 3-month T-bill), TIPS (Barclays Capital U.S. TIPS Index), U.S. Bonds (Barclays Capital U.S. Aggregate Bond Index). Non-U.S. Bonds Hedged (Citigroup Non-U.S. WGBI, currency-hedged), Non-U.S. Bonds Unhedged (Citigroup Non-U.S. WGBI), High Yield (Citigroup High-Yield Market), U.S. Equity (S&P 500 Index), Non-U.S. Equity (MSCI EAFE Index) (MSCI Emerging Markets Free Index).

EXHIBIT 3.11   Foreign Bonds: Thin Left Tail

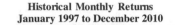

**Historical Monthly Returns
January 1997 to December 2010**

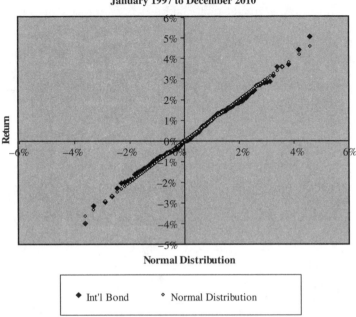

euros). Over time, the relative value of the euro versus the dollar fluctuates. If the euro's value increases 10 percent relative to the U.S. dollar, the currency impact would result in an additional 10 percent gain for the U.S.-based investor. However, currency moves work both ways; a 10 percent *decline* in the euro has the opposite impact. Derivative instruments can hedge out the impact of currency swings (both positive and negative). *Forwards, futures,* and *currency swaps* are used to manage currency risk. This hedging impacts the return as well as the volatility a U.S. investor experiences by owning a foreign security.

Foreign bond managers manage currency in three broad ways. The first is a passive approach, the currency exposure is purely a function of the manager's country-allocation decision. The second approach is defensive, only hedging when a currency becomes extremely under or overvalued relative to its historical trading range. The third approach is *active*, treating currency as a separate asset class. For example, the manager might be long the Japanese yen without holding any Japanese government bonds (JGBs); in other words, they are bullish on the yen, but not the underlying Japanese bonds.

Nonprofits investors must decide whether or not to hire bond managers that hedge currency exposure. Exhibit 3.12 details annual returns for both the Citigroup Currency-Hedged Non-U.S. Dollar WGBI and the Citigroup Non-U.S. Dollar WGBI.

Investors face a dilemma when choosing whether or not to hedge currencies. On one hand, currency hedging significantly reduces volatility leading to higher historical Sharpe ratios (or historical risk-adjusted returns). On the other hand, unhedged

EXHIBIT 3.12   Hedged versus Unhedged Bonds: Calendar Year Returns (1995 to 2010)

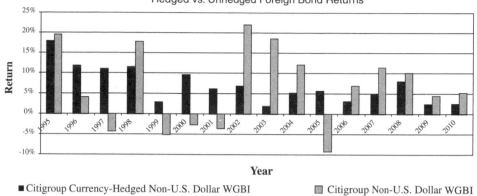

Hedged vs. Unhedged Foreign Bond Returns

■ Citigroup Currency-Hedged Non-U.S. Dollar WGBI   ▢ Citigroup Non-U.S. Dollar WGBI

foreign bond portfolios have had lower correlation to stocks and domestic bonds providing greater diversification. We advocate treating hedged and unhedged bonds as separate asset classes because their risk and correlation profiles are so different By using both, nonprofit investors can get the best of both worlds.

Scale is critical when considering appropriate investment vehicles. In general, commingled funds are most appropriate for allocations under $50 million due to trading and custody costs. Custody costs include *asset-based fees, transaction-based fees, foreign exchange fees,* and the costs of *hedging* (if applicable). Commingled funds pool multiple investors to spread these costs over a greater base.

High-Yield Bonds

High-yield bonds (junk bonds) are securities rated below investment grade (BB or below) by the major rating agencies. Such bonds offer greater yield to compensate investors for their increased credit risk. Before the 1980s, most "junk bonds" came from the decline in credit quality of former investment-grade issuers. These issues were known as *fallen angels.* Today, most high-yield bonds were rated BB or lower at the time of issuance. Any given high-yield bond has substantially greater default risk than an investment-grade bond. However, the higher yield associated with a portfolio of high-yield bonds can more than compensate investors for the added credit risk.

The *Merrill Lynch High-Yield Master Index* is used as a proxy for the high-yield bond universe. The Index is capitalization weighted, comprised of corporate bonds issued by companies rated BB or lower. From its inception in 1984 through 2010, the Index has returned an annualized 9.7 percent with volatility of 9.2 percent (see Exhibit 3.13).

In addition to having higher coupon payments, high-yield bonds offer investors potential price appreciation. If the issuer's debt rating is upgraded due to merger, improved earnings, or a positive industry development, the yield spread over investment-grade bonds may tighten and the bond price rises. Also, if investors become more sanguine about credit risk, spreads can tighten even without a ratings upgrade.

EXHIBIT 3.13 Merrill Lynch High-Yield Master Index (December 31, 2010)

Index Data	
Number of Issues	2,114
Avg. Maturity	8.7 years
Market Value	$1.0 trillion
Avg. Yield to Maturity	7.9%
Avg. Coupon	8.4%
Avg. Duration	4.4 years
Credit Quality	
BB	42%
B	41%
CCC	14%
CC	2%
C	1%
Maturity Spectrum	
1-3 years	9%
3-5 years	25%
5-10 years	57%
10-20 years	5%
>20 years	4%

However, the bulk of historical high-yield bond returns came from the income component. Exhibit 3.14 shows the historical yield relationships between high-yield bonds and investment-grade fixed-income indices.

While default risk is greater for high yield than investment-grade bonds, claims to assets are still senior to equity holders in the event of bankruptcy. But, in the event

EXHIBIT 3.14 High-Yield Bonds versus Barclays Aggregate Bond Index and U.S. Treasuries (1987 to 2010)

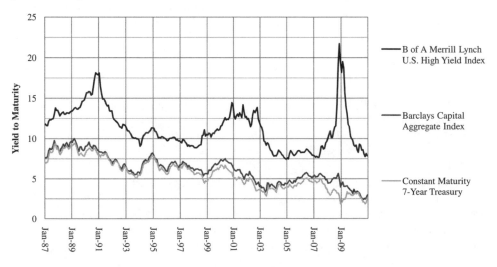

EXHIBIT 3.15 Correlation Matrix: High-Yield Bonds

				Correlation Matrix[1]					
	Cash	TIPS	U.S. Bond	Non-U.S. Bond Hedged	Non-U.S. Bond Unhedged	High Yield	U.S. Equity	Non-U.S. Equity	EM Equity
Cash	1.00								
TIPS	−0.02	1.00							
U.S. Bond	0.06	0.74	1.00						
Non-U.S. Bond Hedged	0.19	0.44	0.71	1.00					
Non-U.S. Bond Unhedged	−0.09	0.49	0.52	0.42	1.00				
High Yield	−0.16	0.25	0.17	−0.12	0.11	1.00			
U.S. Equity	0.01	0.03	−0.01	−0.18	0.10	0.61	1.00		
Non-U.S. Equity	−0.04	0.08	0.02	−0.19	0.30	0.64	0.85	1.00	
EM Equity	−0.12	0.10	−0.04	−0.22	0.14	0.64	0.76	0.84	1.00

[1]Period 3/1/1997 to 12/31/2010. Cash (Citigroup 3-month T-bill), TIPS (Barclays Capital U.S. TIPS Index), U.S. Bonds (Barclays Capital U.S. Aggregate Bond Index). Non-U.S. Bonds Hedged (Citigroup Non-U.S. WGBI, currency-hedged), Non-U.S. Bonds Unhedged (Citigroup Non-U.S. WGBI), High Yield (Citigroup High-Yield Market), U.S. Equity (S&P 500 Index), Non-U.S. Equity (MSCI EAFE Index) (MSCI Emerging Markets Free Index).

of default, high-yield bonds can have low recovery rates. Recovery rates have averaged 46 percent between 2000 and 2010.[5] While riskier on a stand-alone basis, high-yield bonds can still improve portfolio diversification. For example, U.S. Treasury interest rates often rise in the later stages of economic recoveries as inflation becomes a concern for bond investors, making bond prices fall. However, accelerating economic growth makes junk bonds less likely to default, driving their prices up. Exhibit 3.15 illustrates the relatively low correlations of high-yield bonds relative to other fixed-income asset classes. In addition, the correlation between U.S. stocks and high-yield bonds was 0.61, lower than the correlation of 0.76 between U.S. stocks and emerging market stocks.

Like most risky assets, high-yield bond correlations to global stocks rise during periods of stress. High-yield bonds also frequently underperform investment-grade bonds in the early stages of economic recession. Like any other fixed-income security, high-yield bonds have interest rate risk. However, the level of sensitivity to interest rates is lower than their sensitivity to credit spreads. Credit spreads often tighten when interest rates rise. Also, the aggregate high yield bond market typically has a shorter average maturity than investment-grade bond classes. High yield bond liquidity is lower than most investment-grade counterparts. In periods of stress when investors dump high yield holdings en masse, bid-ask spreads can widen dramatically.

Not all high-yield bonds are equal. For example, C-rated securities have the lowest credit rating (barely above defaulted status) and the greatest default risk and volatility. B-rated bonds are in the middle, and BB-rated bonds are the highest quality "junk." As Exhibit 3.16 shows, BB- and B-rated securities have had higher Sharpe

EXHIBIT 3.16 High-Yield Sub-Sectors (October 1988 to December 2010)

	Return	Standard Deviation	Sharpe Ratio	Correlation vs. S&P 500
B of A Merrill Lynch High Yield BB	8.97%	7.31%	0.63	0.60
B of A Merrill Lynch High Yield B	8.33%	9.90%	0.44	0.66
B of A Merrill Lynch High Yield CCC & Lower	8.05%	17.23%	0.23	0.60

ratios or greater return per unit of risk during the sample period. C-rated securities had significantly higher volatility, and they did not, on average, compensate investors for their higher risk during the sample period.

High-yield bonds have exhibited excess *kurtosis* (fat tails) and negative skew (more observations in the left tail) (see Exhibit 3.17). Based on the volatility of high-yield bonds (e.g., a monthly 2.8 percent standard deviation) between January 1998 and March 2009, October of 2008's loss (−16.25 percent) was 6 standard deviations from the mean, which is a 1-in-72-million-year event based on normal distribution assumptions. October 2008's loss was sandwiched between September 2008 (−8.3 percent) and November 2008 (−8.4 percent), which were both approximately 1-in-100-year events based on normal distribution assumptions. During the month of October 2008, high-yield bonds had the "fattest tail" loss of all major asset classes. In other words, high-yield bonds lost more than any other asset class relative to their historical standard deviation. Other asset classes had greater absolute losses, but also had significantly higher standard deviations. High-yield bonds also have high serial

EXHIBIT 3.17 High-Yield Bonds: Fat Left Tail

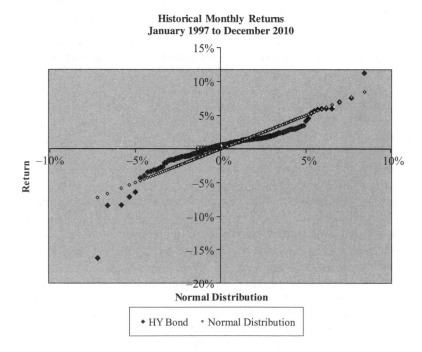

**Historical Monthly Returns
January 1997 to December 2010**

correlation, meaning they tend to trend (positive serial correlation) and mean revert (negative serial correlation) more than most other asset classes.

Global Equity Asset Classes

Stock markets have existed in various forms for at least 500 hundred years. While there's little consensus among historians about the first stock market, some point to the Dutch East India Company's founding in 1602, while others speculate that stock markets existed in ancient Rome.

Common stocks (equities) are ownership shares in companies. Common stock shareholders usually have voting rights that include establishing corporate objectives and electing the board of directors. Unlike bond owners who are lenders to companies, stock owners participate in the profits of a company. Equity ownership is junior in the capital structure, so stocks have higher risk and demand a risk premium over bonds. In the event of liquidation, common stock shares are wiped out first as the company's bond holders and other creditors have senior claims to a company's assets. The total returns for stocks come from a combination of dividend payments and stock price appreciation.

As of early 2011, there were approximately 60,000 publicly traded companies in the world with an estimated \$50 trillion[6] market capitalization. The global geographic breakdown was 44 percent United States, 43 percent non-U.S. developed, and 13 percent emerging market.[7] Each segment of the global stock market serves a different function for diversified nonprofit investors.

U.S. Equity

Most nonprofits have growing long-term spending needs; they need at least some capital appreciation. U.S. equities, of course, play a prominent role. The U.S. equity market is segmented into *large-, mid-,* and *small-capitalization stocks.* Large-cap stocks are those with market capitalizations greater than \$10 billion. As Exhibit 3.18 illustrates, large-cap stocks represent the bulk of the total U.S. equity market (as measured by the Russell 3000 Index). They are also the most liquid segment. The S&P 500 Index, a proxy for large cap, has produced an average annualized return of 9.9 percent from 1926 through 2010. Large-cap U.S. stocks have lower expected returns than smaller-cap or emerging-market equities, but they have historically exhibited less volatility.

Small-cap stocks have market capitalizations of \$2 billion and below. Nearly every large-cap company was once a small cap company. Smaller companies have the ability to grow faster, but the opportunity comes with greater risk. Small-cap stocks lack the liquidity of larger-cap names. They also can have newer and less proven business models and a harder time accessing capital markets.

Mid-cap stocks fall between large and small, and currently have market caps between \$2 and \$10 billion. There is an arbitrary divide between smaller large cap and larger mid-cap stocks, so mid-cap stocks have high correlation to both large and small-cap stocks. One must be aware of the overlap among mid cap, small cap, and large cap portfolios. Many nonprofits invest only with large- and small cap managers, knowing that both managers will invest to some degree in mid-cap stocks.

EXHIBIT 3.18 U.S. Equity Market Capitalization

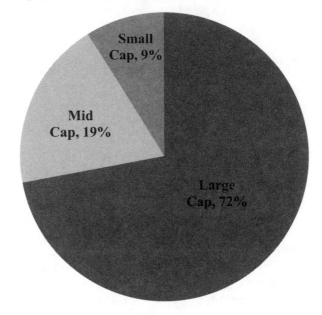

The U.S. equity market can also be divided by *style* (value and growth). Value stocks are relatively cheap based on a valuation metric such as price to book value (P/B) or price to earnings (P/E). Higher dividend yields are another characteristic of typical value stocks. On the other end of the spectrum, growth stocks are supposed to achieve above-average growth as measured by earnings or sales growth. Growth stocks generally have higher P/B and P/E metrics. It is important to maintain exposure to both styles because each cycles in and out of favor. For example, growth stocks significantly underperformed value stocks during the 2000 to 2002 bear market, while value stocks underperformed during the 2008 to 2009 bear market. Some academics argue that over the very long term, value stocks have outperformed growth stocks, but there is considerable debate over whether this is a statistical anomaly, a byproduct of faulty index construction, or a true market inefficiency.

U.S. equities are a core engine of growth in a portfolio. While the United States may not have the highest expected economic or corporate profit growth rates, the U.S. stock market is the most developed and widely traded in the world. U.S. equities can also provide nonprofit investors with a partial hedge against inflation because companies have some ability to pass through inflated input costs to customers. U.S. equities should be core holdings in most diversified nonprofit portfolios.

Non-U.S. Developed Markets Equity

U.S. institutional investors began to invest in foreign-equity markets in the mid 1970s. Over the past 40 years, U.S.-based investors have increased the percentage allocated to foreign stocks, in large part based on the diversification benefits.

Launched in 1970, the Morgan Stanley Capital International Europe, Australasia, and Far East (MSCI EAFE) Index was designed to represent the equity performance

EXHIBIT 3.19 MSCI EAFE Index Country Allocation (December 31, 2010)

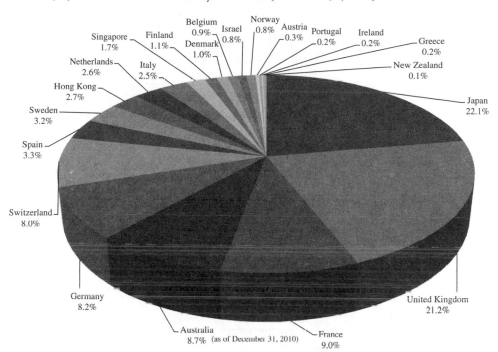

of developed markets, excluding the United States and Canada. The Index consists of the 22 developed-market countries shown in Exhibit 3.19. MSCI categorizes companies by country of incorporation or by principal trading exchange.

World trade has grown dramatically since the 1970s; the trend accelerated in the 1990s. The *North American Free Trade Agreement* (NAFTA), *World Trade Organization* (WTO), and the creation of the *European Union* have all helped spur the forces of globalization. Historically, home market performance was the primary driver of a stock's results. In more recent years, however, globalization has led to greater economic interdependence and higher correlation of stocks across countries. However, diversification benefits persist. Nowadays, investors allocate to non-U.S. equities not only for diversification, but also excess return potential. The 40,000 publicly traded non-U.S. stocks represent a massive opportunity set for U.S.-based investors.

Like U.S.-based indices, foreign-developed equity indices are categorized by size (large versus small) and style (growth versus value). *Large-cap foreign companies* dominate (approximately 70 percent of total market cap), but the small- and mid-cap stocks are prominent as well. Just as in the United States, foreign equity managers are becoming more specialized by strategy.

With greater potential return come additional risks. Although foreign developed equity markets have grown over the years, liquidity is still a factor. For example, Belgium warrants a liquidity premium relative to the larger and deeper markets in Japan and Germany. Currency is also a risk when investing in foreign equities. Currency can hinder (or aid) returns when they are translated back into U.S. dollars.

Foreign equities are highly correlated with some other classes like *emerging market equities*. However, they have had extremely low correlation to asset classes like TIPS and other U.S. fixed-income securities.

Emerging-Markets Equity

Emerging markets are countries whose social or business activity is undergoing rapid growth as they industrialize. Stock markets in emerging-market countries have grown at a blistering pace over the past several decades. The *MSCI Emerging Markets Free Index* was created in 1988. At that time, emerging markets made up about 1 percent of global equity market capitalization. As of early 2011, the index had more than 800 stocks domiciled in 26 developing countries and had grown to about 13 percent of the world equity market capitalization (see Exhibit 3.20).

The economies of many emerging-market countries have evolved dramatically over the past two decades. In the 1990s, emerging-market economies were primarily driven by commodities and exports. Today, many emerging economies have flourishing middle classes and import products from developed and other emerging-market countries. Emerging economies have become a major contributor to global economic growth.

Roughly 50 percent of the emerging-markets universe is large cap. Mid cap and small cap comprise 30 percent and 20 percent, respectively. The delineation of

EXHIBIT 3.20   MSCI Emerging Markets Free Index (December 31, 2010)

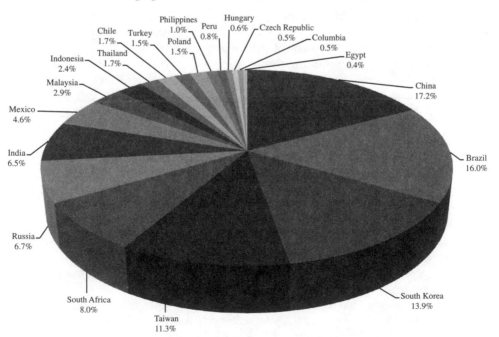

growth and value styles in emerging markets is not as common as it is in developed markets.

Emerging markets have exhibited exponential growth over the past decade. A key driver of higher returns has been higher expected economic growth relative to developed countries. While high GDP growth does not guarantee high equity returns, it is certainly an important building block.

Yet again, diversification benefits are a prime reason for investing in emerging-market equities. Emerging markets can experience above-trend growth at the same time that developed countries experience below-trend growth. An example is Japan versus China over the past decade. Japan has been mired in recession, while China, a close geographical neighbor, has flourished economically.

Emerging-markets currency fluctuations relative to the U.S. dollar can be even more pronounced than fluctuations among developed-country currencies. Currency fluctuation (or even a currency crisis) creates investment risk for an investor in emerging markets. Unstable political environments and less robust regulatory frameworks add to the risks as well.

Emerging-market equities can also be more costly to transact and hold. Thin trading, under-developed exchanges, and other factors add to the expense. Commingled funds are usually the optimal investment vehicle unless the mandate is large.

Conclusion

Traditional asset classes will continue to be core investments in the vast majority of nonprofit fund portfolios. From TIPS to emerging market stocks, traditional asset classes may lack the *cachet* of alternative-asset classes, but they remain effective tools.

Notes

1. Source: Bank for International Settlements. Includes money market instruments, notes, and bonds.
2. Money market funds seek to maintain a stable net asset value (NAV); if a fund's NAV drops below $1.00 it is said that the fund "broke the buck." The Community Bankers U.S. Government Fund and the Reserve Primary Fund broke the buck in 1994 and 2008, respectively.
3. JP Morgan, EM Debt as an Asset Class, January 2004; JP Morgan DataQuery, December 2010. PineBridge Investments, The Rise and Rise of Emerging Market Debt, January 2011.
4. JP Morgan DataQuery, December 2010.
5. Source: Fitch U.S. High Yield Default Index.
6. Bloomberg LP.
7. Dimensional Fund Advisors, February 2011.

CHAPTER 4

Traditional Asset Class
Manager Selection

Once a nonprofit has formulated its asset allocation strategy, the next step is to select investment managers to implement it. Effective manager selection is critically important to ensure the success of the nonprofit's long-term mission, but is not an easy proposition. Despite an investment committee's good intentions, certain factors may overwhelm the process and lead to poor decisions.

First of all, effective manager selection is a time- and labor-intensive process that requires specialized skills. There are thousands of money managers and more starting up every day. Secondly, there is no magic bullet—no single objective metric that assures an investment manager will perform well in the future. The disclaimer "past performance is no guarantee of future results" is a major understatement. "Past performance has almost zero predictive value" is closer to the mark.

Complicating matters further, when overwhelmed by a labor-intensive process the human tendency is to bypass a robust effort in favor of the familiar or the simple—a bank, a local money manager, or a reference from a friend. Managers selected in this fashion are often unqualified or inappropriate for the mandate and can lead to subpar overall results. Asset allocation accounts for the bulk of portfolio return. Therefore, if the nonprofit must opt for simplicity, it is better to opt for passive management of each segment of the portfolio rather than "Old Charlie at the bank."

There are two primary reasons why nonprofits should be prudent and thorough in the selection process. First, ineffective manager selection can result in millions of dollars in opportunity costs. Secondly, the primary duty of a fiduciary is to manage a prudent investment process. Uniform Prudent Management of Institutional Funds Act (UPMIFA) (see Chapter 15) outlines prudent practices for fiduciaries of other types of funds. Failing to follow and document a prudent manager-selection process can have dire consequences for individual fiduciaries.

Manager Search and Selection

Effective manager selection is a laborious multi-faceted process that can be broken down into the following five stages. Each stage has numerous steps, as illustrated by Exhibit 4.1.

EXHIBIT 4.1 Stages of Effective Manager Selection

Stage I - Initial Screens
- ➢ Style analysis
- ➢ Multi-factor risk/return model

Stage II - Qualitative Review
- ➢ Portfolio composition
- ➢ Expenses
- ➢ Assets managed
- ➢ Market capitalization
- ➢ Duration

Stage III - Questionnaire and Analysis
- ➢ Preliminary diligence
- ➢ Custom RFP addressing
  - ▪ People
  - ▪ Process
  - ▪ Philosophy
  - ▪ Performance
- ➢ Risk management
  - ▪ Compliance
  - ▪ Counterparty risks
  - ▪ Securities lending

Stage IV - Deep Dive Research
- ➢ Thorough evaluation of:
  - ▪ The 4 "Ps"
  - ▪ Compliance systems
  - ▪ Trading process
  - ▪ Portfolio construction
  - ▪ Buy/Sell discipline
  - ▪ Composite methodology
  - ▪ Portfolio holdings
  - ▪ Organizational structure
  - ▪ Regulatory concerns
  - ▪ Succession plans
  - ▪ Final analysis
  - ▪ Written profile

Stage V - Finalist Selection
- ➢ Art and science
- ➢ Best fit
- ➢ Defining expectations

Stage I: Initial Screens

The first step is to identify the entire peer group of managers within a particular mandate. For traditional asset classes, managers' names, performance histories, and contact information can be found in databases which can be purchased for a moderate fee. Examples are: Morningstar, eVestment Alliance, and Zephyr Associates. For some of the most populous categories like *domestic large cap growth*, the total number of managers within a peer group may number into the thousands and new managers spring up by the day.

Once all the managers in the peer group are identified, the next step is to perform a style screen in the mandate. If the mandate is domestic large-cap growth, one wants to screen out managers that are not pure to that investing style. A large-cap growth manager who allocates significantly to small-cap stocks, foreign stocks, or bonds is inappropriate because he causes inadvertent overlap with those categories and should be screened out.

The easiest way to win a tomato-growing contest is to paint a pumpkin red and hope nobody notices. A domestic large-cap growth manager whose historical outperformance was generated by investing outside large-cap growth has painted his pumpkin red! The initial style screen is to ensure that only "tomatoes" are entered into the contest.

William Sharpe's returns-based regression methodology plots managers' returns relative to pure style indices. This analysis identifies managers' positions on a *style map*. One should pay particular attention to style drift because this is a key red flag. *Returns-based analysis* may be complemented by *holdings-based analysis.* Returns-based analysis tells how the manager *behaved*; holdings-based analysis looks at the actual positions he or she held. The holdings at various points in time reveal the portfolio's fundamental characteristics and sector exposure relative to the benchmark. Although using both methods paints the most accurate picture, returns-based analysis is easier and cheaper. The data (historical returns) are readily available for analysis.

Exhibit 4.2 illustrates a U.S. equity four-corners-style map. The upper left quadrant represents large-cap value stocks (e.g., Russell 1000 Value Index), the bottom left represents small-cap value stocks (e.g., Russell 2000 Value Index), the bottom right represents small-cap growth stocks (e.g., Russell 2000 Growth Index), and the upper right represents large-cap growth stocks (e.g., Russell 1000 Growth Index). The exhibit shows two managers who categorize themselves as large-cap growth. One manager is named "Tomato" and the other "Pumpkin Painted Red." Managers with style plots located in the upper-right-hand side of Exhibit 4.2 have been pure to their large-cap growth style and should continue to be evaluated. Managers that skew down or to the left have a small cap or value orientation and should be screened out.

As Exhibit 4.2 illustrates, "Tomato" has been pure to a large cap growth investing style over multiple rolling three-year periods. On the other hand, "Pumpkin Painted Red" has skewed left toward value and down toward small cap at times. "Pumpkin Painted Red" should be screened out from the search process because the portfolio already has managers covering small cap and value mandates. Just as a small pumpkin may be larger than a giant tomato, the impure manager may exhibit outsized historical returns because value or small cap were recently in favor. If you don't identify and screen out the painted pumpkin, it will one day disappoint you when the large cap growth style returns to favor and your manager underperforms. If it is a pumpkin, it should compete and be judged against other pumpkins.

Once you have eliminated managers that are not a good fit, the next step is a multi-factor performance screen. The screening metrics can be broken down into the following broad categories:

- *Outperformance.* such as historic excess risk-adjusted returns over a benchmark across multiple rolling periods.
- *Consistency.* such as high batting average versus an appropriate benchmark, good up and down market outperformance, or low tracking error.
- *Consistent outperformance.* such as excess return per unit of tracking error (also known as information ratio).

As already mentioned, strong past performance is a poor predictor for strong future performance. However, managers with consistently *poor* historical risk-adjusted performance over multiple market cycles are unlikely to be strong performers in the future and can be quickly and efficiently screened out. Performance numbers can be useful to screen for managers with certain desirable characteristics, but more importantly, these screens can be used to identify undesirable managers to winnow the list to a manageable size for critical future due diligence.

EXHIBIT 4.2 U.S. Equity Style Map: Painted Pumpkin versus Tomato

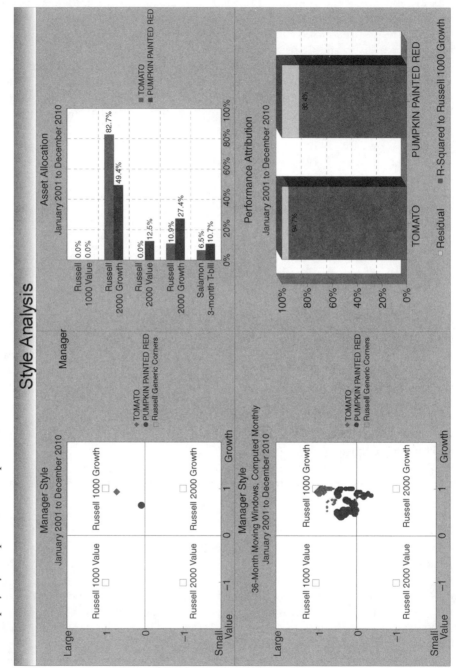

Created with Zephyr StyleADVISOR.

A manager can generate outperformance over a multi-year period with a single terrific quarter, so historical excess returns are not enough for a robust screening process. For example, one strong quarter can keep a trailing three-year performance number looking good for three years. It is unwise to conclude that a manager with a single terrific quarter driving the entire historical outperformance is skillful. A manager who can generate consistent outperformance for a majority of quarters is preferred, which is why *batting average* is an important measure. A high batting average is an indicator of a manger's ability to sustain performance.

The most common mistake made by investors using manager performance screens or ranks is the outsized weight put on the most recent short-term period. Many investors put far too much emphasis on the most recent three-year (or five-year) period. As several DiMeo Schneider & Associates, LLC studies have shown, virtually all of the best long-term performing managers go through three- and five-year periods where they perform poorly relative to their index or peer group. Putting too much weight on the most recent relatively short-term period will cause one to eliminate many good managers from consideration. Worse, it will result in the inclusion of too many bad but lucky managers in the midst of a fleeting winning streak.

Stage II: Qualitative Review

In the second step, one should qualitatively evaluate managers that made it through the initial screens. Research shows that one of the most meaningful predictors of future performance is expense. Managers with the highest expenses are more likely to underperform. Imagine an Olympic gold medalist who had to clear significantly higher hurdles than his less-talented competitors. He would likely lose the race. History shows that screening out high-expense managers is a winning strategy.

Another important screen is *assets under management.* You want your manager to have sufficient size to be viable. A manager who does not attract enough money to become profitable can quickly disappear. Larger asset bases can allow expenses to be dispersed over a wider base. However, too large of an asset base can hinder a manager's ability to effectively maneuver among the markets. This is especially true for small cap and other more capacity-constrained asset classes. Manager performance suffers when assets bloat beyond the strategy's capacity. Make sure that you aggregate all share classes and separate accounts when reviewing a manager's asset balance.

Review the portfolio's allocation to equity, fixed-income, cash, and other asset classes. The cash component of an equity portfolio should be small. After all, you do not pay large fees to manage cash. Also, be wary of domestic equity products with large foreign exposure. Fixed-income portfolios may hold preferred stocks, convertibles, and other nontraditional bonds. Occasionally these securities are used as a tactical play, but should not be a significant component of total assets. In fixed-income portfolios, the use of cash may actually be strategic. The manager may use cash to shorten portfolio duration—a legitimate use.

Finally, look for a stable organization with minimal turnover among investment professionals. The longer the manager's tenure, the more meaningful the track record. A manager should be in place for at least three years and preferably much longer. Discount any quantitative performance analysis of a performance track-record that pre-dates the current manager.

Stage III: Questionnaire and Analysis

The first step of this stage should be to set up a preliminary due diligence call or meeting with the manager. As follow-up to a promising introductory call or meeting, send a request for proposal (RFP) to the manager with heavy emphasis on the "four Ps" (*people, process, philosophy, and performance*).

As a part of the analysis, consider the history and stability of the organization. Review its ownership structure, tenure of personnel, and goals for growth of assets. Can the firm grow substantially without corrupting the investment process? Has the firm been subject to any litigation or censured by a regulatory body? What compliance systems are in place?

How many members are on the investment team, and what is their tenure? Review their credentials to determine investment acumen. Are they knowledgeable in their strategy? How are they compensated? Does the compensation package include incentive bonuses? Are they performance-based or asset-based? How much of their personal money is invested in the product? What is the succession plan if a key member of the team departs?

Does the product have a well-defined investment process? Is management able to clearly articulate the buy and sell disciplines? Is this process driven by an individual or an investment committee? Do the managers and the analysts articulate a consistent message? What are the normal minimum and maximum percentages of a total portfolio that would be invested in any one sector, industry, or stock (both absolute and relative to a benchmark)? Can management override these guidelines? Are checks and balances in place to ensure that the investment process is implemented uniformly across all accounts?

During this stage of the process, it is important to take a detailed look at the manager's performance. Examine performance over various market cycles, including up and down markets. How does a manager perform when his or her style is in favor compared to when it is out of favor?

Stage IV: Deep Dive Research

RFP responses are designed to paint the manager in the best possible light. If a manager cannot make him or herself look presentable in an RFP response, move on to another manager. By this point, one should already have a strong understanding of how the manager performed. The key question is "why?" This is where one needs to verify that their "alpha story" has in fact been the actual source of any historical outperformance (called *alpha*). For example, if a manager states that he is a "bottom-up stock picker", but the firm's historical outperformance was driven by positive sector selection (while stock selection had a negative impact), that's an inconsistency in the alpha story. One should eliminate managers that may look good from a superficial standpoint (e.g., performance, style, fees), but where the alpha story simply does not add up.

Ultimately, the goal is to gain some confidence in the manager's ability to generate outperformance going forward. Decisions should not be made in this meeting; it should be an information-gathering session to answer any gaps raised by the research. This information is then used to put together performance expectations for the manager that can be compared to actual past performance. Review any inconsistencies between the past performance and expectations in follow-up meetings. If expectations are clear and there are no red flags, follow the manager closely. Every month provides another data point to assess and better understand how their process and performance correlate.

One should meet with the prospective manager at least once and usually several times. These face-to-face meetings are a chance to assess aspects of the investment manager that don't fall neatly into a questionnaire response. Do they seem confident? What does their body language tell you? Do they seem to parse their words or are their answers forthright? It is also a chance to ask the difficult questions. Visiting a manager's offices provides access to staff members whose answers may be less glib than those of the marketing team. Both research and operations staff play critical roles in the investment process, but are rarely interviewed and reviewed by investors. The ultimate goal of deep dive research is to produce a short list of quality managers from which to choose.

Stage V: Finalist Selection

By this point the committee should be comfortable that all finalists are high quality. The ultimate selection is a combination of art and science. Which manager's philosophy best aligns with the overall investment strategy of the nonprofit's portfolio? Which manager best complements the other managers in the portfolio? Individual investment committee members will bring different perspectives to the selection process and have their own criteria. Hopefully, these perspectives come together so the manager selected best fits the mandate. This is a highly subjective effort; no two investment committees or members may share exactly the same world view. One investment committee may prefer the bottom-up, theme-driven stock-picking process of Manager A; another may prefer the quantitative model-driven stock-selection approach of Manager B.

At the time the manager is hired, it is essential for the investment committee to have enough conviction in the manager that they will be able to stomach the inevitable performance lulls. Investment committees that gravitate to the hottest-performing manager need to be careful. If you select a manager based solely on strong past performance, you are setting yourself up for disappointment. A combination of unrealistic expectations and disappointment quickly devolves into a destructive "fire at trough and hire at peak" cycle. The investment committee must understand the manager's process and especially the kinds of market environments when that process will be out of favor. Within any specific mandate, there are environments that will favor or punish different sub-styles.

Investment Vehicles

Once one selects a manager, the proper investment vehicle must still be selected. The easiest vehicle is a mutual fund. A mutual fund is a commingled "investment management company" registered with the Securities and Exchange Commission (SEC). Nonprofits that are able to allocate higher balances qualify for institutional share classes that have lower expense ratios.

Other types of commingled vehicles are not as highly regulated as mutual funds and do not necessarily trade daily. However, they may offer the investor the opportunity to invest with a manager who may have a large minimum account size. Commingled funds, as their name implies, commingle investors' assets to provide scale. Commingled funds can use their scale to reduce custody and trading costs and can provide increased liquidity and diversification. Finally, the commingling of assets can allow the manager to reduce fees for each incremental dollar in the portfolio and, therefore, to all the investors in the fund.

For those who want segregated custody of their own assets (and who have the size), a *separate account* offers certain advantages. It allows for some customization such as excluding certain types of investments for socially responsible or mission-based reasons. One can also negotiate management fees on separate accounts, possibly below those of a commingled fund or mutual fund. However, a separate account does have the potential for higher custody and trading fees because it lacks the scale of a commingled vehicle. In addition, a separate account may not have enough assets to provide a fully diversified portfolio of holdings. If a manager can only buy a few securities because of the size of the account, the ability to customize or negotiate fees is negated and the nonprofit investor would be better off in a commingled vehicle.

Active versus Passive Management

Passive management is a low-expense approach that seeks to replicate the performance of a market index. Passive management grew out of the realization that the majority of active managers do not keep pace with market index proxies (after expenses). Since active management is a zero-sum game around the market return, and fees are greater than zero, most investment managers are doomed to underperform. So if you are unable to identify skillful managers, or don't believe investment skill exists, you should simply try to keep pace with the market.

Some asset classes are strong candidates for passive management. In relatively efficient market segments, where index returns are easily replicable on a cost-effective basis and manager persistency is particularly poor, investors should strongly consider passive management. On the other hand, where indexing is costly or replication is difficult, cost-effective active management may be preferred.

Exhibit 4.3 demonstrates one way to view the opportunity-set for active versus passive management. The horizontal axis illustrates the ease or difficulty of replicating the passive returns of an asset class. Many passive investing advocates ignore the fact that in certain categories, index funds do a poor job of replicating an index's return stream. However in many categories, including large-cap U.S. stocks (the S&P 500 Index), passive management is a fairly straightforward proposition; an index fund manager can fully replicate the S&P 500 Index by holding the 500 stocks in proper proportion. The 500 stocks have enough liquidity that managers can minimize implicit and explicit trading costs as cash flows in and out of the fund. There are institutional S&P 500 Index funds with extremely modest expenses.

On the other hand, *high-yield bonds* is an asset class at the opposite end of the spectrum. High-yield bonds are more thinly traded so they are more expensive and

EXHIBIT 4.3 Active and Passive Management Zones

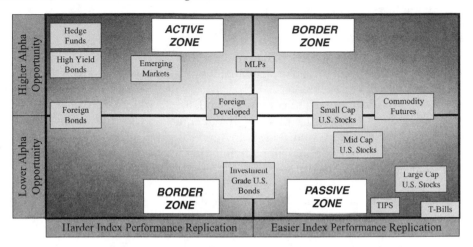

more difficult to trade on a cost-effective basis. A high-yield bond market index may also hold more than 1,500 issues, so attempting to replicate its return stream through a passively managed vehicle can be almost impossible.

The vertical axis in Exhibit 4.3 represents the theoretical opportunity set for a skillful manager to add alpha. The smaller and less liquid areas in the global capital markets are not as picked-over by market participants. They can offer greater opportunities for a skillful manager to exploit security mispricing. For example, high-yield bonds have trading volumes that are much lower than large-cap U.S. stocks and have significantly less analyst coverage.

As Exhibit 4.3 illustrates, there are two key elements required for passive management to work effectively. First, the passive strategy must be employed in a liquid and marketable market segment where low-cost index replication is feasible. Secondly, passive investing makes the most sense in market segments where investors possess fewer informational or trading advantages.

Whether a market index frequently beats active management is irrelevant to the active versus passive debate; what's relevant is whether an index *fund* beats active management. Index funds too have management fees and trading expenses. Some index funds also have significant tracking error to their index (in market segments where replication and trading are challenging). Since an investor cannot actually own an index, the true active versus passive debate should pit the active manager versus an index *fund* rather than the index. In categories where a passively managed index fund is likely to trail an index (by up to 0.50 percent annually) because of replication issues or trading and management expenses, consider this index fund drag when deciding whether to select an index fund or hire an active manager.

If investors cannot be patient with active managers, they should seek passively managed alternatives. The vast majority of long-term top-performing managers experience periods of lousy performance. In March 2010, DiMeo Schneider & Associates, LLC authored "The Next Chapter in the Active versus Passive Management Debate." This study evaluated the persistency of top-quartile mutual funds in

17 different categories during the 10-year period ending December 2009. The following were our key observations:

- 85 percent of 10-year top quartile mutual funds were unable to avoid at least one three-year stretch in the bottom half of their peer groups.
- 62 percent of 10-year top quartile mutual funds were unable to avoid the bottom half during a five-year period.
- Owning the 52nd percentile mutual fund in all 17 categories would have matched the indexed return of a 70-percent equity and 30-percent fixed-income portfolio during the 10-year period. In aggregate, top quartile managers generated +1.6 percent of annual alpha, while bottom quartile managers generated annual alpha of −1.1 percent.
- With few exceptions, the greater an asset class' absolute return during a three-year period, the greater the likelihood and magnitude of median manager underperformance to the index and vice versa. In other words, indices tend to perform better than median managers in up markets and worse in down markets (in part because the managers hold cash).
- Investors often ignored factors that preclude passively managed investment products from keeping pace with the indices they are designed to track. Factors include number of securities in the index, liquidity, and trading frequency to name a few. The impact of each factor depends on the asset class and index. The proliferation of exchange-traded index funds in recent years has allowed us to analyze the impact of these factors in various asset classes.
- For each individual asset class, the active versus passive decision should be viewed as "active manager versus index fund" rather than "active manager versus index." Failure to do so risks overstating the case for passive management.

Falling prey to natural human behavioral tendencies during the manager selection and termination process generally leads to failure. Investment committees need to make better efforts to understand their managers' investment processes, substyles, and investment philosophies before investing to develop the confidence and patience required for long-term success. Otherwise, they should invest passively.

When to Terminate a Manager

Because all good investment managers eventually suffer through poor-performing stretches, knowing when to retain or fire them is just as important (and tricky) as the manager selection decision. Simply terminating managers when they underperform for a short stretch (i.e., three years) is a losing proposition because virtually all great managers will have their dog days. If your termination criteria are solely performance-based, then you're going to one day fire all your managers. As previously discussed, 85 percent of 10-year top quartile managers had at least one three-year period when they finished in the bottom half of the peer group, and 62 percent spent at least one five-year period in the bottom half.

Developing realistic expectations is a critical step in stage V of the manager-selection process. It is important to revisit those expectations during a manager's inevitable performance lulls. Understanding the process and sub-style at the outset arms you with important information to make a wise termination or retention decision. If performance is suffering because the manager's sub-style is temporarily out of favor, that's fine and forgivable; all great managers will one day underperform for this reason. The following are valid criteria to terminate a manager:

- *Philosophy, Process, or Personnel changes.* A sound investment philosophy, a strong repeatable investment process, and the high quality of investment personnel should have all been prime reasons for hiring the manager in the first place. If key members leave the firm or change roles, it is cause for alarm and can be a reason to immediately terminate a manager. If the manager changes his or her stripes (philosophy or process), that should also sound an alarm.
- *Unacceptable Change in Expectations.* When the manager was hired, you should have developed realistic expectations about performance consistency. If you realize that your original expectations are no longer realistic or valid, it is time to cut your losses and move on.
- *Questionable Ongoing Strategy Viability.* The market can evolve away from a historically successful investment strategy, making it unlikely to outperform going forward. For example, a once-unique quantitative model now has too many competitors competing for the same fleeting alpha source
- *Ethical Concerns.* Ethical misconduct is a reason for immediate termination. Fiduciary duty requires holding investment managers to a very high standard.

Exhibit 4.4 presents a helpful framework to determine whether a manager should be terminated for performance reasons. The key determination is whether the underperformance is consistent with expectation. For example, a conservative fixed-income manager who strategically over weights U.S. Treasuries is destined to underperform when corporate bond spreads tighten. At the time you selected the manager, you should have developed an expectation for underperformance when corporate spreads tighten. However, if the manager underperforms when his or her style is in favor, it could be a red flag. If the day to shine came and went and the

EXHIBIT 4.4 Manager Termination Matrix

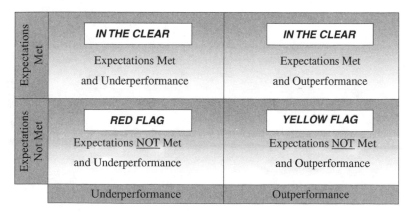

manager failed to keep pace, how is he or she going to perform when his or her style is out of favor?

Conclusion

For eons mothers have chided their peer-pressured progeny with "would you jump off the bridge because your friends did?" Adults are also subject to the herd mentality. Humans are not always logical. We have emotions and the ability to rationalize based on incomplete information.

Many investors become fixated on the money managers with the best absolute performance records. Unfortunately, most investors focus on recent performance with no regard for risk or how that performance was generated. Why is this flawed? Investment styles go in and out of favor, and often the manager with the best recent performance is hired merely because his or her style was in favor or the excessive risk he or she took paid off. All too often managers are hired just as the pendulum swings away from his or her particular sub-style.

If a manager is selected for the right reasons and expectations are properly set, the investment committee will have an easier time making future hire and fire decisions. More importantly, those hire and fire decisions will be in the best interest of the nonprofit's mission. If the manager's style is out of favor at a given point in time, but nothing else has changed, a wise investment committee tends to retain the manager. While nobody likes underperformance, it's worse to make counterproductive knee jerk reactions. Firing a good manager at the low point for performance reasons alone is the classic rookie mistake.

CHAPTER 5

Hedge Funds

University endowments have allocated significant assets to hedge funds over the past two decades. By 2010, the average endowment had 24 percent of its assets invested in hedge funds.[1] In part due to the well-publicized success of some large university endowments, smaller endowments, foundations, museums, libraries, healthcare organizations, and other nonprofit institutions "want to be like Yale." While effective hedge fund investing can help nonprofit investors meet investment objectives, it also brings specialized risks and challenges that must be diligently managed.

Hedge funds have evolved since their introduction 60 years ago. They spread from the United States to Europe, Asia, and the emerging markets. While technical definitions vary across borders, in general, hedge funds are actively managed pools that follow less-conventional investment strategies. They are usually unregistered investment vehicles intended for sophisticated institutional investors and wealthy individuals. In the strictest sense, hedge funds are not an asset class, but rather an amalgam of strategies that invest across asset classes. The term "hedge fund" itself functions as a catchall phrase for private investment partnerships, regardless of whether hedging techniques are actually employed. Like traditional investment managers, hedge funds manage portfolios of securities, have predetermined investment objectives and styles, and employ strategies ranging from conservative to the extremely aggressive. Hedge funds can engage in a variety of investment strategies that include leverage, derivatives trading, and short selling. Unlike traditional active managers, who seek to outperform benchmarks on a relative basis, hedge funds often target positive *absolute* returns regardless of market direction.

The Evolution of Hedge Funds

Alfred Winslow Jones created the first hedge fund in the late 1940s and is widely regarded as the father of the modern hedge fund industry. Jones' inspiration was to combine speculative tools to create what he considered a more conservative or "hedged" investment strategy. He used leverage to buy more shares, but also employed short selling to reduce exposure to market risk. He bought as many stocks as he sold short, so overall market moves up or down offset each other. His objective was to render the overall market's direction irrelevant and generate positive returns by buying and shorting the right stocks.

Jones' pioneering fund avoided the requirements of The Investment Company Act of 1940 by restricting itself to 99 investors in a limited partnership structure and charged a 20 percent incentive fee on gains. However, unlike most modern hedge funds, fees were not levied unless the fund actually profited. The private partnership structure, the incentive fee, and the blending of long and short positions remain core elements of the hedge fund industry today.

Hedge funds spent the 30 years between 1950 and 1980 in relative obscurity. However, by the mid 1980s, *long-short equity* and *global macro* managers dominated the landscape as hedge fund legends Julian Robertson, George Soros, and others grabbed headlines in the financial press. Media attention deified such managers and drove many wealthy investors to seek out hedge funds for the first time. Hedge fund investing became the topic of boastful high society cocktail party chatter.

The industry's growth accelerated considerably in the 1990s. In 1992 George Soros made a famous (and massively profitable short bet) on the British pound that "broke the Bank of England." Long Term Capital Management's infamous and systemically hazardous implosion in 1998 grabbed the spotlight. According to Hedge Fund Research, hedge fund assets grew from $39 billion in 1990 to $539 billion by 2001. Over the same period, the total number of hedge funds increased more than sevenfold from 610 to 4,454.

Modern Hedge Fund Strategies

The first decade of the twenty-first century was eventful for hedge funds. By the end of 2010, Hedge Fund Research counts 9,200 total hedge funds with nearly $2 trillion in assets. Today's hedge fund landscape is crowded with new specialized strategies sprouting up seemingly overnight.

Exhibit 5.1 shows Hedge Fund Research's classification system at the end of 2010. There are five broad categories: Equity Hedge, Event-Driven, Macro, Relative Value, and Multi-Strategy. Each category is composed of several underlying strategies with varying sub-styles. Many of these strategies, styles, and nuanced sub-styles overlap.

Equity Hedge

Equity hedge managers maintain long and short positions primarily in equity and derivative securities. Portfolio selection can be driven by either quantitative or fundamental strategies. Strategies can be broad (global) or narrow (sector specific) and have ranges of net exposures, leverage, holding periods, and concentrations to various market capitalizations.

The equity hedge category has several sub-strategies:

- *Market neutral* managers often use quantitative techniques to build long-short portfolios, but maintain little directional exposure to the market.
- *Quantitative directional* managers are similar to market neutral managers, but they have greater leeway to maintain directional market exposure.

EXHIBIT 5.1 HFR Hedge Fund Strategy Classification

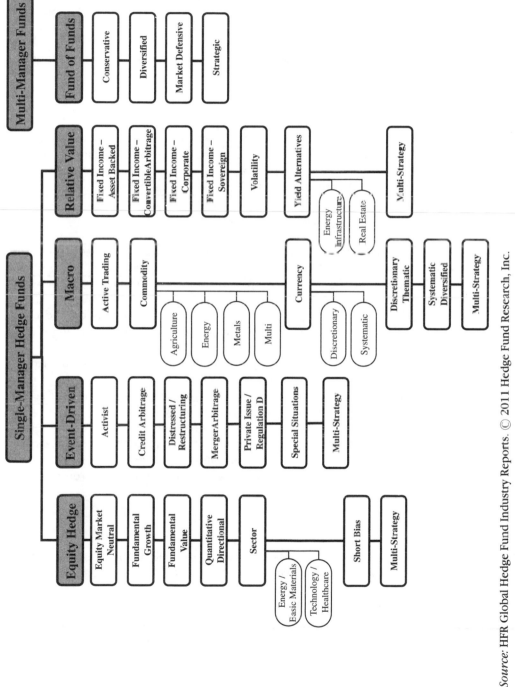

Source: HFR Global Hedge Fund Industry Reports. © 2011 Hedge Fund Research, Inc.

- *Fundamental growth and value* managers follow stock selection processes similar to traditional growth and value managers, but can also employ leverage and short-selling.
- *Sector specialists* concentrate on specific sectors (e.g., healthcare, technology, energy, etc.), but usually maintain net positive market exposure to their sectors.
- *Short-biased* strategies are similar to traditional long-short, but typically maintain varying levels of net short exposure.
- *Multi-strategy equity hedged* managers employ multiple hedged equity strategies within a single portfolio.

Event-Driven

Event-driven managers take positions in companies involved in corporate transactions such as mergers, restructurings, financial distress, tender offers, shareholder buy-backs, debt exchanges, security issuance, or other capital structure events. Security types can range from senior to junior in the capital structure. Such managers frequently use derivatives. Their investment theses are typically fundamentally driven.

The event-driven category has several sub-strategies:

- *Activist* managers seek to gain control to change management or the strategic direction of a company, ostensibly to maximize shareholder value.
- *Credit arbitrage* managers seek to exploit mispricing among debt securities of an issuer.
- *Distressed* managers seek to profit from purchasing deeply discounted credit securities or instruments as a result of a company's actual or impending bankruptcy.
- *Merger arbitrage* managers seek opportunities in equity and equity-related instruments of companies engaged in ownership transactions.
- *Private issue* strategies buy equity and equity-related instruments that are primarily private or illiquid securities of companies.
- *Special situation* managers focus on opportunities in equity and equity related instruments of companies which are engaged in a corporate transaction, security issuance/repurchase, asset sales, division spin-off, or other catalysts.
- *Multi-strategy event-driven managers* employ multiple event-driven strategies within a single portfolio.

Macro

Macro managers take an over-arching economic world view. They engage in strategies where economic change impacts equity, fixed-income, currency, and commodities markets.

The macro category has several sub-strategies:

- *Active trading* strategies employ either discretionary or rules-based high-frequency trading in multiple asset classes.
- *Single commodity* managers trade a single commodity type (e.g., metals, energy, agriculture) using a fundamental, systematic, or technical process.

- *Multi-commodity* managers include both discretionary and systematic commodity strategies. Systematic means that mathematical, algorithmic, and technical models drive portfolio positioning. The systematic commodity trading strategies are often used by Commodity Trading Advisors (CTAs). Discretionary commodity strategies rely on fundamental evaluation of markets, relationships, and influences as they relate to commodity markets.
- *Currency discretionary* strategies rely on fundamental evaluation of market data to trade currency markets. They generally use top-down macroeconomic analysis of variables.
- *Currency systematic* strategies are driven by mathematical, algorithmic, and technical models.
- *Discretionary thematic* strategies trade in equity, interest rates, fixed-income, currency, and commodity markets. They rely on the evaluation of market relationships and influences and a top-down analysis of macroeconomic variables.
- *Systematic diversified* strategies trade multiple asset classes and are driven by mathematical, algorithmic, and technical models.
- *Multi-strategy macro* managers employ a variety of macro strategies within a single portfolio.

Relative Value

Relative value managers seek to exploit value discrepancies between securities. They employ a variety of fundamental and quantitative techniques to develop investment theses. They trade equities, fixed income, convertible bonds, and derivatives.

The relative value category has several sub-strategies:

- *Fixed-income—asset backed* strategies seek to exploit mispriced spread relationships between related fixed-income instruments backed by physical collateral or other financial obligations (i.e., loans, mortgages, credit cards, etc.).
- *Fixed-income—convertible arbitrage* strategies seek to exploit mispricing between a convertible bond and the stock of the issuer. They also may arbitrage spreads between other related instruments.
- *Fixed-income—corporate* strategies seek to exploit the spread between multiple related corporate fixed-income instruments. *Fixed-income-corporate strategies* differ from *event-driven credit arbitrage* in that the former uses general market hedges. Event-driven credit arbitrage typically has little or no net credit market exposure.
- *Fixed-income—sovereign* strategies seek to exploit spreads between a sovereign fixed-income instrument (foreign government bond) and some related instrument (a corporate bond or a derivative contract).
- *Volatility* strategies trade *implied volatility* as an asset class. They use derivative instruments such as options and swaps on the volatility index (VIX) or some other measure of volatility. Volatility exposures can be long, short, neutral, or variable to the direction of implied volatility.
- *Yield alternatives—energy infrastructure* strategies seek to exploit valuation discrepancies between master limited partnerships (MLPs), utilities, or power generators. They typically use fundamental analysis.

■ *Alternatives—Real Estate* strategies seek to exploit the valuation differences between related instruments with exposure to real estate. Strategies are typically fundamentally driven.

■ *Multi-Strategy relative value* seeks to arbitrage spread relationships among any of the above.

Multi-Strategy

A multi-strategy hedge fund allocates capital opportunistically among various strategies and styles. "Multi-strat" managers typically lever the whole portfolio. Total portfolio assets back the obligations of each specific underlying leveraged position. There is an important difference between single multi-strategy managers and multi-strategy fund of funds. Cross collateralization within a single multi-strat manager theoretically allows one errant highly levered strategy or trade to bring down the entire portfolio. A multi-strategy fund of hedge funds allocates capital to several hedge fund firms so this cross collateralization does not occur.

Multi-Manager Fund of Hedge Funds

Funds of hedge funds managers (FOHFs) invest in other hedge funds or managed account programs. A FOHF provides investors with "one-stop shopping" to achieve strategy and manager diversification. A fund of hedge funds may also tactically weight the portfolio toward the strategies and managers they believe are best positioned for the future. The portfolio will typically diversify across a variety of investment managers, investment strategies, and subcategories. However, fund of hedge funds have a double layer of fees.

Why Invest in Hedge Funds?

Why on earth would nonprofit investors want to expose their portfolios to the baffling complexity of hedge funds? Unfortunately, many nonprofit investors invest in hedge funds for reasons that are neither rational nor helpful. A common, and poor, rationale is "Because Harvard and Yale do it." These high-profile institutions have well-trained armies of employees and consultants to vet strategies and managers for the portfolio. Investing in hedge funds without the proper skill and resources is a recipe for disaster. The needed skills and resources are expensive and require significant scale to be cost effective. Depending on the manager and strategy, comprehensive due diligence can cost $50,000 per manager and take several months. A related poor rationale is that hedge funds provide a panacea for dealing with other investment risks. Hedge funds have significant specialized investment risks despite what you might hear from a highly skilled (and incented) hedge fund salesperson.

There are really only two rational reasons to invest in hedge funds. First, you think doing so will improve the risk-adjusted performance of your aggregate nonprofit portfolio. Second, and significantly more importantly, you believe you can do it well. If you can't clear these two hurdles, you would be wise to forgo hedge funds and focus your attention elsewhere.

EXHIBIT 5.2 Efficient Frontiers with and without Hedge Funds (1988 to 2010)

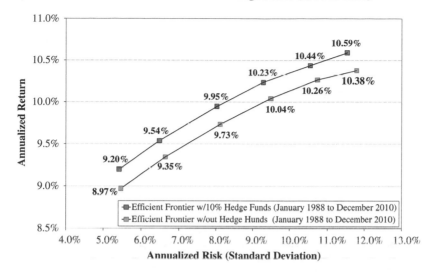

A nonprofit's objective when investing in hedge funds, or any other investment, should be to improve risk adjusted performance. That can either mean increasing expected return without increasing expected risk or reducing expected risk without decreasing expected return. Exhibit 5.2 illustrates a theoretical 23-year performance history (January 1988 to December 2010) for six well-diversified portfolios along two frontiers; one includes and the other excludes hedge funds. The six portfolios on each frontier represent a range from 70 percent fixed income to 11 percent fixed income with the remainder allocated to equities or other non-hedge fund alternative investments. This range is meant to illustrate a spectrum of investment objectives and risk constraints that are applicable to different nonprofit fund pools. Except for hedge funds, both frontiers include the same asset classes; *cash, TIPS, U.S. investment-grade bonds, foreign currency hedged and unhedged bonds, high-yield bonds, U.S. stocks, foreign developed stocks, emerging-market stocks, real estate, energy infrastructure MLPs, and commodity futures.* Indices were used for asset class proxies and monthly rebalancing was used for illustrative purposes (see Exhibit 5.3 for details).

We must note that investing directly in indices is impossible, but for the purpose of this exercise is used to illustrate historical risk-adjusted performance with as few biases as possible. The *HFN Fund of Funds—Multi-Strategy Index* was used as the performance proxy for a diversified portfolio of hedge fund strategies. This index represents a peer group of multi-strategy fund of hedge funds. As we'll discuss later, hedge fund indices have uniquely flawed construction methods that lead to performance biases. Therefore, review the performance history of any hedge fund index with some skepticism.

As Exhibit 5.2 shows, a 10 percent hedge fund index allocation increased the historical returns along the entire frontier by approximately 0.20 percent annually, without increasing volatility. Over a 23-year period, the difference between compounding at a 10.23 percent versus a 10.04 percent annual rate for a $100 million portfolio is

EXHIBIT 5.3 Asset Class Performance Metrics (1988 to 2010)

January 1, 1988-December 31, 2010 Performance Metrics

	Cash	TIPS	U.S. Bonds	Int'l Bonds (50-50 H and UH)	HY Bonds	Large Caps U.S.	Small Caps U.S.	REITs	Int'l Equity	Em. Mkts. Equity	Commodity Future	Hedge Funds Portfolio	MLPs
Geometric Annualized Returns	4.1%	7.6%	7.3%	6.8%	9.0%	9.8%	10.1%	8.6%	5.8%	14.1%	12.3%	10.3%	16.7%
Annualized Standard Deviation	0.6%	5.4%	4.0%	5.4%	8.3%	14.9%	19.2%	19.9%	17.6%	24.2%	17.4%	5.5%	15.0%
Growth of $1 million	$2.5	$5.4	$5.1	$4.6	$7.3	$8.6	$9.1	$6.7	$3.7	$20.6	$14.5	$9.4	$35.1
Maximum Calendar Year Return	9%	18%	18%	19%	56%	38%	47%	37%	39%	79%	46%	26%	76%
Minimum Calendar Year Return	0.1%	−2.9%	−2.9%	−2.0%	−26.2%	−37.0%	−33.8%	−39.8%	−43.1%	−53.2%	−39.5%	−20.5%	−36.9%
Maximum Drawdown (1988 to present)	N.A.	−12.1%	−5.2%	−5.4%	−33.1%	−50.9%	−52.9%	−70.9%	−56.4%	−61.4%	−59.0%	−21.1%	−41.1%
Date Drawdown Began	N.A.	Feb. 2008	Jan. 1994	Nov. 1988	May 2007	Oct. 2007	May 2007	Jan. 2007	Oct. 2007	Oct. 2007	Jun. 2008	Oct. 2007	Jun. 2007
Date Drawdown Ended	N.A.	Oct. 2008	Jun. 1994	May 1989	Nov. 2008	Feb. 2009	Feb. 2009	Feb. 2009	Feb. 2009	Feb. 2009	Feb. 2009	Dec. 2008	Dec. 2008
Duration of Drawdown (Years)	N.A.	0.7	0.4	0.5	1.5	1.3	1.8	2.1	1.3	1.3	0.7	2.1	1.5
2000 to 2002 Bear: August 31, 2000 to September 30, 2002	7.6%	30.4%	23.4%	16.1%	−6.0%	−44.7%	−30.6%	21.0%	42.2%	−34.0%	27.5%	9.7	54.0
2007 to 2009 Bear: October 31, 2007 to February 28, 2009	2.5%	1.0%	6.1%	6.0%	−26.2%	−50.9%	−52.0%	−67.1%	−56.4%	−61.4%	−43.6%	−21.0%	−32.7%
Return from October 31, 2007 to December 31, 2010	2.7%	20.2%	21.3%	19.4%	30.6%	−12.8%	−0.9%	−14.3%	−22.8%	−6.8%	2.4%	−9.4%	46.1%

Historical performance statistics were generated from the following indexes:

Asset Class	Dates Used	Most Recent Index Proxy	Prior Index Proxy	Dates Used
Cash	1/1979-12/2010	Citigroup 3-month T-Bill	N.A.	N.A.
TIPS	3/1997-12/2010	Citigroup Inflation-Linked Securities	Barclays U.S. Aggregate Bond Index	1/1979-4/1997
U.S. Bonds	1/1979-12/2010	Barclays U.S. Aggregate Bond Index	N.A.	N.A.
Int'l Bonds (H)	1/1985-12/2010	Citigroup Foreign Bond (H)	Barclays U.S. Aggregate Bond Index	1/1979-12/1984
Int'l Bonds (UH)	1/1985-12/2010	Citigroup Foreign Bond (UH)	Barclays U.S. Aggregate Bond Index	1/1979-12/1984
HY Bond	12/1984-12/2010	Merrill Lynch High Yield Master	Barclays U.S. Aggregate Bond Index	1/1979-10/1984
Large Cap	1/1979-12/2010	S&P 500	N.A.	N.A.
Small Cap	1/1979-12/2010	Russell 2000	N.A.	N.A.
REIT	1/1979-12/2010	DJ Wilshire Real Estate Sec.	N.A.	N.A.
Int'l Equity	1/1979-12/2010	MSCI EAFE	N.A.	N.A.
Em. Mkt. Eq.	1/1988-12/2010	MSCI Emerging Markets Free	MSCI EAFE	1/1979-12/1987
TIPS/Commodities	1/1991-12/2010	DJ-UBS Commodity Index + Citi Infl-Linked Securities (1997 to present) and Barclays Agg–Citigroup 3-Month T-Bill (1991 to 1997)	Goldman Sachs Commodity Index + Barclays Agg-Citigroup 3-Month T-bil	1/1979-12/1990
Hedge Funds Portfolio	1/1982-12/2010	HFN Fund of Funds - Multi-Strategy Index	HFN Hedge Fund Aggregate Average	1/1979-12/1981
MLPs	1/1991-12/2010	Alerian MLP Index (1996 to present), Atlantic MLP Index (1991 to 1995), Wachovia MLP Index (1950 to 1991)	Goldman Sachs Commodity + Barclays Agg-Citigroup 3-Month T-Bill	1/1979-12/1990

about $37 million. We again stress that it was impossible to have invested directly in indices over the past 23 years, and this analysis is for illustrative purposes only.

During this 23-year period, the HFN Fund of Funds Multi-Strategy Index had an annualized return of 10.3 percent with a standard deviation of 5.5 percent. Over the same period, the S&P 500 Index returned 9.8 percent with a 14.9 percent standard deviation, and the Barclays Aggregate Bond Index returned 7.3 percent with 4.0 percent standard deviation. Hedge funds had an R^2 of 0.18 to the S&P 500 Index, meaning approximately 18 percent of hedge funds' return variance could be explained by large-cap U.S. stocks. Hedge funds had an R^2 of 0.01 to Barclays Aggregate U.S. Bond Index, meaning approximately 1 percent of hedge funds' variance could be explained by U.S. investment-grade bonds. Exhibit 5.3 shows the index proxies used to represent each asset class and their historical performance from 1988 to 2010. Allocating to hedge funds over this period improved the risk-adjusted performance of a portfolio, regardless of where that portfolio falls on the risk-reward spectrum. The historical outperformance was driven by the hedge fund index's relatively high Sharpe Ratio (return per unit of risk) as well as its relatively low correlation to other asset classes in the portfolio.

As a skeptic once quipped, "I've never seen a back-test that didn't work!" So now that you see how hedge funds are *supposed* to add value within a diversified nonprofit portfolio, what's the best way to determine if they really can add value going forward? In order to answer that question, we put together a forward-looking asset allocation model. This model quantifies the expected 10-year forecasted return for various portfolio mixes by aggregating the risks, returns, and correlation coefficients of all underlying assets. The case study in the Appendix has more information on capital market assumptions, including return, risk, and correlation forecasts for each asset class, but Exhibit 5.6 summarizes the (2011 to 2020) 10-year forecast assumptions.

Exhibit 5.4 illustrates a 10-year forecast for the same portfolio mixes illustrated in Exhibit 5.2. In the forecast model, large-cap stocks have an expected return of 8.1 percent. Investment-grade U.S. bonds have an expected return of 2.9 percent, reflecting the average yield-to-maturity of the Barclays Aggregate U.S. Bond index as of December 31, 2010. In Exhibit 5.4, the expected portfolio return for a diversified portfolio of hedge funds is 8.5 percent. If these forecasts are reasonable, hedge funds should improve the expected annualized return of portfolios along the frontier by 0.35 percent to 0.50 percent without increasing risk.

If one believes an 8.5 percent return forecast (after expenses) for a diversified multi-strategy portfolio of "skilled" hedge funds is a reasonable assumption, a 10 percent hedge fund allocation can add significant risk-adjusted performance to a portfolio. On the other hand, if 8.5 percent seems too optimistic, Exhibit 5.5 illustrates the same model, but with a 5.0 percent expected return, while holding all other variables constant (i.e., returns for non-hedge fund asset classes, volatility for all assets, and correlations for all assets). In this illustration, hedge funds, with a 5 percent expected return neither add nor detract significantly from the portfolio in terms of risk or reward. Therefore, one threshold for investing in hedge funds may be whether you believe your diversified multi-strategy hedge fund portfolio will be able to generate *at least* a 5.0 percent return. The greater the hedge fund portfolio's expected return above this threshold level, the stronger the rationale for allocating to hedge funds. This 5 percent return threshold may be applicable in a 2011 capital markets environment, but may not be applicable in the future. Therefore, a good

EXHIBIT 5.4 Efficient Frontiers Forecast (2011 to 2020) with and without Hedge Funds (*8.5 Percent Expected Return*)

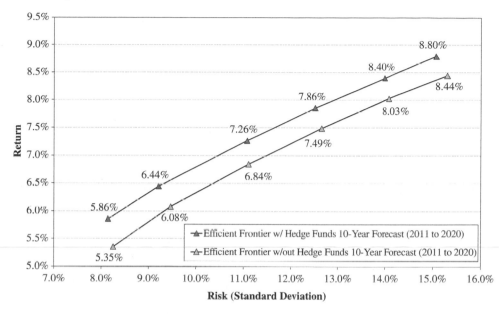

rule of thumb for future market environments is to average the U.S. equity and U.S. investment-grade bond forecasts (currently 5.5 percent). If the diversified hedge fund portfolio cannot meaningfully outperform that proxy (with average volatility) don't invest.

EXHIBIT 5.5 Efficient Frontiers Forecast (2011 to 2020) with and without Hedge Funds (*5.0 Percent Expected Return*)

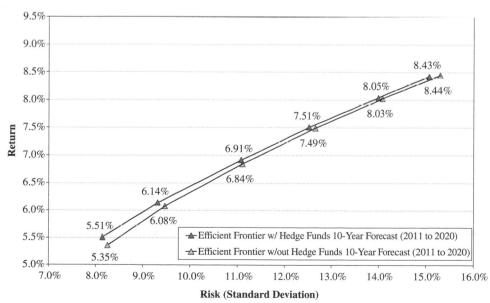

EXHIBIT 5.6 Capital Market Forecasts (2011 to 2020)

Asset Class	Expected Geometric Annual Return*	Expected Risk (σ)	Debt, Equity or Alternative	Cash	TIPS	U.S. Bonds	Int'l Bond	HY Bond	Large Cap U.S.	Small Cap U.S.	REITs	Int'l Equity	Em. Mkts. Equity	Commodity Futures	Hedge Funds Portfolio	MLPs
Cash	0.1%	0.0%	D	1.0	0	0	0	0	0	0	0	0	0	0	0	0
TIPS	2.9%	10.5%	D	0	1.0	0.75	0.56	0.28	0.03	0.00	0.19	0.09	0.10	0.56	0.10	0.10
U.S. Bonds	2.9%	7.2%	D	0	0.75	1.0	0.51	0.28	0.22	0.13	0.20	0.17	0.01	0.32	0.08	0.13
Int'l Bond	2.1%	11.2%	D	0	0.56	0.51	1.0	0.09	0.04	-0.05	0.06	0.40	0.06	0.24	-0.02	0.03
HY Bond	6.0%	16.6%	D	0	0.28	0.28	0.09	1.0	0.57	0.59	0.60	0.51	0.55	0.26	0.46	0.53
Large Cap U.S.	8.1%	18.2%	E	0	0.03	0.22	0.04	0.57	1.0	0.83	0.61	0.65	0.66	0.24	0.52	0.34
Small Cap U.S.	8.9%	21.9%	E	0	0.00	0.13	-0.05	0.59	0.83	1.0	0.71	0.58	0.67	0.21	0.56	0.36
REITs	5.8%	23.1%	E	0	0.19	0.20	0.06	0.60	0.61	0.71	1.0	0.48	0.45	0.24	0.28	0.32
Int'l Equity	8.9%	23.9%	E	0	0.09	0.17	0.40	0.51	0.65	0.58	0.48	1.0	0.68	0.30	0.51	0.33
Em. Mkts. Equity	9.4%	31.4%	E	0	0.10	0.01	0.06	0.55	0.66	0.67	0.45	0.68	1.0	0.29	0.66	0.37
Commodity Futures	5.2%	19.6%	A	0	0.56	0.32	0.24	0.26	0.24	0.21	0.24	0.30	0.29	1.0	0.39	0.29
Hedge Funds Portfolio	Varied	9.3%	A	0	0.10	0.08	-0.02	0.46	0.52	0.56	0.28	0.51	0.66	0.39	1.0	0.31
MLPs	9.8%	20.6%	A	0	0.10	0.13	0.03	0.53	0.34	0.36	0.32	0.33	0.37	0.29	0.31	1.0

Returns & Volatility | Correlation Matrix

Alpha-Beta Framework, Hedge Funds, and Fees

The alpha-beta divide is a confusing and often misconstrued concept. It seems simple; "beta is risk" and "alpha is skill." The term *beta*, (derived from the Capital Asset Pricing Model [CAPM]), describes the component of an investment's total return that is explained by its exposure to a market (systematic) risk factor. For example, if a large-cap stock portfolio has a beta of 1.0 to the S&P 500 index, it has the same market risk as the S&P 500 index. So if this stock portfolio generates a 10.75 percent return when the S&P 500 returns 10 percent, the beta component of total return was 10 and the alpha component was 0.75. Investors can capture beta passively as it requires minimal skill. Beta is viewed as a commodity and should not command a pricing premium.

Hedge funds are at the opposite end of the pricing spectrum from beta-only index funds. Hedge funds have significantly higher fees than traditional active long-only money managers. Are the higher management fees justified? Exhibit 5.7 provides a framework for comparing two managers; *Manager A* is a traditional long-only large-cap mutual fund with a 0.75 percent management fee, and *Manager B* is a long-short equity hedge fund with a traditional 2 percent management fee, plus a 20 percent fee on profits.

In this example, the S&P 500 Index returns 8 percent. Manager A returns 9.0 percent before and 8.25 percent after fees. Manager A has a 1.0 beta, which translates into an 8 percent alpha hurdle and +0.25 percent of net alpha. Manager B returns 7.3 percent before and 4.24 percent after fees. Manager B has a lower 0.40 beta, which lowers the alpha hurdle to 3.2 percent, and generates +1.04 percent of net alpha.

So which manager is more expensive? Manager A has the lower absolute fee (0.75 versus 3.06). However, Manager A has a higher fee if measured in terms of

EXHIBIT 5.7 Hedge Fund versus Mutual Fund Fee Structure

Metrics	Manager A (Long-Only Mutual Fund)	Manager B (Long-Short Hedge Fund)
Manager Fee	0.75%	2% base + 20% on profits
Manager Beta to S&P 500 Index	1.00	0.40
Gross Manager Return (Before Fees)	9.00%	7.30%
Positive Alpha Hurdle (Adjusted For Beta)	8.00%	3.20%
Total Management Fee	0.75%	3.06%
Manager Return (Net of Fees)	8.25%	4.24%
Alpha (Net of Fees)	0.25%	1.04%
Alpha (Net of Fees)/Total Return	3.0%	24.5%
Total Fee/Alpha (Net of Fees)	3.00	2.94
	S&P 500 Index Return	8.00%
	T-Bill Return	0%

fee per unit of alpha. Manager A's fee is 3 times its net alpha, while Manager B's fee is 2.94 times its net alpha. Only 3 percent of Manager A's total return is alpha (or .25/8.25 = 3 percent), while 24.5 percent of Manager B's total return is alpha (or 1.04/4.24 = 24.5 percent). As we mentioned earlier, the beta component of total return is a commodity that can be generated passively and inexpensively. Alpha is the only component of return that warrants a pricing premium. So which manager is actually more expensive? The answer is in the eye of the beholder.

The vast majority of the total return generated by nonprofit portfolios comes from the exposure to the risk premiums of asset classes. These risk premiums, or *betas*, are a valuable and essential component of total return, but they are also fungible commodities that can be inexpensively replicated with passive management. While gaining exposure to betas may not require skill, effectively mixing those betas within a diversified portfolio does (see Chapter 2). Adding an asset class like commodity futures to a portfolio can improve a portfolio's risk-adjusted performance, but asset classes are sources of betas and not sources of alpha.

Time and expense are scarce resources, and they should be deployed efficiently. The best place to deploy these scarce resources is to develop an optimal asset allocation strategy and to find alpha-generating vehicles; beta-generating investment vehicles do not demand a pricing premium or significant time allocation.

This alpha versus beta concept can be the most confusing when it comes to hedge funds because the investor may have a hard time understanding how a hedge fund generates its return. Given the opaque nature of hedge funds, this is a challenge for even the most sophisticated hedge fund allocators. For example, perhaps a hedge fund bets on commodity price increases by loading up on commodities. The fund profits during a period when stock prices fell. When that hedge fund presents its return stream, compared to the S&P 500 index, it might show a significantly positive alpha figure. Is this outperformance really alpha, or is it simply high beta relative to the commodity index (beta "dressed up as alpha")? Without understanding the context, historical returns must be taken with a grain of salt.

If we look at the previous example (Exhibit 5.7), and don't know if Manager B's outperformance is "alpha" or "beta dressed up as alpha," we have a hard time understanding whether the fee per unit of outperformance is a meaningful measure. Manager A is a large-cap mutual fund, and we have access to all its underlying holdings so we know how it generated its alpha (either through sector and/or security selection). The problem with the opacity of hedge funds is that one often doesn't have sufficient information to make an alpha-versus-beta judgment. Investors in hedge funds require far more context about the managers' strategies, styles, and alpha theses to make objective assessments of manager skill.

While a skilled hedge fund manager may generate alpha, a significant portion of return usually still comes from beta. (If hedge funds were alpha-only vehicles, then the average multi-strategy fund of hedge funds would not have lost more than 20 percent in 2008.) Quantifying that beta at the top-down hedge fund industry level is fairly easy. However, it's challenging to quantify it at the individual manager level. Some managers are very skilled at dressing up beta to look like alpha.

Hedge Fund Indices and Benchmarks

A main purpose for any index is to serve as a useful benchmark, enabling investors to objectively evaluate manager performance. It is helpful to understand the minimum requirements for an index to be a "useful benchmark:"

- The index must be representative of the mandate.
- The index holdings and weights within the benchmark must be identifiable and unambiguous.
- An investor should be able to replicate the index benchmark passively.
- The index benchmark's performance must be measurable on a regular basis.
- The index constituents' classification (i.e., strategy) in the benchmark must be formulated from public information and be consistent with market opinions.
- The index benchmark must be constructed before the measurement period begins.

Hedge fund indices seek to represent the performance of hedge fund peer groups. There are two types of hedge fund index categories and both struggle to meet the useful benchmark test. The first type is an *investable index*, which only includes funds that are accepting new capital and excludes funds that are closed. In addition to serving as hedge fund performance benchmarks, investable hedge fund indices are able to be passively replicated. Therefore, they meet at least one of the useful benchmark requirements. However, by excluding managers that are closed to new investment, investible indices do not fully represent the hedge fund peer group. The second type of hedge fund index is a *non-investable index*. Non-investable indices also fail to meet the definition of a useful benchmark. They include hedge funds that are closed to new capital and therefore cannot be passively replicated. While non-investible indices are perhaps more representative of hedge fund peer groups, they suffer from other sorts of biases.

Index providers screen the universe on broad metrics such as assets under management and track record length in order to establish minimum requirements. Once the index providers have applied the initial screens, they classify each fund based on stated investment style (i.e., equity long-short, global macro). Each index provider then applies its own definitions for style screens. Because index providers have differing definitions and methodologies for classifying strategies, the same fund may be placed into different categories. For example, a fund may be classified as "event-driven" by one provider and "merger arbitrage" by another. Further complicating matters, some index providers use equal weights while others use asset-based weightings in their index-construction methodologies. The index providers are also inconsistent on the timing of assumed rebalancing. Some use monthly and others use quarterly or other time intervals.

Due to the private, unregistered nature of hedge funds, databases and indices have several other imperfections. Calculating index returns based on the performance of funds still operating at the end of a reporting period leads to *survivorship bias*. This bias may positively skew index performance because funds no longer operating are often liquidated as a result of poor performance. Established indices typically have less survivorship bias once back-filled data are no longer being used. Once a fund reports to an index, historical returns remain in the index even if they fail.

Liquidation bias occurs when funds in the process of liquidating stop reporting before being fully liquidated; the index loses several months of performance as the hedge fund winds down operation. This bias tends to skew index performance upward as a poorly performing fund is removed from the index before it is done inflicting damage on investors. *Selection bias* occurs because selection criteria differ by index provider and construction methods vary, leading to discrepancy among returns for competing indices that track the same strategy. *Self-reporting bias* occurs because there is no official hedge fund database and participation is voluntary. Managers with poor track records often do not report performance, or only begin reporting once performance has improved. Larger, more successful funds may stop reporting results as capacity is reached. Funds that have performed well may have less incentive to report because they no longer need to attract new investors. *Backfilling bias* occurs when there is a lag between a fund's inception and the date it begins reporting results to a database. This bias can lead to funds entering a database for the first time only after they have established a strong historical performance track record. Presumably, the poorly performing funds may never start reporting, and simply disappear as if they never existed.

Two of the more widely recognized index providers are *Hedge Fund Research, Inc. (HFR)* and *Dow Jones*. HFR was established in 1992 and specializes in hedge fund indices, database management, and analytics. HFR produces more than 100 indices of hedge fund performance ranging from the industry aggregate level down to specific, niche sub-strategies and strategies with regional focus. With performance history dating back to 1990, the HFRI Fund Weighted Composite Index is a widely used benchmark. The HFR suite of products leverages the HFR database to provide detailed, current, comprehensive, and relevant aggregate reference points for all facets of the hedge fund industry. The Dow Jones Credit Suisse Hedge Fund Indexes are a family of hedge fund indexes that include broad market and investable indexes. The indices are constructed from a database of more than 5,000 hedge funds. The database consists of 17 indexes, including a range of geographical and strategy-specific hedge fund indexes.

Hedge Fund Terms and Structures

The most common structures used for hedge funds are limited partnerships (LP) and limited liability companies (LLC). Both structures limit the liability of investors to the value of their investments. Within the LP structure, the general partner is typically the hedge fund manager while the investors are the limited partners. All owners of an LLC are referred to as members; the investment manager is usually the managing member.

Due to tax considerations, hedge funds are structured either as *offshore* or *onshore* funds. Onshore funds may be more suitable for U.S. taxpayers as offshore funds raise complex tax issues. Investing in an offshore fund can be advantageous for tax-exempt U.S. investors because hedge fund leverage can create "unrelated business taxable income" or UBTI. UBTI is taxable even to tax-exempt investors. Offshore hedge fund investors must also make sure the hedge fund structure blocks UBTI. Blocking of UBTI is usually accomplished through a master-feeder structure.

Unlike 1940 Act mutual funds, hedge funds have complicated expense structures. Fees are higher than typical mutual funds, and the general partner (or equivalent) normally shares in profits. However, there are also several less publicized and often meaningful costs born by investors, including research, trading, legal, auditing, and administration expenses. Management fees are meant to cover the manager's operating costs and typically range from 1 to 2 percent of the fund's net asset value (NAV), but can be higher depending on the fund and strategy. Recently, some managers have reduced their fees, particularly if that manager has created a new fund or a share class with more restrictive liquidity terms. However, most pedigreed managers operating at or near capacity are unlikely to reduce fees, and some have actually increased them. Most hedge funds charge a performance fee. Performance fees are calculated as a percentage of the fund's profits over a pre-determined period. Performance fees are customarily 20 percent of the profit, but can range from 0 to 50 percent. Some managers have been pressured into marginally lowering performance fees; that is less common then reductions in management fees.

Most hedge funds must beat a *high water mark* or a previously achieved threshold before they can collect a performance fee; this prevents managers from collecting a performance fee until investors recoup previous losses. This is also sometimes referred to as a "loss carry-forward." Some managers charge redemption fees if investors make withdrawals before a stated predetermined time period.

Hedge funds are typically open-ended vehicles, meaning investors contribute and redeem capital at net asset value on a periodic basis. Most funds allow for contributions at least as often as redemptions. Liquidity terms range from monthly to annually depending on strategy and manager preference. In order to minimize strategy disruption, most managers require notification for contributions or redemptions anywhere from 30 to 100 days in advance of the next liquidity window.

Hedge fund managers often have initial lock-up periods. This lock-up can be specific to each individual contribution or just the initial investment. The lock-up periods vary by manager and strategy, but usually range from one to three years. Funds also can have redemption gates that limit the amount of capital that can be withdrawn on the fund's scheduled redemption date. Gates can be used to delay or suspend withdrawals in order to prevent a run on the fund's capital. During the 2008 financial crisis, many managers imposed gates to the great dismay of investors. However, managers are moving away from *portfolio-level* gates and towards *investor-level* gates, which allow investors to redeem a portion of their assets even under the worst case scenarios.

Fund of Hedge Funds versus Direct Investment

Once a nonprofit investor has made the decision to invest in hedge funds, there are a number of ways to access them. Key criteria are the investor's size and manager evaluation acumen. One option is to invest directly and build a diversified portfolio of hedge funds. Direct investment can make sense when the nonprofit allocates greater than $25 million to hedge funds *and* has the ability to effectively evaluate and monitor hedge fund managers. It can be challenging to build a diversified portfolio of direct hedge funds with less than $10 million regardless of the nonprofit's manager

EXHIBIT 5.8 Direct Hedge Funds versus Fund of Hedge Funds

Characteristic	Direct Hedge Funds	Fund of Hedge Funds (FOHF)
Fees and Expenses	Single layer	Double layer
Manager Evaluation and Due Diligence	Evaluation and due dilligence required for all underlying direct managers	Evaluation and due dilligence required on (single) fund of hedge funds manager who performs underlying manager due dilligence
Diversification	Requires investor to diversify among many managers and strategies	Single fund of hedge funds manager can diversify among many underlying managers and strategies
Liquidity Management	Must be managed by investor	Must be managed by fund of funds
Hedge Fund Portfolio Investment Process	Investor builds and controls hedge fund portfolio's aggregate investment strategy	Fund of hedge funds manager controls overall investment strategy. Investor has no control other than to replace fund of hedge funds manager.
Investment Minimums	Requires significantly higher asset levels to build diversified portfolio	Can diversify with significantly lower asset levels

evaluation and due diligence capabilities. For smaller hedge fund investors, it is preferable to invest through a fund of funds (HFOF) vehicle, where an outside manager selects and diversifies among multiple hedge fund managers and strategies.

For nonprofits allocating between $10 and $25 million to hedge funds, a hybrid "core-satellite" model may be appropriate. This core-satellite approach has a core investment in a HFOF, but also satellite investments in direct hedge funds. This enables the core to be diversified among multiple managers and strategies, while allowing concentration in higher-conviction strategies and managers.

Even if the nonprofit portfolio has sufficient size, the decision to invest directly or through a fund of hedge funds is not clear cut. If an investor elects to invest directly, he only pays one layer of fees. If an investor elects to allocate to a HFOF, he must also pay a second layer of fees. Exhibit 5.8 compares direct and FOHF investing.

Hedge Fund Investment Due Diligence

Hedge fund investors must either have a comprehensive due diligence program to evaluate candidates, or they should forgo investing in the space. The process starts with evaluating the qualifications and track record of the manager. An investor should review the educational and professional history of the portfolio managers and their investment management history. A manager with a background that is incompatible with the current strategy should be eliminated. Also review the education and work experience of all other key analysts and risk-management personnel. Crucial parts of the personnel review process are reference and background checks. Also review the fund's ownership structure to ensure that interests are properly aligned. Finally, the investor should review how much of the manager's own capital is invested in the fund; one wants managers who "eat their own cooking".

The next step of the due diligence process is to understand the strategy of the fund. Investors must understand what *instruments* the fund trades and how its strategy is designed to generate alpha. As a part of the strategy review, the investor should seek to understand the types of market environments that will favor or disfavor the strategy.

Once the investor is comfortable with the strategy, one needs to understand the research process, including how investment ideas are generated. The fund's analysts should walk the investor through the investment process from *idea generation* to *implementation* in the portfolio.

The final investment due diligence step is to understand portfolio construction including *concentration, leverage, liquidity constraints, factor exposures*, and *other constraints* such as maximum sector and position exposures. While it is helpful to have the manager describe the portfolio construction process, due diligence requires a thorough review of historical portfolio construction at various points in time (usually monthly). Historical portfolio construction that doesn't match the portfolio construction story is a major red flag.

Financial leverage inherently increases risk. By definition, leverage amplifies gains, but it also magnifies losses. The appropriate level of leverage varies by hedge fund strategy. *Explicit* leverage requires borrowing, but hedge funds can also *implicitly* leverage assets by buying or selling futures, selling options, entering into swaps, or trading other derivatives. The investor must be comfortable with the level of leverage and understand whether it is appropriate given the strategy.

Because hedge funds often employ leverage, trade derivatives, and invest in less-liquid areas of the market, they can be prone to *fat left tail events*—unlikely but disastrous situations. Certain strategies exhibit return profiles similar to poorly underwritten flood insurance. They collect a steady stream of "insurance premiums," until the flood hits and they collapse. An example of this type of asymmetric risk-reward profile is selling *out-of-the-money* options. Most options expire worthless. As long as the options finish out of the money, they expire unexercised and the seller pockets the premium received. Low month-to-month volatility gives the false impression of low risk . . . until the blow up. Similarly, the non-normality of hedge fund return distributions and unstable correlation coefficients make a single hedge fund or hedge fund portfolios hard to model. The best one can do is to thoroughly understand the strategy and risk-management processes before deciding to invest.

Most successful hedge funds have a robust risk-management process. The ideal is for the fund to have an independent risk-management group that reviews the risks and stress tests the portfolio under a variety of scenarios and market conditions. The risk-management team should provide copies of completed risk reports and be able to demonstrate their process. If a hedge fund exhibits a defect or hole in the risk-management process, eliminate it from consideration.

While a strong performance history is a good starting point, a full quantitative review must be done to ensure an investor fully understands the context of a manager's return stream. Blindly chasing hot performance is a classic rookie mistake. *Return attribution* is important to understand a manager's return profile. The most basic attribution is *long/short attribution,* which shows how a manager has performed on both the long and short portfolio each measurement period. The long/short attribution is vital to see if a manager has been successful on the short side, a requirement for any successful hedge fund manager. Obtain and study return attribution by *security type, market capitalization, geography*, and *sector* to determine other sources of return.

There are many steps in the process to determine if a hedge fund manager is worthy of consideration. The analysts performing the work should document all investment due diligence steps. The nonprofit's investment committee should thoroughly review these analyst investment due diligence reports before including a fund in the portfolio.

Hedge Fund Operational Due Diligence

Hedge funds lack holdings transparency. Rightfully, many nonprofit investors aren't comfortable allocating money to vehicles for which they don't control custody and can't look at positions. As fallout from the 2008 financial crisis, many hedge funds have improved transparency, but still lag their registered competitors. Investors other than multi-billion dollar institutions often cannot access key individuals at the hedge fund. This situation exacerbates concerns. The vast majority of hedge funds don't provide position-level transparency.

However, *operational failure* is also a major risk with hedge funds. Just because a hedge fund manager may be a talented investor does not mean he is necessarily adept or capable of running a business enterprise. Many impatient or preoccupied hedge fund managers lack the expertise and commitment to run a business with proper systems and controls. Outright *fraud* is also a serious risk, given the opaque and loosely regulated nature of the hedge fund industry.

On December 11, 2008, Bernard L. Madoff was arrested and later pled guilty to 11 felonies for running the largest Ponzi scheme in history. Estimates of the fraud have been as high as $65 billion! Madoff asserts his Ponzi scheme began in the early 1990s, but federal investigators suspect the fraud began much earlier, perhaps in the 1970s. As the Madoff disaster demonstrates, longevity and reputation are no substitute for the requisite independent operational due diligence.

As with all successful frauds, Madoff seemed reputable. He was well known in the industry and had even served as the head of Nasdaq. He was well connected, with a reputation for brilliance. He was also affable. However, even a modest operational due diligence effort should have raised numerous red flags. All of the following pieces of information could be found in the marketing materials of at least one of Madoff's feeder fund:

- Madoff's administration, brokerage, and custody were done internally.
- Madoff's firm charged no investment management (or incentive) fee, so it presumably only made money on brokerage commissions charged for trading client accounts.
- Lastly, the auditor was a small and unknown accounting firm.

Without digging any deeper, this short list of operational red flags was more than enough to warrant elimination, but investors relied on word of mouth references. While spectacular failures and frauds like the Madoff debacle make the front page, most hedge fund failures are not spectacular. They result from simple operational failures. Hedge fund managers that are very good at executing their investment strategy may not have the time or expertise to establish and run a well-controlled business. Investors need to perform strong operational due diligence that focuses on the non-investment aspects and the associated risks of running a hedge fund.

An investor must be comfortable with the controls around the process of trading, reconciling, and valuing holdings. Operational due diligence should examine controls across the entire trading process; from the time the portfolio manager initiates the trade with the trading desk, through the settlement and reconciliation process, and ultimately through valuation and the striking of a net asset value.

Outside service providers perform many of the key operational processes. Services providers for hedge funds include the following:

- *Prime Brokers* provide leverage to hedge funds, execute and clear trades, and lend securities (for shorting).
- *Administrators* provide critical middle and back office services, as well as key client-servicing functions.
- *Auditors* examine holdings and provide an opinion as to whether the fund's financial statements meet Generally Accepted Accounting Principles (GAAP).

Due to the importance of these functions, hedge fund investors must determine if the service provider is reputable and has the resources to service the hedge fund's strategy. The investor must then learn the role each plays and understand the reliability and independence of their work. This requires the hedge fund investor to interact with all service providers.

In addition, operational due diligence should also include the other risk-mitigation activities performed by non-investment personnel. As the Securities and Exchange Commission polices insider trading, it has become paramount for hedge fund investors to vet compliance functions. The compliance function must be robust enough to ensure that firm personnel adhere to all regulatory provisions. Also, interview information technology personnel to review the firm's disaster recovery plan. Has it been successfully tested? Also evaluate the operations staff who manages counterparty risk. Determine what plans are in place if a counterparty's financial strength begins to deteriorate. Perform operational due diligence before an investment is made and continue it throughout the tenure of the investment. Eliminate or terminate any hedge fund with material gaps.

Hedge Funds in the Post-2008 World

While market factors since 2008 may have pressured some hedge funds to adapt to new standards of transparency, some top-tier funds have not succumbed to pressure. Still, much has changed. Regulation is the new norm for hedge funds. All funds with greater than $150 million were required to register with the SEC by July 21, 2011, creating additional regulatory burden. These additional burdens may be too much for smaller and emerging hedge fund managers.

Tighter regulation and investor demand will hopefully drive more transparency, including position-level transparency. For HFOF investors, this means a greater look-through to underlying managers and exposures. Many hedge funds that refuse to provide such transparency are losing out in the race for assets with institutional investors.

Since 2008, most hedge funds have increased operations staff to provide more timely response to client demands. Hedge funds also provide greater investment process clarity and more access to senior-level staff. More hedge funds have begun to use third-party risk-aggregation platforms such as *Measurerisk* or *RiskMetrics* to provide clients with useful information. Hedge funds have also increasingly turned to third-party administrators to provide independent monitoring and reconciliation of hedge fund books with prime brokers and custodians.

Gates (exit restrictions) thrown up by hedge funds during the credit crisis have brought liquidity terms to the forefront. Post-2008, many hedge funds provide liquidity terms that better align with the liquidity of their strategies. For example, a U.S. equity long-short manager who trades in highly liquid securities may provide greater liquidity terms. A distressed debt fund that allocates to illiquid credit instruments warrants less liquidity. Hedge fund managers have also begun to offer multiple liquidity options. The share class with the longest lock-up may entice investors with a lower fee structure. Another share class may have a "soft" lock-up that permits earlier redemptions for a fee. There has also been a move toward shorter notice periods for redemptions (i.e., from 90 to 180 days to 90 days or less).

The "Volcker Rule" embedded in the Dodd-Frank bill prohibits banks from engaging in proprietary trading. Although the rule has yet to be implemented as of early 2011, reducing the role of Wall Street trading desks within banks should ultimately reduce hedge funds' competition for alpha.

Since 2008, there has been a shift toward lower fees. A 1.5 percent management fee level has becoming more common for new hedge funds versus the historical 2 percent management fee. However, a 20 percent performance fee remains the norm.

Conclusion

Investing in hedge funds presents unique challenges and risks, but there are compelling arguments for their inclusion in a nonprofit portfolio. However, nonprofit investors should approach hedge funds with sufficient diligence and with healthy skepticism. If your organization does not have the time or expertise to perform the required due diligence, you should either hire someone who does or avoid the strategies.

Notes

1. Source: 2010 NACUBO-Commonfund Study of Endowments. The dollar-weighted average allocation to alternative investments was 52 percent for the 850 institutions surveyed. On average, about 46 percent of the alternative investment allocation was invested in hedge funds, which implies a 26 percent average hedge fund allocation. Hedge funds include marketable alternative strategies (i.e., hedge funds, absolute return, market neutral, long/short, 130/30, event-driven, and derivatives) and distressed debt. The percentage of the alternative investments allocation was positively correlated to endowment size.

CHAPTER 6

Private Equity

Nonprofit institutions have invested in private equity for decades. The *2010 NACUBO-Commonfund Study of Endowments* found that the average endowment fund allocated 16 percent of total assets to private equity.[1] According to a recent survey by Russell Investments, institutional investors, especially those in North America, plan to increase private equity allocations.

There are several key differences between private and public equity. Private equity investments are made in privately owned companies, inherently less liquid than public stocks. Most private equity funds are structured as private placements so that they are exempted from 1940 Act registration. Investment in these vehicles is limited to "sophisticated investors" (institutions and wealthy individuals). The typical private equity partnership structure has two components: the *general partners* (GPs) are the private equity managers and the *limited partners* (LPs) provide the bulk of the capital. The general partner typically supplies little capital, but bears unlimited liability for the fund and is responsible for investment and administrative activities. The limited partners have liability limited to the amount of their capital commitment.

The post-World War II private equity industry has evolved significantly. From 1946 to the early 1980s, *venture capital* dominated the relatively small and fragmented private equity universe. During the 1980s, the *leverage buyout* model emerged, and institutional investors became active private equity participants. In the 1990s, the Private Equity space was further segmented into specialized niche strategies. By the early 2000s, many established private equity firms began institutionalizing their businesses. Several private equity firms announced plans to become publicly traded companies.

Private Equity Investment Strategies

Private equity investments have long investment horizons, often greater than 10 years. In exchange for such illiquidity, financial leverage, and other esoteric risks, investors demand higher expected returns from private equity than from public market investments. Private equity investments typically fall into one of several categories; each has its own unique dynamics, risk, and return profiles.

EXHIBIT 6.1 Venture Capital Stages

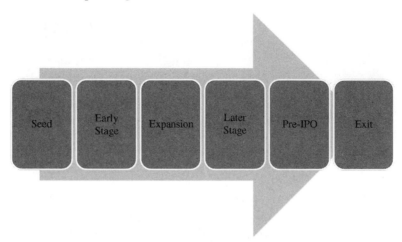

Venture Capital

Venture capital seeds new businesses or provides capital injections in young companies in the early stages of growth. The companies are often too small or lack sufficient operating history to access public capital markets. They also often lack the tangible assets to secure bank financing. In recent years, such companies have often operated in the technology and life science sectors. In addition to providing capital, venture capitalists can facilitate a young company's development by advising on operational and strategic matters. Venture capitalists typically invest in equity or equity-linked investments (e.g., preferred equity, convertible preferred). Unlike other private equity investments, venture capital investments are not typically financed with borrowed money. See Exhibit 6.1 for a summary of the invest stages in venture capital.

Leveraged Buyout

Buyout funds usually acquire *mature* companies or business units with stable cash flows and tangible assets. They use debt-heavy financing from outside lenders. The acquirer may raise funds by issuing non-investment grade debt. The acquisition target may or may not be privately held before the transaction. Cash flow from the company's operations are used to repay the debt. The general partner actively advises management to make strategic and operational improvements to increase future profitability. These improvements are designed to unlock hidden value in the business. Once the value has been "unlocked," the general partner seeks to *exit*, usually via a sale, merger, initial public offering, or recapitalization. While equity holders in successful buyouts can realize high returns, failed buyout investments, especially when significant leverage is employed, can result in large losses or bankruptcy.

Growth Capital

Growth capital investments are equity investments in relatively mature companies seeking to expand, restructure, enter a new market, or finance an acquisition. These companies are more mature than venture capital-funded companies. A *private investment in public equity* (PIPE) is a form of growth capital investing. PIPE investments are often made in the form of a convertible bond or preferred stock investment that is unregistered for a certain period of time.

Distressed or Special Situations

The *distressed* strategy involves investing in the equity or debt of a financially distressed company. Also known *as vulture investing*, an investor may buy significantly discounted debt securities of a distressed company in order to take control of the company when it emerges from bankruptcy. In a *special situation* strategy an investor provides rescue debt and equity financing to a company having operational or financial stress. Private equity and hedge fund managers often overlap in *distressed situation* strategies.

Mezzanine Finance

Mezzanine capital is subordinated debt or preferred equity representing the second most junior claim in a company's capital structure (just above common equity). Mezzanine financing is often used by investors to reduce the amount of equity required to finance a buyout or expansion. Mezzanine capital allows smaller companies that may not be able to access the high-yield bond markets to borrow beyond levels that traditional lenders are willing to provide.

Secondaries

Secondary investments are investments in existing private equity companies. Private equity is inherently illiquid and is meant for long-term buy-and-hold investors. However, investors sometimes need to raise liquidity more quickly than they previously anticipated. Secondary offerings are negotiated directly between the buyer and seller without general partner involvement. Sometimes, secondary investors are able to purchase deals at significant discounts from desperate investors that need immediate liquidity.

Publicly Traded Private Equity Firms and Funds

While still a small segment, there are publicly traded companies that participate in private equity strategies. *The Blackstone Group* (Quotron symbol BX) is one such vehicle. Alternatively, investors can purchase *business development companies* (BDCs). BDCs are closed-end funds that invest in private or thinly-traded public companies through long-term debt or equity capital. While these are not perfect substitutes for true private equity partnerships, they offer liquidity, regulatory oversight, and lower minimums.

EXHIBIT 6.2 Private Equity Strategies

VC	GC	LBO	Distressed or Special Situations	Mezzanine Finance	Secondaries	Publicly Traded
•Financing for startup or emerging companies	•Equity investments in relatively mature companies	•Predominantly debt-financed acquisitions of mature companies	•Equity or debt investing of financially distressed companies	•Private debt and equity financing	•Buying or selling an existing investor commitment	•Closed-end funds •Equities

Exhibit 6.2 compares and contrasts the various private equity investment strategies.

Why Invest in Private Equity?

Unfortunately, there are more bad reasons to invest in private equity than good. A commonly used but poor rationale is "Because Harvard and Yale do it." These high-profile institutions have armies of well-trained employees and consultants to vet strategies and managers for the portfolio. Investing in private equity without the proper skill (and resources) is a recipe for disaster. Skilled talent and other resources are expensive. A nonprofit organization needs to have a significant private equity commitment to justify the expense. Another poor reason to invest is because the investment committee has bought into the "private equity as panacea" hype. Just like any other investment class, private equity has its fair share of warts.

There are really only three rational reasons to consider private equity investments:

1. Your portfolio has a very long time horizon and minimal liquidity requirements.
2. You think doing so will improve the risk-adjusted performance of your aggregate portfolio.
3. You believe that you have access to the required expertise.

If you can't clear all three hurdles, it would be wise to forgo private equity and focus your resources elsewhere.

Theoretically, investing in a privately held and illiquid asset should provide a risk premium over a similar asset that is publicly traded. (A rational investor would avoid the asset class if there were no increase in return expectations.) Therefore, private equity should have a higher expected return (an illiquidity premium) than public equities. However, the evidence is mixed. Several studies have shown that the average private equity investor has received *lower* returns, after expenses, than the public equity markets have generated.[2] And when adjusted for risk, private equity does even worse in some of these studies.

Since the *average* private equity investment may add no value for a broadly diversified nonprofit portfolio, one requires *above average* results, in other words an *alpha thesis*. In plain English, this means that merely achieving private equity asset class exposure (e.g., *private equity beta*) is insufficient. Before deciding to invest, your organization must have confidence that it can be significantly above average at selecting, managing, and, most importantly, accessing quality private equity managers.

Structure and Terms

Private equity funds are typically run by a *general partner* (or manager) on behalf of *limited partners* (investors). An *offering memorandum* describes the terms of a private placement and the types of investments the general partner can make. Most funds are structured as pooled limited partnership vehicles and usually have a fixed life of 10 or more years. Each fund a private equity firm brings to market is a new, unique offering. Investors initially *commit* to a total investment amount but do not have to transfer cash until it is *called* by the general partner. The limited partners face penalties if they do not provide committed capital on a timely basis when it is called.

Private equity funds have an *investment* (or ramp-up) period as well as a *realization* (or drawdown) period. The year that a fund is established or makes its first capital call is classified as its *vintage year*. Limited partners commit capital to a particular fund and are repaid through distributions based on realized profits from underlying investments. Limited partners pay annual management and performance fees. In the early years of a partnership returns are often negative, but are expected to improve over time. This is referred to as the *private equity J-Curve* (see Exhibit 6.3). Start-up expenses lead to initial declining investment values before more positive results kick in and investment valuations have a chance to be revised upwards.

It is difficult for smaller nonprofit investors to access private equity due to the required size of capital commitments. Nonprofits seeking to invest directly should be prepared to allocate anywhere from $5 to $25 million per fund. Obviously, it takes a substantial commitment to develop a diversified portfolio. Most small- to mid-size nonprofits invest through a *fund of funds,* a partnership that invests in a number of separate private equity funds.

EXHIBIT 6.3 The Private-Equity J-Curve

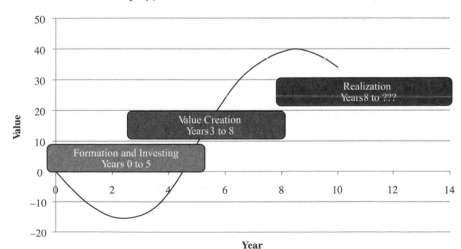

Private equity fees vary by both vehicle type and strategy. The fees are often significantly higher than traditional investments, and the general partner (or equivalent) normally shares in profits. A typical private equity fee might range from a 1 to 2 percent base-management fee with a 20 percent performance fee. Management fees tend to be inversely proportional to fund size. The performance fee, often referred to as the *carried interest*, is not charged until the fund achieves a previously stated hurdle return, and is designed to incentivize the manager. A *clawback* provision gives limited partners the right to reclaim a portion of disbursements made to a general partner for profitable investments if there are losses from later investments in a portfolio. The opposite of a clawback provision, the *catch-up* provision allows the general partner to receive a majority of profits after the limited partners have received their targeted hurdle return. After the catch up returns are paid, profits are split according to the previously agreed arrangement (usually 80/20). Funds also incur other expenses for legal, audit, and other administrative necessities.

Private Equity Risks

Private equity is one of the most *illiquid* asset classes. Therefore, rebalancing and maintaining a target allocation is difficult as the liquid components of a nonprofit portfolio fluctuate in value. A related challenge is that private equity allocations can become overweight within a portfolio if other asset classes are liquidated to fund immediate spending needs. Nonprofit investors should think 10 years ahead and allow a cushion for potential unanticipated liquidity needs.

Smaller investors have difficulty gaining access to top-tier managers. Private equity firms often limit the size of funds they manage. The best funds experience repeat investment from large institutional investors from one fund to the next. There are few slots for first-time private equity investors.

Information on portfolio holdings is quite limited compared with traditional asset classes. Private equity investments have *blind pool risk*, or an inability to preview the portfolio before committing capital. Once capital has been committed, the investor receives minimal reporting that covers only basic portfolio updates. Funds report *lagged* information to investors. Because valuations are only prepared quarterly, investors' information may be as much as 90 days old. This reporting lag makes it exceedingly difficult for investors to evaluate their holdings, particularly in volatile markets or with companies in the midst of significant transformation.

Dispersion risk presents another challenge. There is a huge spread between median returns and top-quartile returns for private equity managers. For example, through December 2009, top quartile funds outperformed median funds by approximately 20 percent over 20 years.[3] Like any other asset class, investors seek top managers. In private equity, however, the difference in performance between the "top" and "average" can mean the difference between feast and famine.

Private equity investors cannot quantify actual performance until portfolio companies are sold. As a consequence, it is highly difficult to accurately evaluate a private equity fund manager's performance until the fund has been dissolved and capital fully returned to investors. Without a willing buyer, it is impossible to know the value of a portfolio company. Valuation estimates reflect the judgment of the private equity manager, a third-party valuation firm, or both. Such estimates are flawed at best.

Private equity also has the basic investment risk of identifying, choosing, and investing in companies. That risk is amplified if the fund uses financial leverage (as most buyout funds do). With venture capital, early stage companies don't have proven business models, and product launches may not be as successful as hoped.

Direct Private Equity versus Private Equity Fund of Funds

As mentioned, nonprofits can invest in private equity directly or indirectly through a fund of funds. Direct investment requires a significant commitment, and it also requires significant expertise. If your organization lacks either, you can outsource the private equity investment to a *fund of private equity funds*. Funds of funds are investment intermediaries that handle all investment and administrative activities for a fee. Fund of funds managers assemble a portfolio of underlying private equity funds. Some provide a diversified portfolio of managers focused on a single strategy, for example venture capital. Others offer a more diversified approach, investing across multiple strategies, co-investing with direct private equity managers, and occasionally investing directly into companies (competing with direct private equity managers for deals).

Premier private equity managers often have by-invitation-only policies for new investors. Successful funds have a high re-up rate for their new funds and little need to source new investors. Without some connection, it can be difficult to get access. The best private equity fund of funds managers are well connected in the industry, so they can provide access for their clients. However, investors must beware. Virtually all private equity fund of fund managers claim to be well connected.

A private equity portfolio should be diversified by *strategy, vintage year, geographic location, industry,* and *manager.* Since some economic environments are better than others for certain private equity strategies, each segment has the ability to outperform at different points in time. Investors need diversification to avoid being over or underexposed to any particular strategy. Large investors can diversify by investing in multiple funds across varied strategies and vintage years. Smaller investors can't. Therefore they need the diversification provided by the fund of funds.

Top-tier (direct) private equity managers often require high minimum investments of $5 to $25 million per investor. For smaller nonprofit investors, building a diversified portfolio of direct private equity funds is untenable. On the other hand, top tier fund of funds managers often have minimum commitments closer to $1 million.

Funds of funds also offer administrative benefits. There is only one set of subscription documents to complete. Capital calls and distributions only need to be managed for the fund of funds rather than numerous individual funds. Thanks to (generally) higher quality reporting, ongoing monitoring is also simplified.

An added layer of fees is one of the main drawbacks to investing in a fund of funds. Direct private equity funds typically charge a management fee of 2 percent of assets plus a 20 percent share of profits. With a fund of funds, the investor incurs a second layer of fees. Investors pay the fees, expenses, and carried interest of the fund of funds and indirectly bear the fees, expenses, and carried interest of the underlying funds. This added layer of fees typically includes a 0.5 to 2.0 percent management fee on committed capital plus a 0 to 20 percent incentive fee. That's a lot of fees! The investor needs to assess value provided by the fund of funds manager and whether their fee is worth it.

Selecting Private Equity Managers

Whether selecting a private equity fund or a private equity fund of funds, investors should look for stable firms with low turnover among investment professionals. Funds of funds should have a global presence. The firm's assets under management should have steadily increased (without growing too large for the niche or strategy). The private equity firm's investors should be a diverse group of sophisticated institutional and high-net-worth limited partners. The investment team should be a cohesive group with access to high quality deal flow. While some degree of flexibility is important, the team should have a disciplined investment process. The performance track record should be consistently upper quartile over an extended period for realized investments. Historical outperformance should be driven by deal selection and operational improvements rather than financial engineering (leverage). The terms and fund structure should reflect industry norms with aligned interests between general and limited partners. The firm should use reputable service providers and have a fully developed back office. Lastly, investors should expect timely and transparent reporting.

A high-quality fund of funds should be able to demonstrate it is able to access top-tier private equity funds. The fund should be large enough to invest with the best, but not so large it becomes a pseudo index. Portfolio investments should be diversified by *vintage years, sectors, geographic regions,* and *underlying managers.* The manager should not chase returns in hot sectors. Most importantly, the team must have relevant experience across each of their target areas. The firm should also communicate on a timely basis and provide useful performance analysis.

Benchmarks

A main purpose for any index is to serve as a useful benchmark, enabling investors to objectively evaluate manager performance. The minimum requirements for an index to be a "useful benchmark" include the following:

- The index must be *representative* of the mandate.
- The index *holdings and weights* within the benchmark must be *identifiable* and *unambiguous.*
- An investor should be able to *replicate* the index benchmark passively.
- The index benchmark's *performance must be measurable* on a regular basis.
- The index constituents' classification (i.e., strategy) in the benchmark must be formulated from public information and be consistent with market opinions.
- The index benchmark must be constructed *before* the measurement period begins.

Because public information is not readily available or sufficiently transparent for most private equity investments, it is impossible to gather all the information necessary to meet most of the above requirements. However, given that a flawed benchmark is presumably better than no benchmark, there are a number of private equity benchmarks currently used by investors.

The two largest and mostly widely used private equity index providers are *Thomson Venture Economics* (VentureXpert) and *Cambridge Associates*. Venture Xpert provides analysis of fund commitments, portfolio company investments, valuations, and fund performance across a variety of strategies. Cambridge Associates only offers quarterly returns for venture capital and the industry as a whole. State Street's *Private Edge Group* and *The LPX Group* are additional, newer options.

Because of the inherent flaws in private equity indices, investors may also use a *public market equivalent* (PME). A PME creates a hypothetical private equity benchmark based on the returns of public equity market indices (with nominal adjustments) and the timing of the private equity investment's cash flows.

Conclusion

Private equity's illiquidity, complexity, and *very high* expense structure makes the category inappropriate for many nonprofit investors. However, nonprofits who decide to invest should be sophisticated long-term allocators who are able to dedicate meaningful resources to the space. Given its illiquid nature, most nonprofit investors should only make modest allocations unless the investor has tremendous foresight about future portfolio liquidity needs. And the nonprofit investor must be convinced it can gain access to exceptional managers.

Notes

1. Source: 2010 NACUBO-Commonfund Study of Endowments. The dollar weighted average allocation to alternative investments was 52 percent for the 850 institutions surveyed. On average, about 30 percent of the alternative investment allocation was invested in private equity, which implies a 16 percent average private equity allocation (including venture capital). The size of the alternative investments allocation was positively correlated to size. For institutions in excess of $1 billion in assets, the average allocation to alternative investments was 60 percent. For institutions between $101 and $500 million, the average allocation to alternative investments was 35 percent. For institutions under $25 million, the allocation to alternative investments was 12 percent.

2. Gottschalg, Oliver, and Phalippou Ludovic, 2006. "The performance of private equity funds." (HEC Paris, Jouy-en-Josas cedex, France)

3. Based on 20-year pooled return data from Thomson Financial Venture Economics as of December 31, 2009.

CHAPTER 7

Real Assets

R eal assets include *commodities, real estate, infrastructure assets, natural re-sources, farm land, art,* and countless other examples. In the simplest terms, real assets are things you can touch that are intrinsically valuable. *Intrinsic value* can be derived from productive value or other more subjective considerations. For example, land has intrinsic value because it can produce food, shelter, or natural resources; a piece of art has intrinsic value because it is unique. While gold lacks significant industrial productive application, humanity has long considered it valuable for its scarcity, beauty, and relative portability.

Many nonprofit investors recognize the unique role real assets play in diversified portfolios. According to the *2010 NACUBO-Commonfund Study of Endowments,* the average endowment fund had 12.5 percent allocated to real assets.[1] Unlike stocks, bonds, and other financial assets, *real assets* have intrinsic value, which is not derived from claims on an institution's future cash flows. Real assets can be critical diversifiers. Because intrinsic value is not based on nominal cash flow, real assets are more impervious to inflation shocks, irresponsible governmental economic policies, or geopolitical crises. In the most extreme case, real assets retain value even if fiat currencies become valueless (to the extent ownership rights are protected under such a dire circumstance). A bond interest payment or a stock dividend has no value if the money has no value.

The main categories of investable real assets are commodities, various real estate and land types, infrastructure, and natural resources. Additionally, Treasury Inflation-Protected Securities (TIPS) provide an inflation hedge like real assets. Strictly speaking, TIPS are not a real asset because they have no intrinsic value. Value is derived from a *contractual* obligation between borrower and lender, the classic definition of a financial asset. However, they do have some unique properties giving them a closer association to real assets (see Chapter 3).

Investors face many challenges in the decades ahead. However, one clear and present danger outshines all others. As of early 2011, annualized U.S. federal government budget deficits exceeded $1.5 trillion, and the U.S. federal government debt-to-GDP ratio had rapidly accelerated beyond 100 percent. The total U.S. government debt is more than $14.5 trillion. Moreover, unlike corporations which are required to include *unfunded* liabilities in their debt ratios, the U.S. government ignores unfunded liabilities for social security, Medicare, and Medicaid. According to the *Wall Street Journal,* the *true* debt is closer to $65 trillion. Possible remedies for this unsustainable fiscal condition include confiscatory tax increases (which would impair economic growth), *significant* spending cuts to entitlement programs (that risk political instability), or default either explicit or implicit. (Debt monetization by the Federal Reserve is a form of implicit default.) The ultimate remedy may include all three elements. Fiscal policies are controlled by Congress and the political process, while monetary policy is controlled by the Federal Reserve. Too often, nations that cannot muster the political will required to rein in unsustainable deficits and debt have turned to debasing the currency (and the nominal value of debt) through inflationary monetary policy. While the Federal Reserve is supposedly an independent institution, unsustainable deficits can force the Federal Reserve to finance debt with printed money as an alternative to explicit sovereign default. *Quantitative easing* (QE I and II) is a euphemism for such money "printing."

Real assets can serve as a hedge against such currency debasement. Other distinctive attributes of real assets include a total return that rises with inflationary forces; hedges against geopolitical and certain economic and financial risks; and enhanced portfolio risk-adjusted performance when combined with financial assets. Traditional financial asset classes like stocks and bonds have generally performed poorly during accelerating inflationary environments or periods of geopolitical, financial, or economic instability.

Commodities

A commodity is *a raw material* used in the production of other goods. While definitions vary, the commodity asset class can be divided into two broad categories: *hard commodities* are normally mined, while *soft commodities* are typically farmed. Soft commodities include corn, coffee, and wool. Soft commodity prices tend to be volatile due to spoilage and weather-related risks. On the other hand, hard commodities are removed from the ground or extracted from other natural resources. Once extracted, they are commonly processed to create other types of commodities. For example, gasoline is refined from oil. Hard commodities are key ingredients in the industrial production process and generally do not spoil. Examples include oil, gold, and copper.

There are multiple ways to gain commodity exposure. A common way is through forward (or futures) contracts. A commodity futures contract is a standardized agreement to buy or sell a commodity at a predetermined price and date. Commodities producers (for example, natural gas producers) often sell a commodity futures contract to lock in a certain future sale price for their product. Buyers of commodity futures usually include commodity consumers (like power plants) that wish to lock in a future purchase price today and speculators who bet on rising commodity prices.

Instead of buying futures contracts to gain exposure to commodity prices, investors can also buy the stocks of commodity-producing companies. However, a commodity stock is not a pure commodity play. For example, the company may have hedged its commodity price exposure or have idiosyncratic risks such as deteriorating financial conditions or labor disputes. An investor could also buy and take possession of physical commodities. This approach may work for large companies that use the commodity, but nonprofit investors generally do not want to manage storage and transportation.

The most practical route for most nonprofits is through the futures market. There are three components of total return for commodity futures, *changes in spot prices*, the *roll return*, and the *collateral return:*

1. *Changes in Spot Prices*. As the *spot price*, or current price, of a commodity increases or decreases, the close-to-maturity futures price rises or falls. This component of total return captures the impact of commodity price inflation over time.

2. *Roll Return*. The roll return component is the most difficult to measure and requires assumptions about the motives of so-called hedgers and speculators. Longer-term futures contracts frequently have large discounts from the spot prices. This condition is known as *backwardation*. In backwardation, buying and holding a futures contract can earn a positive return as the spot and futures price converge at maturity of the contract (the futures price increases to match the spot price). A natural hedger, for example a heating oil distributor that owns the physical commodity, is already exposed to fluctuations in the commodity price. This heating oil distributor may want to insulate itself from falling future prices by selling a commodity futures contract. They risk missing out on higher profits if the commodity's spot price increases, but they have locked in the sale price ahead of time and protected themselves against a potential price decline. The distributor prefers a slightly lower, but certain profit today in exchange for a slightly higher expected (but also uncertain) profit later. *Speculators* take the other side of the trade (they "go long") on the futures contract. Hedgers transfer *price risk* to speculators, who may have an expected positive roll return (risk premium) for taking the commodity price risk. Over time, speculators achieve higher returns if this risk premium exists.

3. *Collateral Return*. Collateral return is interest earned on the collateral posted for the *futures contract*. When buying a futures contract, there is no immediate transfer of cash, rather collateral is posted to assure the future payment. Because only a minimal *margin requirement* is needed to establish a futures position, commodity futures can be fully collateralized with a variety of fixed income securities. The total return earned from this collateral provides additional returns to the investor. Historically, this component of total return has been significant for commodity futures indices. Commodity futures index returns are calculated as if the collateral was invested in three-month T-Bills. If one invests the collateral in some other security, say TIPS, excess return can be earned over the index (albeit only if the TIPS collateral outperforms T-Bills).

Commodity futures indices represent the total returns of holding long positions in agriculture, metals, energy, and livestock commodities. There are some limitations in constructing investable commodity indices. Not all commodities have futures markets, so it is impossible to construct a fully comprehensive commodity index using only futures markets.

Commodity indices differ in a number of ways. These differences include variations in selection and weighting criteria, as well as rolling mechanisms and rebalancing periods. The following compares two widely used commodity indices; the *Dow Jones (DJ)-UBS Commodity Index* and the *S&P Goldman Sachs Commodity Index (GSCI)*.

Dow Jones–UBS Commodity Index

The DJ-UBS Commodity Index is comprised of 19 physical commodity futures contracts and is designed to provide diversified exposure to commodities as an asset
class. No related group of commodities (e.g., energy, precious metals, livestock,
grains, etc.) may constitute more than 33 percent of the index. The liquidity of a
commodity futures contract and the level of production of the underlying commodity are factors used to determine the weight of each contract within the index. No
single commodity may constitute less than 2 percent of the index. Commodities represented in the index include *natural gas, crude oil, unleaded gas, heating oil, live
cattle, lean hogs, wheat, corn, soybeans, soybean oil, aluminum, copper, zinc,
nickel, gold, silver, sugar, cotton, and coffee.*

S&P GSCI

The GSCI is *world-production weighted;* the weight of each commodity in the index is
determined by the average quantity of production in the last five years. This weighting scheme makes the GSCI one of the most popular measures of commodity investment performance. The index is composed of physical commodities only, and energy
generally represents more than 60 percent of its weight (approximately 66.5 percent
as of December 31, 2010). There is no index rebalancing. Since it has no rebalancing,
rising prices cause a commodity to have an increasing weight in the index.

Commodities are major inputs in the production process. Therefore, the prices
of commodities, which are determined primarily by near-term events, should be positively related with the inflation rate. Specifically, higher commodity prices should
ultimately result in higher inflation. Stock and bond prices that are based upon discounted cash flow expectations can react negatively to inflation, especially in the
short term. Therefore, commodities can help protect a portfolio from the adverse
impact of unanticipated inflationary pressures.

Due to low correlations with stocks and bonds, commodities provide significant
diversification benefits. Instability in the Middle East, wars, and supply disruptions
due to natural disaster like hurricanes, earthquakes, droughts, and floods may adversely impact the supply of certain commodities driving prices up. Meanwhile,
most of these events negatively impact stock prices.

Equity Real Estate Investment Trusts and Private Real Estate

Equity real estate investment trusts (REITs) are companies that own and actively
manage income-producing commercial real estate properties. As of February 2011,
there were 128 publicly traded equity REITs, representing $392 billion in total market
cap. In 1960, President Dwight Eisenhower signed into law the Cigar Tax Extension,
which included a favorable tax provision allowing REITs to avoid taxation. In order
for a REIT to qualify for the favorable tax treatment, it must invest at least 75 percent
of its assets in real estate, generate at least 75 percent of its income from property
leases, and distribute at least 90 percent of annual taxable income as dividends
to shareholders.

While equity REIT shares constitute ownership interests in businesses, their high correlation with each other and low correlation with other types of stocks warrants their classification as a separate asset class. The liquidity and favorable tax treatment of publically traded REITs offer advantages over non-REIT private real estate ownership. Because nonprofit investors are tax exempt, they escape both direct and indirect income taxation. Another benefit of REITs over private real estate is that publicly traded REITs are registered and regulated by the Securities and Exchange Commission (SEC) and must adhere to corporate governance and financial reporting standards.

While all real estate represents real tangible assets, many commercial and residential properties derive significant value from their ability to generate cash flows from the rents of residential and commercial customers. So unlike farmland, which has intrinsic value because of its productive capacity to grow food, real estate properties in population centers demand valuation premiums because tenants are willing to pay for location. That location premium can be tied to the health of the economy, employment, and other local factors. When economies enter traditional recessions, the relatively long life of real estate leases can provide a revenue buffer; the economy hopefully recovers before many leases expire or renters default. REITs earnings are still tied to the sustainability of healthy economic activity. Lease contracts only have value to the extent that businesses and residential tenants have the capacity to honor their leases.

Private real estate and publically traded REITs both provide exposure to the same asset class. Private real estate is often touted as providing greater diversification benefits than REITs because REITs have some positive correlation to the stock market. However, private real estate has no readily observable market price, so correlation to stocks cannot be precisely measured over short intervals. An inability to measure correlation does not prove an absence of correlation.

Private real estate and public REITs have more fundamental differences than liquidity. REITs are usually comprised of well-established income-generating properties and do not typically invest in development projects or major property improvements. The best argument for investing in illiquid private real estate instead of REITs is that a skillful manager has greater flexibility to add value through development or major renovations and improvements. Private real estate investments also have greater latitude to use leverage, which can multiply returns (although with increased risk).

Farmland

Farmland investors acquire and rent land to farmers to produce crops. Farmland supply is constrained due to urban sprawl, limited expansion, and low turnover. High-quality farmland has historically produced uncorrelated, competitive returns with less volatility than equities. Returns are comprised of cash flows generated by producing and selling agriculture products and the long-term capital appreciation of the land. Farmland is an inefficient asset, meaning a skillful manager can add significant value.

Historically, farmland has been owned and operated by individual farmers—the quintessential "Mom and Pop" operation. However, modern farming has become more institutionalized. First, there is a growing trend toward the separation of owners and operators. Long gone are the days of "40 acres and a mule." Modern farm equipment is huge . . . and expensive. A combine may cost half a million dollars. Operators need to farm thousands of acres to rationalize the use of such equipment. Secondly, farming has become more technologically advanced. Laser land leveling, genetically engineered seed, advances in irrigation techniques, and insect control have enabled yields to rise dramatically over the past 20 years. Finally, many non-operators who inherit farms want to sell to realize the cash value of their land. There is a growing trend toward institutional ownership. The California Public Employees Retirement System (CALPERS) is one example of such an institutional owner.

Farm management companies exist to oversee the farms for absentee landlords. They can help with the acquisition of the land, identifying and contracting with the operator, selling the commodities, and stewardship of the land. Some of these companies are large, overseeing thousands of individual farms and employing hundreds of individuals. The individual managers typically hold a Bachelor of Science in Agriculture, have extensive farming experience, and are accredited by organizations like the *American Society of Farm Managers and Rural Appraisers* (ASFMRA).

Farmland has historically produced a cash return of 3 to 5 percent plus appreciation. Over long periods of time the appreciation component has been about 1 percent above the inflation rate. Often a good farm manager can enhance the total return by suggesting improvements to the land. Examples of such improvements include: *laser land leveling* (to eliminate low spots that may flood), installing *drain tiles*, building on-site *grain storage or drying bins,* drilling wells, or adding center-pivot irrigation systems.

Farmland owners receive income through one of these methods:

- *Cash rent*—The operator pays a fixed price, for example, $200 per acre. This method is the least risky for the owner and therefore, usually has the lowest return potential.
- *Share crop*—The owner and operator split input costs (seed, herbicide, pesticide, etc.) and share the proceeds of the crop sale.
- *Custom farming*—The owner pays all input cost and pays an operator to plant, weed, and harvest the crop. The owner receives all profit from the sale. This method has both the greatest risk and return potential.

Farmland returns are virtually uncorrelated with stock and bond returns and so can enhance total portfolio risk-adjusted return. The land can be acquired on either a *cash* basis or a *leveraged* basis. Risks of farm ownership include commodity price fluctuation, weather (drought or flooding), operator disappointment, insects, and fuel inflation. As with all investments, it is best to diversify both geographically and by crop type. Crop insurance is a must.

In addition to direct ownership of farmland, a nonprofit can purchase shares in an *agricultural partnership,* structured much like a private equity fund. Limited partners own shares in a diversified pool of farmland assets; the general partner oversees the pool and contracts with farm managers and operators. This structure allows for diversification with a smaller amount of capital but adds an extra layer of fees.

Energy Infrastructure Master Limited Partnerships

Master Limited Partnerships (MLPs) are publicly traded partnerships that were born out of tax-friendly legislation in the 1980s. The Tax Reform Act of 1986 enabled companies organized under the MLP structure to pass all income, losses, gains, and deductions on to limited partners *without* corporate taxation. Fearing that many corporations would rush to adopt the tax-friendly MLP structure, Congress followed up with The Revenue Act of 1987. The Act limited the MLP structure to companies where at least 90 percent of their income was considered "qualifying income," defined as "income and gains derived from the exploration, development, mining or production, processing, refining, transportation (including pipelines transporting gas, oil, or similar products), or the marketing of any mineral or natural resource including fertilizer, geothermal energy, and timber." As a result, the majority of modern day MLPs own and operate energy infrastructure assets such as pipelines that transport crude oil, natural gas, and other petroleum products. As of December 2010, the 50 largest MLPs represent a total market cap of $206 billion. Approximately 70 percent of the MLP market is dedicated to the (midstream) transportation of petroleum products and natural gas. Less than 7 percent are dedicated to exploration and production.

MLPs are traded like shares of stock on public exchanges and are regulated by the Securities and Exchange Commission. However, unlike ownership interests in traditional corporations, MLP ownership interests are divided into two groups, a *general partner* (GP) and *limited partners* (LP). The GP typically has a 2 percent stake, manages the partnership, and has *unlimited* liability. On the other hand, the LPs provide the capital and receive cash distributions from the partnership. The LP's risk is limited to their invested capital. Also, the LP's ownership interest is structured as "units" rather than as "shares" and the cash flows to the LPs are called "distributions" rather than "dividends."

In the 1980s, MLPs were involved in a variety of businesses, including risky oil and natural gas exploration and production companies. These exploration and production MLPs fell victim to falling energy prices and depleting reserve bases and often relied heavily on exploratory drilling to sustain cash flow. Without reinvestment, many of these MLPs were self-liquidating partnerships and were ultimately unable to sustain their distributions. In the late 1980s and early 1990s, large energy companies started transferring their low-growth physical pipeline assets (that generated "qualifying income") to the more tax-efficient MLP structure. MLPs were reborn, largely as midstream energy infrastructure assets that transported, processed, and stored natural gas, crude oil, and refined petroleum products. So unlike the exploration and drilling MLPs of the prior era, today's MLPs focus on energy transportation, refining, and storage and are relatively insulated from volatile energy prices.

Beginning in the late 1990s, many MLPs began making significant acquisitions, pursuing growth projects, and aggressively raising distributions. This change in focus was largely due to the continued availability of midstream energy transportation assets as large diversified energy companies (mainly C-Corps) divested their mature assets to redeploy capital to higher growth opportunities. MLPs were able to take advantage of their tax-exempt structure, which affords them a lower cost of capital and allows them to produce higher after-tax returns than traditional corporations.

Modern day MLPs mainly own midstream energy infrastructure assets like pipelines that generate "tariffs" for the transportation of crude oil and refined petroleum products (jet fuel, gasoline, and distillate fuel oil). These tariffs generate fee income, like a toll road. Most pipelines that cross state lines are regulated by the Federal Energy Regulatory Commission (FERC). The FERC regulates the rates that pipelines can charge, usually building in annual *inflation adjustors*. Therefore, the fees generated are usually not tied directly to changes in the price of the transported commodity, but rather simply to the quantity and distance of the transported good. This fee income tends to be fairly stable over time. As the volume of the commodity transported increases with demand growth (and inflation increases), the fee revenues increase.

Because MLPs distribute virtually all available cash to unit holders, they must access the capital markets to finance growth. This dynamic causes MLPs to be disciplined acquirers, at least compared to traditional corporations because management teams must demonstrate to unit holders that acquisitions and projects are immediately accretive to earnings.

From 1996 to 2010, the Alerian MLP Index generated a compounded total annual return of 16.8 percent. Over the same period, the S&P 500 Index returned 6.8 percent and the Barclays Capital Aggregate U.S. Bond Index returned 6.0 percent. More importantly, the Alerian MLP Index's correlation was 0.34 to stocks and 0.05 to bonds.

Looking forward, MLPs offer distributions (or yields), plus the potential for distribution growth. As of January 2011, the MLP market's average yield was 6.2 percent. While the high historical growth rate for the last 15 years may be difficult to duplicate over the coming decade, a 3 to 5 percent growth rate may be sustainable in the foreseeable future due to the continued growth in demand for energy in the United States and the inflation adjustments in some MLP contracts. Moreover, C-Corps continue to hold a significant number of (non-core) qualifying assets that are potentially available for divestiture. MLPs can also increase distributions organically by connecting existing pipelines and building new ones. Combining the current 6.2 percent distribution yield with a potential 3 to 5 percent distribution growth rate means an expected 9.2 to 11.2 percent annual return does not seem unreasonable. In an era of low interest rates and relatively low equity risk premiums, a 9.2 to 11.2 percent potential annual return is attractive. Of course, since MLPs are publicly traded, their prices can go down as well as up. Since their total market cap is relatively small, buying or selling pressure can move prices precipitously.

Broad Infrastructure Investing

In the early 1900s, con artists "sold the Brooklyn Bridge" to gullible victims. Beginning in the 1990s, governments sold bridges and other infrastructure assets to private institutional investors. The *global private infrastructure* investing asset class was born.

The potential global infrastructure asset base is massive (an estimated $20 trillion). So far, only a tiny fraction is owned by private investors, but cash-strapped cities and states have begun to sell. Infrastructure assets are tangible structures, networks, and facilities that perform important functions for economic activity.

Infrastructure includes *transportation* assets such as bridges, toll roads, railroads, tunnels, seaports, and airports. It also includes *communication* assets like television and radio towers, wireless networks, cable systems, and satellite networks. Additional infrastructure assets can include electricity transmission lines, utilities, water systems, hospitals, prisons, schools, courthouses, and even parking meters.

Private infrastructure investments share some characteristics with other asset classes. The structure, liquidity, and (relatively high) fees of investment pools are similar to those of private equity investments. The significant cash yield component is like fixed income. Like commercial real estate, a significant portion of value comes from the structures built on the land rather than just the land itself. Unlike many investable assets, the intrinsic value of many infrastructure assets is relatively impervious to economic cycles. Whether the economy is in expansion or contraction mode, society presumably needs core infrastructure assets in order to function.

Infrastructure assets can be attractive for many reasons. Most perform critical functions and face little or no competition so they have stable cash flows, asset values can be protected against inflation as revenues are implicitly or explicitly linked to inflation (i.e., utility rate setting, toll road rates), and leases or concession agreements typically range up to 99 years providing a long expected asset life.

However, infrastructure investments face a variety of esoteric risks. Assets are often controlled directly or indirectly by government entities and can face political pressures or regulatory risk. Illiquidity is a significant risk as there is essentially no secondary market. The newness of private infrastructure investing creates some concern. There is not yet enough history to teach us what *can* go wrong. Valuation uncertainty creates auditing challenges. The uniqueness of each asset makes performance benchmarking difficult. Physical risks such as natural disasters or terrorist attacks can impair value, depending on insurance policies and each circumstance. Lastly, operation of many infrastructure assets can be complex, and the lack of skilled operators might pose problems.

For nonprofit investors with a very long time horizon and low liquidity needs, private infrastructure investments offer the ability to generate inflation-protected investment returns along with significant diversification benefits. However, given private infrastructure's complex, small, and fragmented nature, manager selection and access to the highest quality assets are critical to success.

Timberland

Over the past 20 years, endowments, foundations, and pensions have made timberland investing a part of their "playbook." Global institutional investors now own about $35 billion of timberland, including $25 billion in the United States, representing about 8 percent of total investable timberland. However, about $150 billion worth of timberland remains owned by private non-industrial landowners. Landowners and forest products companies continue to divest timber holdings, creating opportunities for increased institutional ownership.

Timberland differs from virtually all other investable assets in that its primary source of total return is derived from organic growth. Trees grow as long as rain falls and the sun shines. As an investable real asset class, timberland offers several attractive characteristics, including historically attractive risk-adjusted returns compared to traditional asset classes and significant diversification benefits independent of capital market forces.

Trees grow in size into higher-valued assets. For example, in the southern United States, young trees begin as lower-valued *pulpwood*, but grow into a combination pulpwood and *saw timber trees*, which range from 9 to 12 inches in diameter. As these trees continue to grow beyond 12 inches in diameter, they become even more valuable because they can be used for lumber products. As tree growth continues, the value of their product classes increases as well. The negative impact of waiting to harvest (*the time value of money*) can be offset by the increasing size and value of the trees. When timber prices fall due to adverse economic forces, the timber investor can simply delay harvesting. This is very different than growing an agricultural commodity which must be harvested each year regardless of market prices.

Due to soil and climate conditions, geographical regions favor different types of trees. Expected returns and risk vary substantially by region and species of tree. The U.S. timber market is typically divided into three regions: the *Northwest, Northeast,* and the *South.* The Northwest and Northeast typically produce superior hardwoods (cherry, oak, maple, and ash), while southern timberland properties generally produce softwoods (pine, fir, and spruce). Additionally, one can diversify globally with timber investments in places like New Zealand and British Columbia, Canada.

There are strong demographic reasons to believe timber prices may continue to rise, adding another potential component to total return. Demand for timber has been rising fast, especially in emerging-market countries. This trend may continue as the middle class in emerging-market countries expands. Furthermore, international political pressure to protect publicly owned forests may further enhance timber values by creating supply shortages.

Timberland can generate income throughout the life of an investment as trees on the land are periodically harvested and sold. The income varies based on the investment and management strategy for different timberland properties, but can be a meaningful component of total return. The land used to grow the timber may also contain mineral resources, and be sold at a premium for its natural resources value. In other cases, timberland may be converted to a "higher use" (i.e., commercial real estate development as cities expand). At the very least, timberland tends to appreciate with inflation.

The *NCREIF Timberland Index* is a composite of investment performance of a large pool of individual timber properties acquired in the private market for investment purposes only. All properties in the Index have been acquired in whole or in part by institutional investors. All properties are held in a fiduciary environment. Between 1987 and 2010, the NCREIF Timberland Index returned 13.5 percent annually, compared to 9.6 percent for the S&P 500 Index. Over the same period, the NCREIF Timberland Index had an 11.4 percent annual standard deviation compared to 18.6 percent for the S&P 500 Index. Furthermore, the annual correlation between the two indices was 0.24.

However, these compelling numbers should be taken with a grain of salt. While the timberland index performance is calculated quarterly, most appraisals are performed annually. This gives the illusion of seasonality with most of the returns appearing in the fourth quarter. Appraisal data skew volatility and correlation measures as well. For example, the lagged correlation, or the correlation between the S&P 500 in year N and the timberland index in Year N+1 was 0.32 during this period. This illustrates a "lagged beta" effect due to the illiquid nature of timberland. In other words, if timberland were publicly traded, it would likely show a higher correlation.

As with any investable asset, higher returns come with corresponding risk. Illiquidity is a prime risk; cash commitments typically exceed 10 years and some investments may take up to 20. Therefore, nonprofit fiduciaries should carefully consider their cash-flow requirements before investing. Natural disasters like fire and insects pose another risk, but these losses for industrial managed forests in the United States have historically been less than one half of one percent per year. Another risk is that timber prices can fall, but that risk is mitigated long-term by "storing the timber on the trunk" (delaying harvesting until conditions improve). Supply shocks are possible if the governments create new legislation to protect threatened or endangered species. The spotted owl crisis of the early 1990s is a prime example (although bad for loggers, it was actually good for aggregate timberland investors because it led to higher timber prices).

Most institutions invest in pooled vehicles due to the cost and time horizon involved. Pooled funds are managed by *timberland investment management organizations (TIMOs)*. The typical investment structure is a limited partnership investing in a portfolio of properties diversified by location, timber market, tree age, species, and end product. Similar to private equity investments, timberland management fees are relatively high (one to two percent with an incentive fee above a hurdle rate).

However, a good timber manager can add value in several ways, including property due diligence, negotiating purchases and sales, diversifying the portfolio by species and geography, and ongoing forest management to maximize timber output per field. Investors should focus heavily on the quality, experience, and depth of the management team. Managing timberland investments is a highly specialized niche and very labor intensive. Experience matters.

While illiquidity can be an issue and timberland is full of esoteric risks, effective timberland investment offers returns competitive with equities as well as significant portfolio diversification benefits, especially protection against rising inflation. Timberland is most appropriate for nonprofit investors with very long time horizons and manageable liquidity needs.

Gold

While gold is just one of many commodities, it has played a unique role in human history as a preferred store of value. In modern times, global financial markets have played a key role in shaping the relevancy of gold. In 1944, the *Bretton Woods Agreement* set the price of one ounce of gold at $35 U.S. dollars. This price remained virtually unchanged until 1971 when the United States went off the gold standard. Most major countries followed the U.S. example in the early 1970s and adopted floating exchange rates, and thus gold fell out of favor, taking a back seat to world currencies, equities, and bonds.

Following its decoupling from the U.S. dollar, gold prices climbed throughout the 1970s, culminating in a January 1980 intraday price high of $850 per ounce.

Similar to the most recent run-up in gold prices, the oil crisis of the late 1970s, coupled with inflation concerns, resulted in a peak in gold prices. Gold eventually fell back to $300 per ounce by late 1982. Gold traded mostly sideways for the next 20 years (1982 to 2002), hitting a bottom of $252 per ounce in August 1999. The terrorist attacks of 9/11 and the subsequent wars in Iraq and Afghanistan triggered renewed interest in the precious metal, and it began its current rise. As we've witnessed throughout history, global conflicts and civil unrest often result in a flight to gold as investors seek wealth preservation in times of geopolitical uncertainty.

Investors have a variety of options to gain portfolio exposure to gold. The most straightforward option is through the physical purchase of gold either in coin or bullion. However, this can be an inefficient method of investing, as gold dealers typically charge a commission of several percentage points over the spot price, and investors then must store and protect the bars.

Exchange-traded funds (ETFs) offer perhaps the most cost-effective structure to gain exposure to gold. However, in order to access the value of a gold ETF, the investor must one day convert the ETF shares back into the U.S. dollar-dominated cash. Gold investors who seek to protect themselves from the risk of U.S. government insolvency and the death of the U.S. dollar may find the need to convert gold back into the fiat currency problematic.

Investors can gain indirect portfolio exposure to gold by investing in gold mining companies. Mining company stocks, however, are not only sensitive to the price of gold but also the underlying company performance and general market movements. Mining companies make vast capital expenditures on exploration and extraction, and the company's performance is ultimately determined by the relative success or failure of such projects. The futures market offers investors another method to gain portfolio exposure to gold.

While gold affords investors a hedge against inflation and some geopolitical crises, there can be other, lower-risk ways to insulate against such risks, such as investing in TIPS. Of course, the one advantage of physical gold over TIPS is that the U.S. Treasury could theoretically "explicitly" default on its obligations, rendering TIPS worthless. However, under that extremely dire circumstance, the gold owner must also be prepared to protect his or her valuable metal as government protections, property rights, and order break down. If one wants to invest in physical gold to hedge against the "Mad Max" scenario, one may also want to consider investing in a mercenary army to protect against looting mobs!

Other Investible Real Asset Categories

Other real asset subsectors offer nonprofits varying degrees of inflation protection, return potential, and diversification. *Water* is another precious resource that investors have reexamined over the past decade. While information is incomplete, it is hard to deny the compelling supply-demand story. Only about 3 percent of the world's water is fresh. Unlike oil, water has few, if any, suitable substitutes. Demand is not projected to decline any time soon, and the development of the world's emerging markets will continue to pressure supplies, potentially driving prices higher. Investing in water has historically been difficult since there is no water futures contract. Instead, water investment is usually indirect through water utility companies that maintain and develop water networks and infrastructure around the world.

Collectibles such as stamps, antiques, artwork, and baseball cards are loosely defined as rare assets. Collectibles are relatively illiquid assets and do not generate income. Depending on the type of asset (e.g., a Picasso painting versus a collectable child's toy from the early 1900s), the liquidity and marketability can vary dramatically. While an expert may be able to predict the future value of a collectable, it is difficult to determine where such an investment fits within a diversified institutional investment portfolio.

Conclusion

Real assets can serve multiple purposes within a diversified nonprofit portfolio. Many nonprofits have spending needs that are implicitly or explicitly tied to inflation. While each underlying real asset class has its own unique risks, the inflation-protected nature of intrinsically valuable assets can improve portfolio diversification, especially when the portfolio is heavily allocated to financial assets like stocks and bonds.

Note

1. Source: 2010 NACUBO-Commonfund Study of Endowments. The dollar-weighted average allocation to alternative investments was 52 percent for the 850 institutions surveyed. On average, about 24 percent of the alternative investment allocation was invested in real assets, which implies a 12.5 percent real assets (timberland, real estate, natural resources, commodities, infrastructure, etc.) allocation. The size of the alternative investments allocation was positively correlated to size. For institutions in excess of $1 billion in assets, the average allocation to alternative investments was 60 percent. For institutions between $101 and $500 million, the average allocation to alternative investments was 35 percent. For institutions under $25 million, the allocation to alternative investments was 12 percent.

CHAPTER 8

Performance Measurement and Evaluation

Performance measurement and evaluation are essential components of fiduciary oversight for nonprofit investors. Performance measurement quantifies investment performance. Evaluation provides the context for that performance so the investor can determine if it is at an acceptable level. The current regulatory climate and increased scrutiny of fiduciaries reinforces the importance of performance measurement and evaluation. Nonprofit fiduciaries must ensure that investment managers adhere to their stated styles and investment policy guidelines. Effective performance monitoring and evaluation allow fiduciaries to make proactive rather than reactive decisions.

Why Monitor Performance?

Evaluating investment manager performance appears straightforward. After all, good managers are those that consistently outperform their benchmarks, right? Unfortunately, it is not that simple. Thoughtful performance evaluation is essential to distinguish skillful managers from those that are just plain lucky. Your written *investment policy statement* (IPS) should set performance guidelines, objectives, and risk constraints. The IPS should also lay out a process for the selection, hiring, and monitoring of investment managers. Those guidelines enable one to measure the manager's performance versus stated goals. Such comparisons enhance understanding. Comparison metrics typically include an appropriate *index benchmark* and a *peer group* of similar investment managers. Performance should also be evaluated on a *risk-adjusted basis*.

Performance Calculations

Performance measurement begins with calculating a rate of return for the investment manager. The total rate of return can be calculated on a *dollar-weighted* or a *time-weighted* basis. The dollar-weighted method, also known as internal rate of return, includes the impact of the timing of cash flows on total performance. A limitation of dollar-weighted returns is that performance depends largely on the timing of cash flows. For example, if the nonprofit fund invests additional funds with a manager just before the market falls, the dollar-weighted return magnifies the impact of that loss through no fault of the manager. Since cash flows are outside the manager's control, dollar-weighted returns are not useful when comparing performance to index returns or the returns of other managers. Investors use the time-weighted method as the standard performance measure because it is not sensitive to the timing of cash flows like the dollar-weighted method. The time-weighted method determines the rate of return between cash flows and links the returns to calculate longer period performance. This isolates a manager's performance from the timing of cash flows and allows for a more consistent measure of a manager's performance relative to other managers and indices.

Investment returns can be presented *gross* or *net* of management fees. "Gross-of-fees" performance results do not reflect the deduction of management fees. If a manager is reporting performance "net of fees," the reported results include the deduction of management fees. Net-of-fee performance reflects the actual return earned by the investor. However, because investment managers typically charge investors varying management fees based on asset size or other factors, gross-of-fees comparisons are generally more appropriate when comparing performance relative to other managers or indices. However, it is obviously important to consider the impact of fees on performance.

Benchmarks

Benchmarks enable investors to evaluate the relative performance of investment managers. Absolute performance results without the reference to a benchmark reveal little about *why* a manager performed as he or she did. Any benchmark should meet certain minimum standards: the benchmark should be widely followed, have a clear construction methodology, and represent the appropriate asset class and investment style.

Using the wrong benchmarks for evaluation purposes can result in misleading or incorrect conclusions about manager performance. It can lead nonprofits to terminate a good manager, and it can lead to the retention of a manager who should be terminated.

Market Index Basics

A market index is a *basket of securities* representing an asset class. Market indices can be *broad* and include all listed securities in an asset class, or *narrow* such as market capitalization or sector-specific subsets. Market indices exist for virtually every asset class, country, style, sector, and sub-sector.

One needs to understand index construction methodologies because they drive security weights, return calculation, index rebalancing, and ongoing constituent changes to the index. In a *market cap-weighted* index, each security is held in proportion to its capitalization relative to the entire market. In an *equal-weighted* index, each security is assigned an equal weight regardless of market capitalization. Index vendors periodically reconstitute the underlying securities to reflect market changes and corporate actions such as mergers and spin-offs. For example, Russell reconstitutes its indices annually, while S&P indices are done on an as-needed basis.

Because stocks trade on exchanges and prices are readily available, the major indices are maintained by stock exchanges such as the Nasdaq and New York Stock Exchange (NYSE) or publishing companies such as Dow Jones. The prices of fixed income securities are less transparent. As a result, the most commonly used indices are those created by large institutions that participate in the fixed-income markets such as Bank of America Merrill Lynch, J.P. Morgan, Barclays Capital, and Citigroup. Barclays Capital now oversees the former Lehman Brothers indices that were rebranded under the Barclays name in November 2008 after Lehman's bankruptcy.

It is important to select the right market index for a benchmark. The index benchmark should be consistent with the manager's investment style, to facilitate apples-to-apples comparisons. The closer the index fits the style of the manager, the more useful it is for evaluation purposes. It is important to compare your results over various time periods to help identify past trends in performance relative to the index and peer group as they emerge (see Exhibit 8.1).

Investment Style

Vendors construct equity indices based on both market capitalization and *investment style* (e.g., *growth* or *value*). Growth companies are expected to grow earnings and revenues faster than their peers. Growth stocks tend to have higher price/earnings (PE) and price-to-book (PB) ratios. Value stocks have low prices relative to their intrinsic values. They tend to have low PE and PB ratios and higher dividend yields. For example, the domestic U.S. large-cap Russell 1000 Index is sorted into growth stocks and value stocks (the Russell 1000 Growth and the Russell 1000 Value indices). Style-based indices are further broken down into mid- and small-cap components. The Russell Midcap Value, Russell Midcap Growth, Russell 2000 Value, and Russell 2000 Growth indices perform similar functions for mid- and small-cap stocks. In the international markets, several indices such as the *MSCI Europe, Australasia, and Far East (EAFE)* Index are further broken down into growth and value segments. They are also segmented by size.

The most important distinction among equity managers is *investment style*: growth and value. When one of these styles is favored by the market, the other tends to be "in the doghouse." Exhibit 8.2 shows relative performance of the Russell 1000 Growth and Value indexes relative to the Russell 1000 (the center line).

Fixed-income indices are constructed based on the sector, maturity, and credit worthiness of the issuer. Indices exist for virtually every bond segment, including *government, mortgage-backed, high-yield, foreign, and investment-grade corporate securities*. Fixed-income indices are more difficult to replicate than equity-market indices. They hold a large number of issues, some of which may not even trade on any given day. For example, the *Barclays Capital U.S. Aggregate Bond Index* had about 8,000 government, corporate, and mortgaged-backed securities as of early 2011.

EXHIBIT 8.1 Performance versus Index (various time periods)

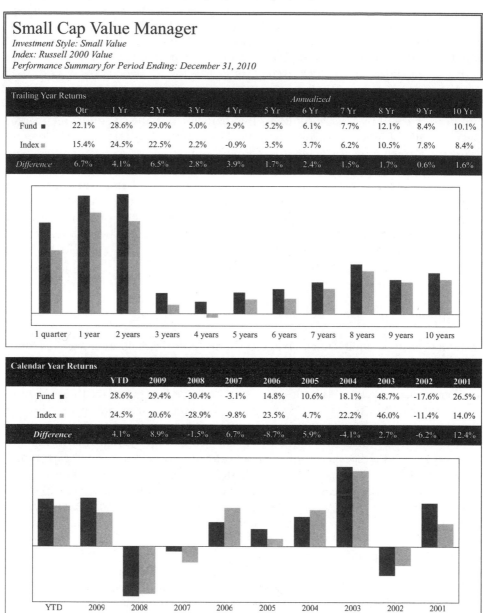

Small Cap Value Manager
Investment Style: Small Value
Index: Russell 2000 Value
Performance Summary for Period Ending: December 31, 2010

Trailing Year Returns							Annualized				
	Qtr	1 Yr	2 Yr	3 Yr	4 Yr	5 Yr	6 Yr	7 Yr	8 Yr	9 Yr	10 Yr
Fund ■	22.1%	28.6%	29.0%	5.0%	2.9%	5.2%	6.1%	7.7%	12.1%	8.4%	10.1%
Index ■	15.4%	24.5%	22.5%	2.2%	-0.9%	3.5%	3.7%	6.2%	10.5%	7.8%	8.4%
Difference	6.7%	4.1%	6.5%	2.8%	3.9%	1.7%	2.4%	1.5%	1.7%	0.6%	1.6%

Calendar Year Returns										
	YTD	2009	2008	2007	2006	2005	2004	2003	2002	2001
Fund ■	28.6%	29.4%	-30.4%	-3.1%	14.8%	10.6%	18.1%	48.7%	-17.6%	26.5%
Index ■	24.5%	20.6%	-28.9%	-9.8%	23.5%	4.7%	22.2%	46.0%	-11.4%	14.0%
Difference	4.1%	8.9%	-1.5%	6.7%	-8.7%	5.9%	-4.1%	2.7%	-6.2%	12.4%

There are also specialized sector and industry-specific indices that track narrow sectors of the market. Numerous country and regional indices focus on a single country or region of the world. For example, the *MSCI Japan* and *MSCI Pacific* are widely used as market-index benchmarks for investment managers that focus their investments in Japan or the broader Pacific Region.

EXHIBIT 8.2 Shifting Favor of Growth versus Value Styles

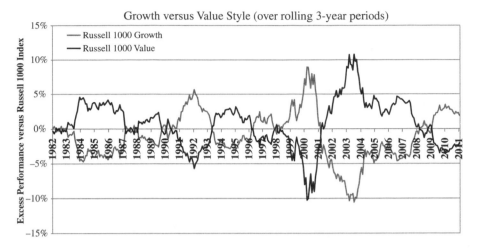

Socially responsible indices (SRI) or ethical indices are also available. These include only those companies that satisfy certain social criteria. For instance, these indices may ban holdings in the index based on things such as exposure to alcohol, tobacco, firearms, gambling, or countries like the Republic of the Sudan. See Chapter 11 for more information about socially responsible investing.

Major Market Indices

The major index providers for the U.S. equity markets include Standard & Poor's (S&P), Russell Investments, Wilshire, and Dow Jones. The granddaddy of all broad-based benchmarks is the Dow Jones Industrial Average (DJIA). Established in 1896, it is the oldest and most frequently quoted index in the world. While widely followed, the DJIA only tracks the performance of 30 large "blue chip" U.S. stocks. The second most widely known index is the S&P 500, which represents 500 companies considered to be industry leaders. Russell Investments is among the most commonly used family of style-specific and market-cap-weighted U.S. equity indices.

Barclay's Capital and Citigroup boast some of the better-known fixed-income indices. Flagship benchmarks in the Barclays Capital platform include both the *U.S. Aggregate*, which is often used as a proxy for the entire investment grade bond market, and the *U.S. Treasury Inflation Protected Securities (TIPS)* Index. The *Barclays U.S. Corporate High Yield* and the *Citigroup High Yield Market* are widely used high-yield indices. These indices represent below-investment-grade securities, also known as "junk bonds." As U.S.-based-investor demand for foreign fixed income has grown, providers have created currency *hedged* and *un-hedged* foreign fixed-income indices.

MSCI is a leading provider of both broad-based and country-specific indices for both international developed and emerging markets. The MSCI EAFE Index is the pre-eminent benchmark for developed international equity performance and comprises the developed markets outside of North America. The MSCI Emerging Markets Index measures performance in emerging markets equities.

There are indices for less-traditional asset classes, including hedge funds, energy infrastructure master limited partnerships (MLPs), Real Estate Investment Trusts (REITs), commodities, timberland, private equity, and other asset classes (see Chapters 5 through 7).

Determining the Right Index

An index may be a useful benchmark only if it is *investable* and its performance is *measurable*. The index should be transparent and have securities that can be purchased in the market. Investors should use a market index benchmark that has a high *R-squared* to the investment manager. R-squared quantifies how closely an investment manager's returns are correlated with those of the index. A high R-squared (1.00 is the highest) implies a high explanation value between the index and manager. A low R-squared (0.00 is the lowest) means that very little of the manager's return variance can be explained by the index. The higher the R-squared between manager and index, the more useful is the index as an evaluation benchmark.

Style analysis of the investment manager is a valuable tool when choosing the appropriate index benchmark. Given that investment styles cycle in and out of favor, performance evaluation must be normalized for style factors. An investment manager may have a style that has been out of favor. If a manager's investment strategy crosses multiple asset classes or investment styles, a blending of multiple indices may be appropriate.

Peer Group Universes

Peer group comparisons play an important role in manager evaluations. They show how a manager has performed relative to a group of similar managers. Unlike an index's single performance number, a peer group consists of multiple return streams that can be ranked from the top- to bottom-performing manager.

When a universe is defined too broadly, the investment characteristics may not reflect the manager's mandate and will not yield meaningful information. Therefore, peer groups should be appropriate to the manager being evaluated or the analysis can become a counterproductive "apple-versus-orange" exercise. A peer group is reported with percentile rankings. For example, a percentile ranking of 1 is best, and 100 is worst. A ranking of 50 means the manager outperformed half of the peer universe. A ranking of 25 means the manager was in the top quarter of the universe. Obviously, one desires high rankings over all time periods. However, it is more important to rank well over longer rather than shorter periods (see Exhibit 8.3).

Universes (or peer groups) have limitations. They are *not* investable and they are not specified in advance of the performance period (they are only quantified by looking back). Universes also tend to have "survivorship bias," where poor performing managers drop out of the universe. Underperforming managers are often liquidated or merged with more successful managers. When this happens, only the successful manager's track record is maintained in the peer group, and the poorly performing manager's record disappears as if it never existed.

EXHIBIT 8.3 Performance versus Peer Group

Trailing Year Universe Rankings

	Qtr	1 Yr	2 Yr	3 Yr	4 Yr	5 Yr	6 Yr	7 Yr	8 Yr	9 Yr	10 Yr
Fund ●	22.1%	28.6%	29.0%	5.0%	2.9%	5.2%	6.1%	7.7%	12.1%	8.4%	10.1%
	1	30	44	43	34	37	25	37	33	61	40
Index ◆	15.4%	24.5%	22.5%	2.2%	-0.9%	3.5%	3.7%	6.2%	10.5%	7.8%	8.4%
	53	68	90	72	81	70	69	73	65	73	72
5th Pctl	19.5%	34.6%	47.0%	9.3%	5.8%	8.5%	8.3%	10.0%	14.2%	11.4%	12.4%
25th Pctl	17.2%	29.6%	32.7%	6.3%	3.6%	6.5%	6.2%	8.6%	12.6%	10.0%	11.3%
Median	15.4%	26.1%	27.9%	4.2%	1.8%	4.4%	5.0%	7.0%	11.3%	8.6%	9.5%
75th Pctl	13.8%	23.2%	25.2%	2.0%	-0.4%	2.6%	3.5%	5.9%	10.1%	7.6%	8.4%
95th Pctl	10.1%	17.7%	20.7%	-0.6%	-2.7%	0.7%	0.6%	3.9%	8.5%	5.8%	7.0%

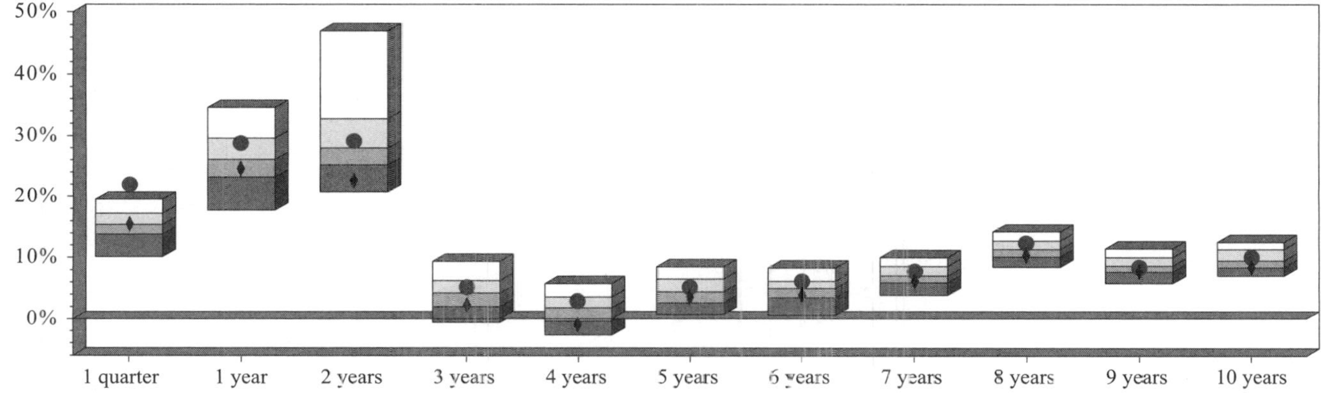

Modern Portfolio Theory Performance Metrics

An underpinning of *Modern Portfolio Theory* (MPT) is that expected returns of various asset classes are related to their risks. The greater the expected volatility or *systematic* risk, the greater return investors should expect for taking that risk. MPT uses statistical concepts to define risk and reward:

- *Beta* measures systematic risk relative to the benchmark. A portfolio with a beta of 1.0 has risk equivalent to that of the benchmark. If the market is up 5 percent, one would expect the portfolio to be up 5 percent. A portfolio with a beta greater than 1.0 has more risk than the index. For example, a portfolio with a beta of 1.5 would be up (or down) about 50 percent more than the index. In other words, if the market were down 10 percent, the manager would be down 15 percent.
- *Alpha* measures the return adjusted for beta. Positive alpha implies that the manager's decisions added value.
- *R-squared* measures the dispersion of the manager returns relative to the benchmark. The higher the R-squared, the more reliable the alpha and the beta statistics. (R-squared may range from 0 to 1.00.) Beta, alpha, and R-squared are derived from statistical regression analysis using the manager and the index benchmark returns as the dependent and independent variables respectively.
- *Standard deviation* measures the total volatility of the manager by measuring the dispersion of returns. Unlike beta, which measures risk relative to a market proxy, standard deviation is a measure of absolute risk. A high standard deviation means greater volatility.
- The *Sharpe ratio* measures return per unit of standard deviation. Developed by William Sharpe, the Sharpe ratio is simply the ratio of the portfolio return in excess of the risk-free rate (Treasury bills) to the portfolio's standard deviation. The higher the Sharpe ratio, the more return per unit of risk.
- A similar method, the *Treynor ratio,* was developed by Jack Treynor. The Treynor ratio is the ratio of the reward, defined as the portfolio return minus the risk-free rate, divided by the portfolio beta. Again, a higher Treynor ratio is better.
- *Batting average* measures a manager's ability to consistently meet or beat a benchmark. The batting average is calculated by dividing the number of months or quarters in which the manager beats or matches the index by the total number of months or quarters in the period. For example, a manager who outperforms the index in 10 out of 20 quarters would have a statistical batting average of 50. The longer the time period, the more statistically significant the measure becomes.
- *Up-market/down-market ratios* measure how the manager performed in both up and down markets by segregating the performance for each time period into the quarters in which *the index was positive or negative.* A simple arithmetic average of returns is calculated for the manager and the index based on the up and down quarters. For example, an up-capture ratio of 115 indicates that the manager has outperformed the index by 15 percent in periods

when the index has risen. A down-capture ratio of 80 would indicate the manager has declined only 80 percent as much as the declining index, indicating relative outperformance. Ideally, a manager would have a greater up-market-capture ratio than down-market-capture ratio.

Style Analysis

Managers' investment styles lead to discernable and predictable differences in performance. U.S. equity markets are differentiated by size (large-cap and small-cap stocks) and valuation (growth versus value stocks). Mid-cap stocks (value and growth) split the difference between large- and small-cap stocks. Growth style managers seek to identify companies with the best prospects for rapid earnings growth; value style managers seek to buy stocks at a discount to their true value. As mentioned, both styles may work, but they typically work at different times.

One form of style analysis is holdings-based style analysis, which examines the stocks held in the portfolio and maps these into styles at different points in time. In order to perform holdings-based style analysis over multiple time periods, it is necessary to have historical security holdings, which can be both time consuming and expensive. Another approach is returns-based style analysis. This is a technique that regresses a manager's historical returns against a family of style indices and determines the combination of indices that best explains the manager's performance. For example, this analysis may show that a particular large-cap growth manager's return stream was best explained by an 80 percent allocation to the Russell 1000 growth index (large-cap growth), a 10 percent allocation to the Russell 2000 growth (small-cap growth), and a 10 percent allocation to the Russell 1000 value (large-cap value).

The four primary style corners for U.S. equities are large-cap value, large-cap growth, small-cap value, and small-cap growth. An important benefit of style analysis is the ability to easily identify "style drift." Style drift refers to a manager's deviation from the expected investment style. This drift often occurs gradually—for example, when a small-cap manager starts gradually buying larger capitalization companies as its assets grow because it's becoming capacity constrained, but has opted not to close to new investors. By looking at this manager's style history over rolling periods, you would be able to see it drift more to mid- and large-cap stocks, which may mean the manager is no longer appropriate for the mandate (see Exhibit 8.4). See Chapter 4 for more information about style drift.

Style analysis can be used for market segments other than U.S. stocks. For example, a similar growth-value and large-small cap grid can be used to delineate investment styles for foreign equity investment managers. Also, one can evaluate additional dimensions of style, including emerging markets to analyze foreign-developed managers that may allocate to emerging-markets stocks. Similarly, one can also employ returns-based style analysis for fixed income. Dimensions of fixed income style include *duration*, *credit quality*, and other dimensions depending on the manager's mandate.

EXHIBIT 8.4 Style Drift

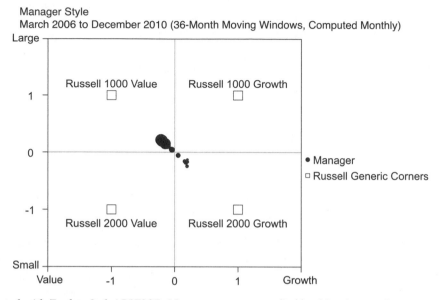

Created with Zephyr StyleADVISOR. Manager returns supplied by: Morningstar, Inc.

Portfolio Analysis

Attribution analysis disaggregates the components of a manager's investment decisions. Attribution analysis attempts to identify and quantify the contribution of *asset allocation, stock selection, currency, country, sector weightings,* and other factors to overall performance. Identifying *how* a manager's excess (or under) performance was generated gives one valuable insight into his skill level. Knowing *why* a manager performed the way he or she did gives more actionable information than just knowing *whether* he or she underperformed or outperformed a benchmark.

Manager database programs usually have attribution analysis features that allow one to evaluate manager decisions. Attribution analysis measures a manager's securities holdings versus the benchmark and differentiates allocation from selection decisions. Attribution analysis allows you to decompose a manager's performance. For example, if a manager's value-added acumen is supposed to be security selection, but all historical excess returns were driven by sector selection, there is a contradiction in the alpha thesis implying that the manager may have been more lucky than skillful.

Performance Reporting

At a minimum, investment managers should be reviewed quarterly. While three months is insufficient to make a "fire" or "retain" decision, ongoing quarterly attribution reports with manager commentary allows an investment committee to build context over time. This context can be crucial if a manger one day falls under consideration for termination for performance reasons. Quarterly performance reports should provide a clear and concise quantitative and qualitative summary. In addition to the quantitative measures discussed, commentary regarding a manager's security or sector positioning can provide insight into the manager's skill level. Their investment theses are ultimately proven correct or incorrect.

One should also constantly evaluate investment managers for *organizational, legal, regulatory,* or *investment-style* issues. Committees should have a procedure for "watch listing" managers. While the term "watch list" is a misnomer because presumably all managers should be watched, it has evolved into a catch-all term for managers on the verge of termination. For lack of a better analogy, a watch-listed manager has two strikes—one more and he or she is out. Triggers for adding an investment manager to "watch-list" status include but are not limited to:

- Trailing index benchmark over a three- or five-year period
- Poor peer group rank over a trailing three- or five-year period
- Style or strategy drift
- Deviation from investment process or philosophy
- Departure of key investment professional(s)
- Organization change, including ownership change
- Legal, regulatory, or compliance issues.

Depending on circumstances, one could skip the "watch-list" phase altogether and terminate an offender immediately. See Chapter 4 for more information about when to terminate managers.

Conclusion

Performance measurement and ongoing manager evaluation are critical elements of a sound decision-making process. While quarterly evaluation can be labor-intensive and the next actionable steps are not always apparent, the practice forces nonprofit committees to build context around manager performance. While past performance alone is a poor predictor of future performance, unless we have a crystal ball, all empirical information is based on what has *already happened.* Understanding the full context around a manger's past performance allows an investment committee to make better judgments about a manager's ability to perform well in the future. Bear in mind, the vast majority of good managers go through periods of underperformance. Without ongoing robust monitoring and evaluation, a nonprofit committee may lack the context to retain a good manager going through inevitable performance slumps.

CHAPTER 9

Structuring an Effective Investment Committee

The most effective investment committees focus on the organization and how their decisions impact its long-term mission. A well-written investment policy statement, an engaged investment committee, and a focused chairperson are all critical elements. However, they do not assure success. Volunteer investment committee members are usually smart, accomplished, and generous, but they are also typically time constrained. Most investment committees are limited to quarterly meetings that last an hour or two. To be productive, the committee needs a clearly defined scope, well-prioritized agendas, and a disciplined decision-making framework.

Procedures

In advance of each quarterly meeting, committee members should receive meeting materials, including reports, minutes from the prior meeting, and a detailed agenda. These materials should be provided at least a week in advance to allow ample preparation time. Well-prepared committee members are more likely to stay on track and on time. Competent staff or consultants need to follow up and report back in a timely fashion.

At the beginning of the meeting, the committee chair should present the agenda. An effective agenda lists each discussion topic, presenter, and the allotted time. An effective agenda helps ensure that all topics are covered and all required decisions are made.

An investment committee meeting agenda should include *approve prior meeting minutes.* While often a formality, voting to approve the prior meeting's minutes can jog memories and keep a committee on task. The chairperson should recruit a staff member or one of the committee members to keep these minutes. The minutes should include a list of those present. It should also include the topics discussed and references to any presentation materials. Most importantly, the minutes should include a summary of the decisions made by a committee, including the rationale and a reference to presentation materials relevant to the decision. These notes document the committee's prudent process. However, avoid excessive or irrelevant details that can make the minutes more difficult to understand or interpret at a later point. Topics for future discussions should be noted and prioritized in the minutes.

Historical meeting minutes can provide valuable perspective to new committee members. It's not time efficient to use the quarterly investment committee session to bring new members up to speed. A separate meeting with the committee chair, a staff member, or a consultant is usually better.

The agenda should certainly include an *investment review*. Review the aggregate portfolio and individual managers based on the parameters outlined in your Investment Policy Statement (IPS). Even if a manager performs well and is inside the bands of policy guidelines, it is still ideal to discuss all managers. A complete review helps the committee build context about a manager if (or when) performance starts to falter. Investment committees with ineffective agendas tend to allocate too much time to investment reviews. While reviews are important, the group needs to allocate time to more forward-looking topics. For example, at least once a year, discuss the organization's *three levers* (see Chapter 1), the investment policy, and asset allocation strategy.

It is critical for the committee to allocate agenda time to *additional topics for discussion*. This broad category often has the greatest impact on the portfolio. But because these topics can be so varied, they may not fit a standard bullet point in a quarterly agenda template. These could be topics that arose during a committee meeting, but that were tabled because of time constraints or a lack of presentation materials. Examples include a formal review of the IPS, introduction of new asset classes, expense analysis, or a discussion of regulatory changes that may impact the portfolio.

The agenda should also include the *date and time for the next committee meeting*. This serves as a good reminder and allows people to anticipate potential scheduling conflicts. It is ideal to schedule all four quarterly investment committee meetings at one time, or schedule them based on a predetermined rule (e.g., "the second Tuesdays in February, May, August, and November"). It is frustrating for volunteer investment committee members to arrive at a meeting to find they don't have a quorum.

A strong investment committee establishes processes for overseeing the organization's assets, and, more importantly, follows that process. Failing to follow the procedures laid out in an IPS can be worse than having no IPS at all.

Committee Structure

Large nonprofit funds generally have more volunteer investment committee members and internal staff members then do smaller organizations. They have greater ability to attract volunteers due to community scope or alumni reach. However, larger committees are not necessarily better. There can be too many cooks in the kitchen. The larger the committee, the broader the representation of world views . . . and biases. Although there are positives, these vastly different opinions clog up the decision-making processes. An effective committee needs to both make and implement decisions.

The ideal committee is big enough to offer diverse opinions, but not so large that unending discussion and disagreement leads to gridlock. Efficient investment committees typically have an odd number, ranging from five to nine members. The odd number ensures that decisions can be made by majority vote if no clear consensus emerges. Committees larger than nine members often become unwieldy. For example, it takes an hour of meeting time if 15 committee members each take the floor for four minutes. (And such meetings are often only budgeted for an hour.) Clearly, this can be a problem. On the other hand, committee members who habitually don't provide perspectives or input probably shouldn't be on the committee in the first place.

Some organizations have a charter that imposes terms limits to control the tenure of committee members. Term limits can be a double-edged sword. On one hand, particularly with smaller organizations, it may be difficult to recruit volunteers to take the place of departing members. And if you have a relatively small, but engaged and effective committee, why turn members over arbitrarily? Continuity and perspective are valuable. On the other hand, without term limits, an investment committee's perspectives may become stale, and without a stimulating environment committee members may lose interest, disengage, or even stop attending.

A hybrid term limit approach may be ideal. Term limits may be suggested but the committee has the flexibility to retain key individuals beyond the targeted tenure. Regardless of the approach, the object should be to retain members long enough to profit from their experience, but to facilitate enough turnover to prevent "groupthink." A term length of three to five years is often a good target. If an organization decides to implement term limits, it is better to *stagger* the entrance of new committee members rather than to have complete turnover. This way the committee preserves continuity and historical perspective while new members are brought up to speed.

Committee Makeup

Having a financial background can be beneficial, but there are arguably other more important traits for effective committee members. Members who bring leadership experience from military service, other volunteer activities, or sports can be valuable. Smart people who are passionate about the institution and understand its long-term mission usually make the most effective committee members, regardless of experience. Good interpersonal skills and the ability to "play well with others" are ideal. A commitment to work hard and make a positive impact on the institution is also a must.

It usually makes sense to look first within the organization. There are certain roles that should be represented (even if they are not voting members of the committee). It is critical that each member understands the institution's three levers (inflows, outflows, and required investment returns). Usually, no one is more aware of the organization's overall financial condition and obligations than the CFO or the treasurer; they should have roles.

The CEO or president also may provide a valuable perspective. For a college or university endowment, recruiting respected professors from the finance or economics departments is a "no brainer." However, be aware that there may be unintended consequences. Committee members need to feel comfortable about openly sharing their opinions. In the presence of superiors or respected intellectuals, some members may defer to the so-called "experts." Even without trying to impose their wills, the CEO or professor may end up becoming the voice of the committee. For an investment committee to function optimally, all members must feel free to express their opinions and to trust that those opinions will be given fair consideration.

As we mentioned, financial or investment expertise are ideal, but some of the most effective investment committee members make up for the lack of direct investment experience with a natural aptitude and the desire to educate themselves. They may enter the arena free from preconceived notions. Those who are new to a topic may ask more basic but invaluable questions. Some of the best questions begin with, "I'm no expert, but why . . . ?" Often a provocative question that challenges long-held assumptions can sweep away ineffective practices that have been in place for years.

With smart, opinionated, and passionate people, there is always the risk that discussions may lose focus and meander off onto tangents. Therefore, it is imperative that a strong chairperson is in place to facilitate both discussion and timely decision making. The chairperson does not need to be an investment expert, but does need to have the ability to prioritize the most important topics and know when to end discussion and compel the committee to make decisions. It's a good practice to follow *Robert's Rules of Order*. Those formal procedures have kept decision-making groups on task for decades.

When an Investment Committee Needs Outside Help

Especially in the beginning, overseeing investments may be an afterthought. The portfolio may be small and provide minimal support for the organization. But as assets grow, portfolio oversight takes on greater importance. At some point an investment committee is formed to provide that oversight. Their tasks include setting investment policy, designing asset allocation, hiring and firing investment managers, identifying a custodian, and rebalancing the portfolio. Fiduciary prudence mandates a formal process and documentation. At this point, the organization generally hires an outside consultant to provide the knowledge, experience, time, and resources necessary.

An experienced consultant has probably already dealt with challenges similar to those that your organization faces. Even if committee members have investment expertise and the time to devote to the task, they still may not have all the necessary resources. It is a full-time job to understand and analyze dozens of asset classes and thousands of investment managers in the context of volatile market conditions. Selecting custodians and negotiating fees requires highly specialized knowledge. The best consulting firms have the necessary tools, data, and most importantly, the skilled professionals to handle the role efficiently and effectively (see Chapter 12).

Effective Use of the Consultant

Once you have engaged a consultant, how does your organization get its money's worth? The key is to consider the consultant as an extension of staff. Help the consultant understand what is expected. He or she should help crystallize the organization's objectives and deliver a work schedule detailing timing and events. Delegate as much of the work as possible, and make it the consultants' duty to explain any specific tasks for which they do not assume responsibility. Good consulting firms often provide support beyond investment analysis, for example responding to donor inquiries, handling incoming investment manager solicitations, evaluating spending policy approaches, coordinating and facilitating interaction among auditors, custodians, and investment managers, and providing fiduciary education for committee members.

The consultants should assume the lead role in portfolio oversight. They should be proactive rather than reactive. Use their experience and leverage their knowledge. However, the relationship should not be one sided. The investment committee must be open-minded about new approaches. A good consulting firm should add value many times its fee by:

- Improving investment performance;
- Helping committee members satisfy their fiduciary responsibilities;
- Reducing expenses;
- Providing continuity for a committee with changing members;
- Supporting the administrative components of portfolio oversight; and
- Helping to increase donations to the nonprofit by communicating well-founded investment and spending policies.

Traditionally, investment consultants provide their services on a *non-discretionary* basis. That is, the consultant provides input and makes recommendations, but it ultimately remains the committee's responsibility to make the final decisions. However, nonprofit committees are increasingly reevaluating this traditional consulting relationship.

Portfolio oversight requires significant time, attention, and, increasingly, swift action. Investment committees sometimes suffer from the inability of members to meet regularly. Committee members may find it difficult to make timely decisions due to the absence of key members, or maybe simple reluctance to make a change . . . even one that they know in their hearts is necessary. Decision paralysis can severely damage a portfolio.

Unfortunately, we have all seen these scenarios play out: Personal biases may limit the use of needed asset classes, or committee members may be reluctant to terminate a failing manager because of a personal relationship. Many other roadblocks can derail a committee's ability to make effective portfolio decisions . . . even in the face of a consultant's strong recommendation.

More and more nonprofits have adopted a *discretionary* relationship with their consultants. The consultant assumes authority to shift asset allocation within defined ranges, hire and fire managers, and rebalance the portfolio. In Chapter 10, we discuss the concept of *Outsourced Chief Investment Officer Services*.

Conclusion

Managing nonprofit assets can be a daunting task. The trend for nonprofit investment committee oversight is going in only one direction: toward greater complexity.
With *macro-level* tasks that align investment policy to the mission and *micro-level*
tasks like performance analysis, effective investment committees need to use time
and resources efficiently. The difference between effective and dysfunctional investment committees often separates those nonprofits that meet objectives from those
that fail miserably.

CHAPTER 10

Outsourced Chief Investment Officer Services

S kip loved his job at a Midwestern health care organization. For 20 years he had been the go-to guy for anything to do with the organization's investment pools. He went to investor conferences and networked with his peers; he was especially interested in the approaches used by university endowments. Private equity and hedge fund managers called on him and occasionally his fund invested with them. Skip was proud of the fact that the hospital's $500 million nonprofit fund had a 12 percent allocation to alternatives; he always referred to the asset allocation as "cutting edge." Somewhere along the way he had been given the title Chief Investment Officer (CIO). The Chief Financial Officer (CFO) and other members of the investment committee deferred to Skip's obvious expertise. In fact, some of the committee members seemed to have little interest in stocks and bonds . . . and virtually no understanding of their distressed debt fund and other alternative investments.

At the age of 62, Skip decided to take early retirement, surprising the CFO. Being a "good corporate citizen" he agreed to work part-time until a suitable replacement could be found. The problem was that no one else in the management group had the expertise to step in; furthermore no one had the time or inclination to get up to speed, particularly on alternative investments. Administration began a search but was shocked to find that experienced CIO candidates wanted close to a million dollars a year in compensation, and required sizable support staff!

One of the board members mentioned, "There might be a solution. I sit on the board of a private college. We just outsourced the entire CIO function to an investment advisory firm for significantly less cost. Maybe we should explore that option?"

Overview

Outsourced Chief Investment Officer Services, also called *Fiduciary Management*, or *Discretionary Management*, is rapidly gaining traction among nonprofit organizations. Simply put, the organization hires a Registered Investment Advisory (RIA) company to oversee portfolio investments on a discretionary basis.

The practice began with university endowments as a way to cope with high turnover in the CIO position. (It turns out that successful and knowledgeable CIOs are frequently recruited by consulting and investment management firms at salaries beyond the budgets of most schools.) In 2009 total outsourced assets in the United States were approximately $195 billion. By 2012 that amount is estimated to grow to $510 billion, according to Casey Quirk, an institutional consulting firm.

Why Outsource?

There are a number of valid reasons that more and more nonprofits elect to outsource the function:

- First and foremost, there is the question of *core competency*. As one client put it: "We know how to run a hospital; we are not investment experts. We look at the material presented, debate the pros and cons, and then follow our consultant's advice 95 percent of the time, anyway."
- Second, there are *time constraints*. Most committee members wear a number of hats. Important investment decisions may take a back seat to other pressing matters. It is not unusual for an investment committee to invest millions of dollars based on a presentation shoehorned into the last 15 minutes of a two-hour meeting.
- Then there are *cost considerations*. To build an in-house capability that is truly competitive requires an annual outlay north of seven figures. (And in the challenging world of asset management one does not want to be less than world class.) An experienced, knowledgeable CIO alone typically commands more than half a million dollars annually. That person also needs to be supported by a team that includes analysts (CFA charterholders with six-figure salaries) and administrative staff. Specialized technology adds to the cost. Portfolio reporting systems, electronic custodian interfaces, database services, and other software do not come cheap.
- *Alternative investments* demand an exponentially higher level of due diligence. Hedge funds, private equity funds, and even more esoteric investing strategies are not the province of amateurs. A committee member does not want to start the day by turning on the morning news only to see his hedge fund manager led off in handcuffs. Out-and-out frauds like *Madoff, the Manhattan Fund,* or *Beacon Hill Asset Management* were avoided by astute investors who did the legwork.
- Hiring a consulting firm to manage the fund on a discretionary basis is probably a *higher use of their expertise*. The firm can spend its time on investment research and management rather than relationship management.
- An outsourcing firm can more easily *make the tough decisions*. For example, committees find it almost impossible to hire a good investment manager whose style has recently been out of favor . . . thereby missing the chance to profit when the substyle returns to the fore.
- There is also an *explicit fiduciary role* and a *higher level of accountability* than with the traditional consulting relationship.

Outsourced Services

What exactly is outsourced? While there are no hard and fast rules, outsourced CIO services generally include certain areas of investment oversight:

- *Allocation to sub-asset classes.* The broad equity/fixed income mix may be set at the board or committee level, but decisions regarding the mix of growth and value, large and small cap, foreign and domestic, Treasury Inflation-Protected Securities (TIPS) and nominal bonds, and so on usually fall to the CIO firm. These decisions are typically the most important source of performance.
- *Portfolio rebalancing.* As discussed in Chapter 2, rebalancing decisions can be a critical source of performance.
- *Manager selection.* The CIO firm usually chooses the mix of active and passive strategies as well as specific managers. A good consulting firm can typically match up managers with complementary styles more easily than investment committees (who are often attracted to "the hot dot" on a performance chart).
- *Alternative-strategy review, analysis, and implementation.* As mentioned, alternative investments require a much higher level of due diligence than do traditional strategies.
- *Ongoing manager oversight and (if necessary) replacement.* Once the game plan has been established, it is important to make sure it stays on track. The outsourcing firm is charged with the responsibility of making timely decisions.

Of course, your investment committee can retain some of the above responsibilities. For example, in some arrangements only *alternatives oversight* is outsourced. In other cases, the committee may delegate *manager selection* and *portfolio rebalancing* only. One important area that is virtually *never* outsourced is the ability to withdraw assets.

What Is Done in Conjunction with the Committee?

While most of the day-to-day work is outsourced, key oversight responsibilities remain. Since the *Three Levers Exercise* (see Chapter 1) and the resulting broad asset allocation determine the overall risk budget of the fund, they should remain committee decisions. Likewise, broad investment policy is a committee decision. Finally, the committee should meet quarterly to review overall performance. While the daily work is delegated, the committee should stay in the loop.

Potential Benefits

Potential benefits to outsourcing the CIO function include:

- Enhanced risk-adjusted performance
- Cost-effective infrastructure

- More coherent approach
- Reduced time commitment for the investment committee and in-house staff
- Timely response to changing market conditions
- Improved accountability

Finding a Firm

Once you've made the decision to delegate the CIO function, you'll find no shortage of companies willing to "manage" your fund. How do you separate the players from the pretenders? Since, as yet, there are no associations or database of outsourced CIO firms, how does one develop a list of candidates?

We'd suggest a few cuts to winnow the field. To avoid potential conflicts you might want to eliminate broker/dealers, money managers, and banks. Such firms have a history of offering the hot financial product du jour . . . frequently with less than satisfactory results. Besides they often want to funnel your money into proprietary investment products. Perhaps they can objectively evaluate their in-house products alongside other potential money managers, but there's little upside in making that bet.

A better place to start is with a list of independent investment consulting firms. *Pensions and Investments Magazine* publishes a list of the top firms, as does *Standard and Poor's Money Market Directories*. Of course, one can Google "Outsourced CIO services" and come up with hundreds of hits. A law firm or accounting firm may also be able to provide recommendations. (But be careful. They may provide a list of banks, money managers, and brokers.) However one obtains a candidate list, the next step is to conduct phone interviews to narrow the list.

Characteristics

As you interview firms, remember the goal is to *eliminate* nonstarters. You want to send a request for proposal (RFP) only to legitimate candidates. You might want to screen for the following characteristics:

- *Conflict-free advice.* The firm's primary source of revenue should be client fees paid for advisory services. Commissions, "revenue sharing," and investment-management fees on proprietary products are all red flags.
- *Experience.* You probably don't want them reinventing the wheel just for you. (But be aware that since this is a relatively new approach, even experienced firms may have only a handful of outsourced CIO clients.)
- *Expertise.* The firm should be able to demonstrate a high level of knowledge in all aspects of fund oversight including asset allocation, manager selection, portfolio rebalancing, and the analysis of both traditional and alternative assets.
- *Research capability.* In the evolving capital markets, cutting-edge strategies or insights can add significant value.

- *Transparency.* You want a clear understanding not only of fees, but also of procedures and policies in all areas. Beware of "black boxes."
- *Risk management.* Ask them to describe their policies and procedures.

The RFP

Send the *RFP* only to a manageable list of candidates. Remember, someone still has to read the responses and put together an apples-to-apples comparison. Shorter is better. We'd suggest that you put "deal-killer" questions up front. For example, if you don't want a firm that sells any proprietary products you might tell the candidates "Do not continue with this RFP if your firm sells financial products." It's better to save their time and yours.

The RFP should provide greater insight into the firms' philosophy, process, and people. How do they think they'll add value? Look for specific answers. Share information about your fund; ask for their observations and thoughts. They probably won't "give away the store" but if they take the time to give specifics about your fund it at least shows that you're important to them. (See Chapter 13 for a comprehensive investment consultant RFP that includes Outsourced CIO questions.)

Interviewing Finalists

We'd suggest narrowing the list to no more than four semifinalists. Make certain that most of each firm's presenters are the actual people who will work on your account. Use the face-to-face interviews to clarify any issues raised in the RFP process. Since assets will be managed on a discretionary basis, you should clearly understand how decisions are made and implemented and what risk controls are in place. If the firm's decisions are made by an investment committee, arrange to interview one or more members of that committee. We suggest that you also talk with the firm's compliance officer to understand safeguards. At the end of the interviews you should be able to narrow the field to two finalists for the next step.

It's always a good idea to conduct an on-site visit. When considering a firm to provide discretionary oversight, it's a must! Plan on spending at least half a day with each finalist. Start the onsite by having them walk you through the steps they will follow to bring your account up to speed. Ask for demonstrations of the tools, technologies, and processes they will use to oversee the funds. Ask to see the internal reports and tools used to monitor client accounts. Have the firm's compliance officer explain and demonstrate client safeguards. Don't limit your conversations to the senior professionals; meet the analysts and the support people who will do the "grunt work."

By the end of the onsite you should have developed a preference for one of the firms. But don't neglect to check references. Ask for current and *former* clients. (Because these are relatively new services, the firm may not yet have lost any clients . . . but that's good information too.) One hint: A useful reference checking technique is to say, "What do they do particularly well?" Followed by: "We all have areas that we need to improve. What would you say that is for XYZ firm?" It's human nature to soft peddle criticism; phrasing the question that way gives the reference permission to be more direct.

Fees

It's advantageous to negotiate fees *before* you hire the CIO firm. Discretionary management fees are three or four times comparable consulting fees. While there is not a lot of information about specific fee levels, anecdotally in 2010 a $500 million public fund hired an outsourced CIO firm at 85 basis points (bp) (0.85 percent) of plan assets. A consulting fee for a fund that size would have been in the 0.05 to 0.10 percent range.

CIO firms point out that fee levels are commensurate with greater labor intensity, fiduciary exposure, and the potential added value that such an arrangement can bring. One way to create alignment of interest is for the client to pay a reduced base fee plus an incentive fee for achieving certain benchmarks. If you enter into such a fee arrangement, make certain that you don't inadvertently encourage the advisor to "swing for the fences" if they're having a bad year. For example, you could establish a three-year average performance versus the benchmark or establish a *high-water mark,* which must be exceeded before the firm can earn the bonus.

The Contract

Once you have decided on a firm, you need to enter into a formal agreement. They may present you with their standard contract. We strongly suggest that you have *your* attorney review the document. Contracts will typically include the following sections:

1. A section appointing the advisor as your organization's agent to hire and fire managers, and execute transactions on your behalf. Typically there is language that says actions shall be done in accordance with the Investment Policy Statement. (Often a copy of the IPS is inserted as an addendum.)
2. Responsibilities of the client. These usually include directing accountants, trustees, custodians, and legal advisors to provide information to the outsourced CIO firm. There is often language specifying that the client needs to inform the advisor in writing of any change in investment objectives or policy. If the client has established custody or brokerage arrangements, there is language directing the advisor to utilize those relationships on the client's behalf, unless to do so would cause the advisor to breach its fiduciary duty to the client.
3. Responsibilities of the advisor. This is a list of the services that the firm agrees to provide, typically asset allocation, manager selection and oversight, portfolio rebalancing, and reporting. There may also be a mention of services that will *not* be provided (e.g., proxy voting).
4. Fees. This section defines the basis and timing of fee payments to the advisor.
5. Termination. Typically, either party may terminate the agreement with 30 days written notice.

Reporting

Once the CIO firm has been appointed and has begun oversight of the fund you still need to monitor its performance. A point person (usually the controller or CFO) within your organization will review the monthly custodial statement. Quarterly or at least semi-annually your investment committee should still meet with the firm to review progress. Since the CIO firm is responsible for manager oversight, your reviews can be shorter and higher level. At a minimum you want to know:

- The fund's results versus the benchmark.
- Actions taken and the rationale.
- Any actions contemplated.

Of course, any recommendations that require committee action should also be discussed; for example, changes to permitted investments, new asset classes, and so on.

Conclusion

More and more frequently, nonprofit organizations have decided to focus on their core competency and outsource the CIO function in the hopes of achieving better risk-adjusted return, more cost-effective infrastructure, and greater time efficiency.

CHAPTER 11

Environmental, Social, and Corporate Governance-Focused Investing

M any nonprofit investors want to tailor their investment portfolios to be consistent with their organization's mission. *Environmental, social, and corporate governance-focused investing* (ESG) has increased significantly in recent years. According to the Social Investment Forum Foundation, assets in ESG strategies were $3.07 trillion in 2010, up significantly from $639 billion in 1995. This 380 percent increase exceeded the 260 percent growth of professionally managed assets over the same period.[1] It's easy to infer that ESG's market share has grown significantly. Exhibit 11.1 shows the growth in assets under management for various ESG strategies since 1995.

History and Evolution

ESG, also known as *socially responsible investing* (SRI), has evolved considerably from what was once the province of religious organizations. In 1760, John Wesley, co-founder of Methodism, wrote his famous sermon "The Use of Money," in which he shared his vision for how "Christian wisdom" should apply to the "right use of money." This included avoiding investment in businesses that caused harm to others. In the late 1700s, Quakers showed their opposition to slavery by avoiding doing any business with companies using slave labor.

Over time, the focus of ESG has expanded. Some investors' religious beliefs and advocacy of peace and non-violence led them to avoid investments in products such as *alcohol, tobacco, armaments,* and *gambling.* During the 1960s and 1970s ESG investors focused on *Civil rights, women's rights, the environment,* and *nuclear concerns.* The anti-apartheid movement and opposition to the Vietnam War, in particular, increased awareness of ESG.

More recently, investors are concerned not only with the financial and economic performance of companies, but also how company policies and practices contribute to society. ESG now includes *environmentally themed investing, labor relations, shareholder advocacy, community investing,* and concepts such as *program-related investing.*

EXHIBIT 11.1 Socially Responsible Investing in the United States from 1995 to 2010 (in Billions)

	1995	1997	1999	2001	2003	2005	2007	2010
ESG Incorporation	$162	$529	$1,497	$2,010	$2,143	$1,685	$2,098	$2,512
Shareholder Advocacy	$473	$736	$922	$897	$448	$703	$739	$1,497
Community Investing	$4	$4	$5	$8	$14	$20	$25	$42
Overlapping Strategies	N/A	($84)	($265)	($592)	($441)	($117)	($151)	($981)
Total	$639	$1,185	$2,159	$2,323	$2,164	$2,290	$2,711	$3,069

Data Source: Social Investment Forum Foundation

Many investors may think of ESG purely in terms of screening that excludes companies that don't fit the desired social criteria. However, there are other methods to effect social goals. ESG generally follows three main strategies: *screens, shareholder advocacy, and community investing*.

Negative Screening

The exclusion of stocks or *negative screening* based on social criteria is the oldest and most common method of ESG implementation. This strategy helps nonprofits avoid investments that oppose the organization's beliefs and values. Common exclusions include *alcohol, tobacco, gaming, militarism, birth control,* and *environmentally unfriendly* companies. Other exclusions may involve *human rights, labor relations/employment equality, abortion,* and *pornography*.

Positive Screening

Positive screening produces a list of companies with policies that agree with an organization's mission. The investors actively seek out companies with corporate policies that have a positive impact on the environment or society. Positive screens include workplace or environmental standards above those mandated by federal or local laws as well as community reinvestment or involvement.

Shareholder Advocacy

Some socially conscious investors pursue a more active strategy of *shareholder advocacy*. While it is estimated by the Social Investment Forum that only 20 percent of ESG money is used in shareholder advocacy, it can be a powerful force when used properly. Often called the muscle of ESG, the three main components of an activist shareholder strategy are *corporate dialogue, shareholder resolutions,* and *proxy votes.*

Corporate dialogue is generally the first step. Shareholders convey their concern on social issues to the company. By articulating the position in a thoughtful and consistent manner, investors have the potential to shape policy. Lobbying shareholders need to be persistent. It may take several years of dialogue to change a given policy. However, it can be a successful strategy to convince the company that the issue is worth incorporating. If the company takes no action the next step is to threaten a shareholder resolution.

A *shareholder resolution* is a formal request made to a company by a current shareholder seeking action by the company on a specific issue. According to the Social Investment Forum Foundation, from 2008 to 2010, more than 200 institutions controlling $1.5 trillion in assets filed or co-filed shareholder resolutions. The peak was 1,050 resolutions filed in 2003 in the wake of the Enron and WorldCom bankruptcies. Those resolutions were mainly focused on corporate governance changes. The Securities and Exchange Commission (SEC) has set forth certain regulations regarding the eligibility, timing, and filing of shareholder resolutions. Each shareholder is limited to one resolution per year, so it is quite common for several shareholders to join together and coordinate their resolution efforts, choosing a designated sponsoring shareholder.

The initial goal of a shareholder resolution is to place the issue on the proxy statement so that all shareholders can vote on it at the company's annual meeting. Depending on the shareholder vote, the company may move to adopt or change their policies in accordance with the resolution. However, regardless of total shareholder support, the resolution is generally not binding on a company's board of directors. They can simply choose to ignore it. Conversely, it's possible for a resolution to be successful with as little as 10 percent of the shareholder vote if the board believes the recommendations have merit.

The *proxy voting* process provides an opportunity for shareholders other than the resolution's sponsor to voice their opinion, either for or against the resolution. Voters need to understand the company-specific proxy issues in order to vote in a manner that reflects the values of their organizations. Keeping track of numerous proxy voting issues can be a daunting task. Several organizations such as *Institutional Shareholder Services* (ISS, www.issgovernance.com) and the *Interfaith Center on Corporate Responsibility* (ICCR, www.ICCR.org) provide research and recommendations on proxy voting issues. They can also be helpful resources in building a network of support.

If corporate dialogue and shareholder resolutions fail to bring about the desired change in policy, shareholders can always sell their shares. Small single shareholders will not have much impact, but a group of shareholders, especially larger institutional investors, command attention.

Community Investing

Though generally not the centerpiece of most nonprofits' ESG programs, *community investing* plays a small but meaningful role. Community investing supports low-income and disadvantaged communities by providing financial services, loans, and capital to individuals and small business enterprises that may not otherwise have access. Investment options are generally available through four types of vendors: *community development banks, credit unions, loan funds,* and *venture capital funds.*

The simplest form of community investment is for the nonprofit to open an account at a community development bank or credit union. These deposits can be levered by the community bank to fund small business loans and worthwhile projects in the community.

Another method for community investing is through *community development loan funds* that pool investors' resources to extend loans that are generally below market interest rates. These investments are not federally insured and usually require an investment commitment of several years. Because these loans may produce lower returns than comparable risk investments, there is an opportunity cost for nonprofits who want to "prime the pump" of grass roots capitalism in this manner.

Program-related investing (PRI) is available for foundations to support charitable activities that involve the potential return of capital within an established time frame. Foundations use PRI to encourage private-sector innovation and encourage market-driven efficiencies. These investments commonly include debt instruments such as loans to non-governmental organizations or financial institutions. They may also include equity investments in funds or purchases of stock. While a significant amount of investment supports affordable housing and community development, PRI commonly focuses on projects which manage environmental risks and promote green technology and renewable energy.

Strategy Considerations

Before adopting an ESG strategy, an organization must prioritize the values it wants to emphasize. Once the organization identifies the areas of social concern, the process of screening may seem straightforward. However, a company's practices regarding an ESG issue may not be black and white. Many larger companies have businesses in diverse industries and geographical regions. Subsidiaries may manufacture products unrelated to the parent company's primary business lines. At any given point in time, a conglomerate may have a business line involved in activities that violate a nonprofit's stated ESG policies. For example, General Electric's (GE) military equipment division, nuclear power businesses, or even the content on GE's NBC Universal television shows may cause it to be negatively screened. On the other hand, ESG investors focused on positive screening may look at GE's solar and hydropower divisions or medical equipment businesses and their positive impacts on society.

Reasonable allowances can be built into an ESG policy, so that companies with significant non-compliant activities are screened out, but companies with small non-compliant activities are tolerated. For example, perhaps companies that derive less than 2 percent of their revenues from certain non-compliant activities might be allowed. The nonprofit's investment consultant or investment managers can help establish criteria that are consistent with the mission while not being onerously prohibitive.

Investment Selection

MSCI created a group of ESG indices that include the USA ESG Index, World ESG Index, USA IMI ESG Index, and the MSCI Global Environment Index. These MSCI indices focus on general themes such as alternative energy, sustainable water, pollution prevention, clean technology, and green building.[2] The ESG factors and how they are used vary among indices and managers. An organization needs to research a manager's specific ESG factors and understand how technical and tactical applications are used.

Separate Accounts

Depending on the overall size of an ESG portfolio, *separate account management* may offer significant advantages. Separate accounts can be tailored to follow specific screens selected by the nonprofit. The nonprofit can set limits on cash, foreign exposure, sector weights, acceptable credit quality, and other non-ESG constraints as well. In addition to customization, if you have sufficient scale separate account expenses can be lower than mutual funds or commingled trusts. Most investment managers are willing to run custom ESG portfolios in a separate account if the portfolio meets a minimum size threshold.

Mutual Funds

If an ESG portfolio is relatively small, mutual funds may be the most practical solution. Although the universe of ESG mutual funds is not nearly as large as the universe of ESG separate account managers, the number continues to grow. According to the *2010 Report on Socially Responsible Investing Trends in the United States,* there are 250 socially screened mutual funds, up from 200 in 2004 and 139 in 1997. These funds have more than $300 billion in assets.

ESG mutual funds use varied screening criteria. Common screens include tobacco, alcohol, weapons, employment issues, and the environment. Other less common screens include human rights, pornography, abortion, nuclear power, gambling, and animal testing. Many ESG mutual funds use five or more individual screens; most use at least two. One drawback is that it can be difficult to find a fund with the exact screen(s) the organization wants. If screens in one area are important, the organization may have to accept screens in other areas it considers irrelevant. Most ESG mutual funds use a broad range of screens to increase their appeal to the widest number of socially conscious investors.

Commingled Funds

Some investment managers offer commingled ESG products to clients who are too small for separate account management. Similar to a mutual fund, the manager pools investors' assets and runs the portfolio according to a uniform set of guidelines. As is the case with mutual funds, custom screens are not available through a commingled product. Commingled funds also can offer less than daily liquidity, and some products may have monthly or quarterly liquidity.

Exchange-Traded Funds

There are an increasing number of *exchange-traded funds* (ETFs), which track U.S. and international ESG indices. Various ETFs incorporate screens for companies that show a commitment to corporate-governance, religious principles, and environmental concerns. An ETF, similar to an index mutual fund, is structured to replicate a clearly defined subset of bonds or stocks. ETF subsets can be as broad as the entire stock market (e.g., S&P 500 Index) or as narrow as a specific sector such as technology. Unlike separate accounts, mutual funds, and commingled funds, ETFs are priced intraday on various stock exchanges. Like index funds, ETFs have relatively low expenses compared to actively managed investment vehicles.

Because these ESG ETFs are structured to track indices, avoiding industries such as gambling or tobacco may lead to significant overweights in other sectors. To maintain a low tracking error (avoiding wide deviation in performance relative to the index) an ESG ETF may invest in a company that passes a "best practices" screen. For example, an ETF may have exposure to a consumer-related company that follows certain "best practices," but may also manufacture a small amount of tobacco-related products.

Alternative Investments

Managers have started to create *ESG alternative investment vehicles* including hedge funds, hedge fund of funds, and private equity. Hedge funds use a variety of tools and strategies including leverage, derivatives, and short-selling. A nonprofit may allocate to a hedge fund of funds for diversified exposure to several hedge fund strategies and managers. According to the Social Investment Forum Foundation's Trends report, there are 177 alternative investment vehicles that follow ESG guidelines. The report also shows alternative investment vehicles incorporating ESG criteria increased 285 percent since 2007, faster than any other segment of ESG vehicles, while assets increased 613 percent.

Some critics argue that hedge funds cannot follow ESG principles. Hedge funds often trade rapidly. Critics argue that excessive turnover is not in the best long-term interest of any company, shareholder, or society as a whole. Proponents counter that hedge funds improve market efficiency, and that applying ESG principles to hedge fund investing may encourage responsible corporate behavior.

New funds following quantitative models based on ESG factors are in their infancy. "Quant" investment managers blend ESG factors into multi-factor models which also incorporate a company's business data and traditional financial measures such as volatility or growth forecasts.

According to Hedge Fund Research Inc., ESG quant funds have trailed other alternative investment classes, especially hedge funds, in attracting assets since

2005.[3] Nonetheless, work continues in this area. MSCI ESG Research is developing frameworks that compare data across several factors such as *carbon emissions* or *executive compensation practices.*

Performance Impact of ESG

Some nonprofit investors believe it is critical that their portfolios reflect their values. Others nonprofit organizations fear being "penalized" with lower returns for following socially responsible guidelines. However, much of the research over the past 10 to 15 years finds no discernable ESG penalty. ESG screens often result in portfolios having *smaller average market capitalizations, higher betas,* and *more growth* (versus value) style characteristics. When market forces favor these factors, ESG portfolios benefit.

Rob Bauer, Koedijk Kees, and Roger Otten wrote a paper titled "International Evidence on Ethical Mutual Fund Performance and Investment Style" in January 2002. Bauer, Kees, and Otten analyzed a database of more than 100 socially screened mutual funds using multifactor models to examine returns and investment style from 1990 to 2001. Their research affirmed that ESG mutual funds tend to be more *growth* than *value* oriented. However, their research also found that after accounting for investment style, there was no significant difference in returns on a risk-adjusted basis between ESG strategies and traditional strategies. Bauer, Kees, and Otten concluded that ESG (or ethical) funds "do not under-perform relative to conventional funds."

A different but favorable hypothesis was reached in a 2008 paper by Michael Barnett and Robert Salomon. In their paper, Barnett and Salomon determine that using only a few social screens hurts financial performance, but as more screens were introduced, performance improved. Their conclusion was that the loss in diversification from broad social screens was offset by the selection of better management teams and more stable companies.

Through December 31, 2010, the MSCI KLD Social Index and the MSCI USA Catholic Values Index outperformed the broad market indices by nearly 1.5 percent annually over the trailing three-year period. Over the trailing five- and 10-year periods, the MSCI USA and S&P 500 Indices were essentially in line with the ESG indices.

The Social Investment Forum's review of 160 socially responsible mutual funds from the 22-member group showed similar long-term return results. When analyzing the universe of large-cap funds, the largest category in the review, approximately 50 percent outperformed the S&P 500 Index over a trailing three-year period and nearly 63 percent outperformed the Index over a trailing 10-year period ending December 31, 2009.

Incorporating ESG into Investment Policy

A nonprofit's approach to ESG should be incorporated in the Investment Policy Statement (IPS). ESG IPS language can be basic or detailed depending on the complexity. The level of complexity is determined by several factors, including the number and level of screens and whether separate accounts or commingled funds are used. If the portfolio's size allows for the use of separate accounts, and the nonprofit organization subscribes to various research and proxy-voting services, they may have access to company-specific data that would allow the formulation of a list of individual company restrictions to be included in the IPS. However, such a process can be too time consuming, costly, and cumbersome for many nonprofits. For this reason, broader language is often used to convey the types of business and activities that should be restricted. Besides relying on their own research, separate accounts managers often subscribe to software and various research services to ensure that the holdings in the portfolio adhere to the IPS constraints. You should provide ESG separate account managers with an individual IPS that lays out restrictions. Any separate account manager engaged should sign the IPS, acknowledging that he or she understands the guidelines.

Mutual fund or commingled trust investments will be screened according to pre-determined criteria identified in the fund's prospectus. Since investors have no control over a mutual fund's ESG screens, the IPS should avoid overly specific language. Organizations should understand the ESG screens used by a mutual fund or commingled trust before selecting that fund. Make sure to reconcile any conflicting IPS language before investing.

Each manager or fund should be incorporated into the main IPS. The criteria for oversight, selecting managers, and ongoing evaluation should be listed. The same performance measures that are used to evaluate traditional managers should be applied to ESG managers. For instance, a large-cap value manager following ESG guidelines should be measured against the Russell 1000 Value Index or S&P Barra Value Index and against a peer group of other large-cap value managers.

The inclusion of screening criteria in the IPS helps ensure that the values and beliefs of the nonprofit organization are consistently reflected in the portfolio. The investment committee should periodically review the ESG criteria. Many nonprofits believe their organization's mission and beliefs warrant the additional effort and cost of overseeing an ESG portfolio.

Conclusion

Many nonprofit investors feel strongly that they *must* tailor their investment portfolios to be consistent with their organization's mission, values, and conscience. ESG investing has increased significantly over the past 15 years, and that trend is likely to continue for the foreseeable future. Through *positive screening, negative screening, shareholder advocacy,* or *community investing,* socially conscious investors have more tools than ever to reflect their values through the structure of their investment portfolios.

Notes

1. Social Investment Forum Foundations: 2010 Report on Socially Responsible Investing Trends in the United States.

2. MSCI ESG Indices, www.msci.com/products/indices/thematic/esg/

3. Cui, Carolyn. "Funds Unite Do-gooders and Quants." *Wall Street Journal.* November 3, 2010.

CHAPTER 12

Selecting Vendors

I n addition to all the investment decisions, your nonprofit organization may also need to select a *custodian* (or trustee) for the investment portfolio, a *record keeper or administrator* for charitable trusts, *brokers* to execute investment manager trades, or a *transition manager* when you terminate investment managers or make broader allocation changes.

A *custodian* holds most, if not all, of the fund assets. Custodians are typically financial institutions such as *banks* (local, regional, or global), *trust companies*, and *brokerage firms*. They hold the securities in safekeeping, facilitate or execute transactions, and provide an accounting of assets and activity in your accounts. Many banks and trust companies also provide *trustee* services. Trustee status means that they assume a fiduciary role in the oversight of the funds. The use of such an outside trustee provides some comfort to your nonprofit organization's decision-makers.

A *record keeper* can be a bank, trust company, mutual fund company, or independent *third-party administrator*. Record keepers handle the administration of charitable remainder trusts and other annuity trusts that may be gifted to your organization. They track individual accounts and process distributions.

A *broker/dealer* executes investment manager trades and clears transactions. It may also sell investments and custody assets. However, you need a complete understanding of the services offered, the broker's capabilities, and any potential conflicts of interest.

Finally, a *transition manager* is a broker that seeks best price and execution when a nonprofit transitions from one investment manager to another, or when a portfolio makes a broader asset allocation (or investment strategy) change. Transition managers tend to specialize in the execution of large block trades.

Custodians

The first step, of course, is, to completely assess your organization's needs. There are various types of custodians, with different areas of specialization. It is important that you have a clear sense of exactly what help you need before embarking on the search process. There is no "one-size-fits-all" solution; it is rare that one vendor excels in providing all services. For example, a firm that handles custody may not even provide record keeping for charitable trusts. Many vendors offer ancillary services only so that they can manage the investments. Since money management and banking are where the profits lie, other services may be less than state of the art.

Assuming that your organization needs trust and custody services, you can consider a number of different types of firms. Perhaps your local bank provides these services. If your needs are more complex, larger regional and national banks or trust companies may offer more robust trust and custody operations and provide these services for large numbers of clients. Make sure you will receive the appropriate level of service if a vendor is willing to discount trust and custody services based on using their investment-management or banking products. Such multi-service firms are potential recipients for your request for proposal (RFP).

The next step is to draft the RFP. Your specific needs determine if the RFP should be short and simple, or if it needs to include great detail. In general, the smaller the portfolio, the simpler your trust and custody needs may be, particularly if the portfolio predominantly holds mutual funds. If your portfolio is larger, or you use separately managed accounts, you may need more robust capabilities. Separate accounts holding foreign securities add another layer of complexity and costs.

The RFP should address a few broad areas, with detailed questions in each section. You need to understand the *background* of each firm and their experience in providing trust and custody services. How many clients do they service? How much revenue does their group generate as a percent of the overall company revenue? How many clients does it have that are similar to your size and needs? How committed is this firm to the trust/custody business? Has it achieved critical mass, or is it likely to exit this business?

Along with the firm background, it is important to learn about the *individuals* who will service your account. What is their average industry experience and how long have they been with the company? What is the level of personnel turnover? How do they compensate these people? What incentives do they have to provide superior service to clients?

A second area of importance relates to the capabilities of the potential custodian. Can they provide *master trust administration*? In other words can a portfolio be managed as one large pool, even though the custodian has the capability to track several subaccounts as individual segments? Does the custodian have global custody capabilities?

For larger portfolios, can the candidate facilitate *securities lending*? (Securities are loaned to brokers in exchange for a fee. Securities lending can provide an additional source of revenue to your fund.) Although securities lending may provide additional revenue, it does not come without risk as many found out during the Lehman Brothers and Bear Stearns collapses. (Several banks invested lending proceeds in money market funds that were heavily weighted in commercial paper issued by the two brokerage firms. It took months to free up the supposedly liquid funds.) You need a good understanding of all components of the lending program before you enter into an agreement. What is the minimum account size they'll consider for lending? Generally, the individual separate accounts need to be fairly sizeable ($50 to $75 million or more depending on the asset class).

If you have a small portfolio, can the custodian work with a large universe of mutual funds? Do they have the capability to take custody of and place transactions in *any* publicly traded mutual fund or only a finite list? What do their statements look like? Do they provide the level of reporting that you desire? How often are the statements generated and how promptly after each period will you receive yours?

A third area you need to examine is *technology*. How much does the firm invest annually in technology? Can clients access account data via the Internet? What functions can you perform via the Internet? How are your data protected? What are their disaster-recovery contingency plans? What new capabilities are on the horizon?

The fourth major section of the RFP should address *fees*. Describe your expected investment structure. Provide an estimate of the number and types of separate accounts and mutual funds; this will allow the potential vendor to gauge the complexity of their trust/custody duties. The vendor may propose a flat-dollar fee, a percentage of assets, or transaction fees. If the fee is a percentage of assets, it should include break points. The RFP should require details of any transaction fees. This is especially important if your separate account managers are active. A roundtrip transaction on a 2,000 share trade at $0.02/share costs the portfolio $80. This may not sound like much . . . until you consider that your managers could be executing thousands of trades a year. For how long will they guarantee their fees? Is there a service guarantee?

The fifth section of the RFP should include a request for *references*. Ask for references that are similar to your organization. Presumably they face many of the same issues that you do. Three or four current client references should be sufficient. Ask for a reference from a *former* client.

Send the RFP with a brief introduction. Describe your organization, its history, and mission. Include specific instructions about how and to whom to respond. It is a good idea to clearly set a response deadline no later than three weeks from the date you send the RFP. Also communicate the name and contact information for a point person who can respond to vendors' questions. Clearly state that any questions should be directed only to the point person. (This will prevent vendors from hounding board members.)

When the RFP responses are received, it is helpful to place the individual vendor responses into a matrix. This will make it easier for you to compare and contrast vendors' responses, question by question. This method is particularly helpful when reviewing proposals in a committee setting. Time may be limited, and efficiency is important. You will find it easier to compare vendors if you set up a grid where each type of fee is broken out line by line. When preparing this analysis, carefully consider any transaction-related fees. Estimate a total annual fee. Compare those bottom-line numbers side by side. Also, estimate any asset-based fees based on a recent market value of the portfolio. With this information in hand, your committee's review will be more organized and efficient.

Using this summary information, narrow the field to three or four semifinalists. Invite the semifinalists to present to the committee. It is best to have the vendors in one after the other or, at worst, on two consecutive days. The presenting firms should be encouraged to bring along the people who will serve you. Presentations should be limited to an hour and allow sufficient time for questions. If possible, provide the vendors with topics that are most important to the committee. It can be helpful to distribute a rating sheet to the committee members before the presentation. This rating sheet covers the major elements you'll use to judge the vendors and allows committee members to score each vendor on a scale of 1 to 5. This is an especially helpful tool when you must listen to three or four presentations over the course of a day.

After the vendor presentations are complete, try to narrow the field to two custodians for specific follow-up questions. Consider on-site visits. Many nonprofit organizations later regret that they selected a winner on the basis of presentation skills. On-site visits are particularly helpful if the field has been narrowed to two vendors but the committee has no clear preference. On-site visits typically involve a half or full day of tours and meetings at the vendor's service or operations facility. However, the information gained is well worth the effort. Committee and/or staff members can get a look at the vendor's infrastructure, view the service team in action, and can spend more time getting to know the people who will service the plan.

Check references when you've decided on the finalists. Depending on staff resources, you may perform this reference check yourself or delegate it to your investment consultant. Before placing calls, formulate a list of reference questions. Make sure you pose the same question to each reference. You'll get more information if you "loosen up" the reference. Start out with general information such as the person's position and details about the fund size and complexity. Then ask about particular services that the vendor provides. First, ask the reference to describe the vendor's strengths. Then ask "Where is there room for improvement?" (People generally don't like to start out by saying anything bad about someone.) It is also helpful to know how long the reference has worked with the vendor. If they have recently gone through the RFP process as well it will provide a good opportunity to ask about any transition problems or what encouraged them to make a change.

Probe specific areas such as *conversion, transition management, audit assistance,* and *inquiry-response time.* How have problems been resolved? Does the main contact keep a log of outstanding versus resolved inquiries? Has there been turnover among the individuals working on the account? Have they increased fees? If so, what was the rationale?

As part of fee negotiations, also discuss related issues such as asset management, cash management, performance measurement, or credit/banking services. If the vendor won't budge on the overall fee structure, perhaps there are additional services that they could include? This is the time to address any element of the proposal that you don't like.

Ideally, fee negotiations should take place before the winner is selected. This is your time of maximum leverage; use it to your advantage.

Record Keepers and Administrators

You may also need an administrator for gift annuities that have been donated to the organization. Donors often make gifts that ultimately pass to your nonprofit organization but provide the grantor with an income stream in the interim. The grantor enters into a contract that stipulates the amount to be paid to the grantor as an annual annuity. These irrevocable gifts may pay income for life or a specific period of years. The payments are generally fixed. When both the grantor and surviving beneficiary pass, the remaining funds become the sole property of the nonprofit organization. There are tax advantages for the grantor as well as the comfort of a steady income stream.

While such gifts are appreciated, they come with responsibility to oversee the investment strategy, remit payments, file tax-reporting forms, and issue statements to the donors. Administration of these annuities can be complex, particularly if you oversee a large number. It's possible for the annual payments to represent taxable income, taxable capital gains, or even nontaxable income to the grantor. A nonprofit organization has to either hire staff to administer these annuities or find a record keeper or administrator to perform these duties for them. Outsourcing is a growing trend because many schools, hospitals, and religious organizations recognize the liability and complexity in servicing annuities.

Large trust company or bank custodians may provide software to help you manage the accounting and general administration. But if the process has become too cumbersome, you may want to search for a vendor to take over the administration.

The search process can begin with local financial institutions that have trust-servicing capabilities. But generally only large banks with significant operations offer these planned-giving services. If your bank says that they offer this service, ask for a list of clients they currently serve. Some smaller trust companies may claim that they perform these duties, when in fact they are geared to service individual trusts and are not structured to administer a hundred or more annuity trusts for one client.

Modify the custodial RFP to focus on the key services needed to administer annuities. How will the bank perform tax reporting? How timely can they process payments to donors? How often will statements be sent to donors? What do the statements look like? What type of investment flexibility is allowed in annuity accounts? Is there a proprietary investment requirement?

Fees for this service can be paid directly out of the annuity trusts. The workload relief can actually reduce your institution's costs. Fees are generally quoted as a percentage of assets.

Large nonprofit organizations that hold hundreds or even thousands of annuity accounts may find that larger financial institutions with great processing capabilities are the best fit. However, if your nonprofit organization only has a few, banks and trust companies below that top tier may also work.

Broker/Dealers

You may also consider using broker/dealers for some of these functions. When considering using a broker's services, it's important to understand the nature of their businesses and how they are compensated. Individual brokers are, first and foremost, sales people. Most are paid based on transactions. These transactions generate a commission on a stock purchase or sale, the markup or spread on a bond that is purchased or sold, or the front-end loads (sales charge) that are assessed on mutual fund transactions. If it seems as though a broker (or anyone for that matter) offers a host of services at little or no cost, chances are that there may be hidden fees or commissions.

When considering a broker for custody services, be conscious of the fact that while the custody may be "free," you need to keep a close eye on trading costs. You should make a distinction between *institutional* brokers and traditional *retail* firms. The institutional firms are generally accessed through independent registered investment advisers or money managers. They are characterized by salaried service people. The retail Wall Street firms tend to actively pursue your business. They are characterized by commissioned sales people. (More and more firms now seek to compensate their sales people via a "wrap fee" as a percentage of assets.)

Transition Managers

When your portfolio needs to change investment managers, shift asset-allocation strategy, or merely has large cash flows in or out, it may make sense to consider the services of a *transition manager* to help control costs and reduce risks associated with large transactions. Transition managers quarterback the transition process for separately managed accounts and can even assist with implementation when a portion of the assets involve mutual funds. Not only can transition managers help reduce the explicit costs (commissions) associated with transitions, they often can help reduce implicit costs (market impact, spreads, and volatility). The implicit costs of a transition event are often much greater than the explicit costs.

For simplicity, we'll refer to *equity* transitions in this section but fixed-income transitions are also common. Transition managers can add value with fixed-income transitions in many of the same ways as with equities. However, fixed-income transitions are not generally subject to the same level of volatility risk and often there is less liquidity as compared with equities.

One of the biggest risks associated with a transition is having assets that are invested for a long-term purpose remain out of the market for an extended period while the transition is being completed. It is an unintended circumstance and one that can either help or hurt the portfolio based on market movements during that period. (However, since markets have gone up more than they have gone down, being out is statistically more likely to harm portfolio results.) The transition manager greatly reduces or even eliminates that uncertainty by staying fully invested for as much of the transition as possible.

If a transition manager is not used, the current (or newly fired) manager may be asked to liquidate the account. Liquidation by the investment manager generally creates higher commission costs. Investment managers often trade at commission rates that are higher to pay for ancillary services for the manager such as stock research provided by the broker. Investment managers may trade at commission rates of $0.03 to $0.05 per share but transition managers often trade at $0.01 to $0.02 per share or less. This can have a dramatic impact on cost depending on the size of the transition and the number of shares traded. In addition, a newly fired investment manager does not have the best alignment of interests in liquidating your account. Knowing that the relationship is ending, the newly fired manager may make ongoing client accounts a greater priority. They may even use your commission dollars to "reward" a broker/dealer who has referred business to them.

Allowing the new investment manager to purchase the stocks for the new portfolio may also result in higher commissions. In addition, the new investment manager may take a longer time to build the new target portfolio, creating a *benchmarking* issue. (Since a large portion of portfolio may remain in cash with no market exposure, the transition period provides a convenient excuse for tracking error.)

A transition manager can act as a "project manager" to help oversee this entire process. He or she can be expected to liquidate the existing portfolio in short order and simultaneously purchase the securities for the target portfolio. The transition manager coordinates the trading and movement of securities with the custodian, delivering a fully invested target portfolio for the new investment manager within a narrow window of time—typically a day or two.

Transition manager evaluation and selection is likely uncharted territory for most nonprofits. There is no standard means to measure transition manager track records, and trading concepts and terminology may make investors' eyes glaze over.

If possible, it is important to start the process of identifying potential appropriate managers well in advance of the actual transition event. At the very least, do some preliminary screening so that you have a short list. Portfolio changes need not be delayed by transition manager due diligence and selection.

Begin with a *Request for Proposal* tailored to your specific needs. Potential recipients may include your custodian bank (if they have the in-house capability) or some of the established transition managers. Since the 2008 financial crisis this group is somewhat smaller in size. It primarily consists of large banks and brokerage firms with significant trading operations.

Transition managers begin by comparing current holdings detail for the legacy (existing) investment managers and the holdings list for the new investment managers' target portfolios. The managers then run complex algorithms to simulate the transition and potential trading impacts. The transition manager summarizes the impacts in a detailed pre-trade analysis. This spreadsheet estimates total explicit costs (commissions) and implicit costs (market impact, spreads, and volatility).

These pre-trade estimates may seem confusing. As you review these estimates from the various transition managers, it's human nature to be drawn toward the firm that shows the lowest commission cost or lowest estimate of total transition cost. However, remember that the commission costs are just one small piece of the overall transition cost. More importantly, the pre-trade reports are simply estimates based on the assumptions used by each firm. Compare total cost estimates *and* the underlying assumptions (and risk factors) used. Know that managers have a psychological incentive to understate market impact and spread costs.

It is probably more important to understand the qualitative aspects of each transition manager, including their access to liquidity sources, infrastructure, experience, philosophy, and continuity of personnel. In many ways the decision to select a transition manager is similar to evaluating a traditional investment manager. Certainly consider their experience in executing transitions in particular market segments and presence in those markets. Choosing solely based on the lowest-cost pre-trade estimate is not a reliable predictor of future success.

Additional factors:

- Assess the transition manager's ability to manage the project.
- Review a draft timeline including individual steps, timing, and the responsible party.
- Thoroughly review the cost estimates and be sure to ask questions if they seem confusing.
- Do they provide full transparency regarding their sources of revenue?

- Are they prepared to work directly with your custodian?
- What is their approach to trading the portfolios?
- Understand the trading venues recommended and rationale for choosing each.
- What are potential risks or worst-case scenarios?
- Will they provide status updates to you and/or your consultant each day until the transition is completed?

Once you know the differentiating factors, the decision still may be subjective. *What firm do we most trust to look out for the nonprofit's best interests?* There is no single quantitative formula or statistic that can answer that question.

After the transition event, you should receive a post-trade analysis from the manager. This synopsis should compare the actual costs to the estimates and provide detail of the trade activity. It's important to review this analysis and discuss variances from the pre-trade report with the transition manager. Understand the drivers of lower/higher actual cost. Were any of those within the manager's control? This information is useful in assessing the success of the transition event and in planning future transitions.

Conclusion

Whether you are searching for a *custodian, record keeper, administrator, broker,* or *transition manager,* it can be challenging to cut through the pretenders and find the right partner. Many of the functions these vendors perform are critical, but they can also be relatively thankless; these types of vendors often only get noticed when something goes terribly wrong. Finding the right partners can be a critical component of fulfilling fiduciary duties, and hiring the wrong vendor(s) can have dire circumstances.

CHAPTER 13

Hiring an Investment Consultant

A nonprofit organization's ability to fulfill its mission is almost always constrained by its financial resources. Better investment performance translates directly into accomplishing more of the mission. Therefore, when a nonprofit fund crosses a certain threshold, probably in the $10 million range, its investment committee should consider seeking outside assistance. Unless individuals at your nonprofit possess knowledge, experience, and resources in *all* of the following areas, it probably makes sense to hire a consultant:

- *Investment Policy.* Is the appropriate investment objective clear to the committee? Once the objective is clear, does the committee have confidence it can formulate an effective investment strategy to meet the objective? Is the committee confident that its investment objectives, investment strategy, and spending needs are all compatible? Does the committee understand the fund's risk, liquidity, regulatory, and other constraints?
- *Asset Allocation.* Do committee members have experience and skill at developing capital market assumptions and asset allocation strategies? Can they devise effective rebalancing strategies? Does the committee have the ability to estimate, quantify, and manage market risk?
- *Investment Manager Selection.* Does the committee have the time, resources, and expertise to investigate thousands of investment managers spanning the spectrum from fixed income to hedge funds? Does it have the skills and resources to source, evaluate, and perform investment and operational due diligence on investment managers?
- *Fiduciary Stewardship.* Is the investment committee confident that its investment and oversight process is prudent and being appropriately documented?
- *Vendors and Expense.* Does the committee understand the changing landscape of pricing structures and vendor services? Are committee members certain that the fund is getting fair value for fees paid? Are they capable of negotiating favorable terms with investment managers and other vendors?
- *Time.* Do committee members have the requisite time (and staff) to perform all of the above tasks?

The Investment Consultant

Imagine how difficult it would be to construct a home by haphazardly hiring tradesmen without a clear understanding of the role each plays. Although each carpenter, plumber, and electrician may be a skilled worker and possess strong professional references, they may not be right for the specific assignment. Is there any rationale as to when and how each subcontractor should be hired? Are they capable of following the blueprint? Who coordinates all of this? Every well-run construction project has a general contractor. In the investment world, an investment consultant is the general contractor. An effective investment consultant will help to:

- Understand the fund's "three levers" and crystallize the organization's objectives and priorities.
- Develop the investment policy "blueprint" including investment objectives, asset allocation, and oversight procedures.
- Hire "subcontractors" such as investment managers or custodians.
- Monitor progress and performance to ensure that objectives are met.
- Negotiate fees with investment managers and other vendors.
- Coordinate the various parties and hold them accountable.

Simply put, an effective investment consultant should help the nonprofit organization to achieve its goals with less time, cost, and burden. An effective consultant is impartial; there should be no axes to grind or products to sell. Each and every recommendation must be the result of independent analysis. Finding the best solution should be the only objective.

Overseeing the management of a nonprofit fund is complicated and time consuming. The stakes are high. An experienced consultant has probably already dealt with every challenge the organization faces. There's no substitute for objective advice and an experienced perspective. Even if committee members happen to be experts and have the time to devote to this task, they still may not have all the resources needed. Effective consulting firms have the necessary tools and intellectual capital.

Identifying a Qualified Investment Consultant

Once you have made the decision to seek outside help, you soon learn that every salesperson with a financial product to sell now calls himself a "consultant" or "adviser." (Whatever happened to all the brokers?) So how can a fund fiduciary identify the real thing?

It's relatively easy. A true consulting firm derives virtually all of its revenue from consulting; it is not a part-time occupation. A true consultant does not recommend proprietary investment products. And, perhaps most importantly, the firm can access the full universe of investment managers and products . . . not a limited "wrap fee" product stable. The firm should be able to provide numerous references from current clients similar in structure.

The following is a sample of a comprehensive consulting firm request for proposal (RFP). The more focused the RFP is on the key areas the nonprofit will use to differentiate firms, the better. For example, the *Outsourced Chief Investment Officer (CIO) services* section of this sample RFP should only be included if the nonprofit is considering that particular service.

Sample Investment Consultant RFP

Consulting Firm Profile

A. Provide the full name of your firm, the address and telephone number of your main office, along with the location of other offices. Also, indicate which office would service our nonprofit organization.
B. Provide a brief summary and history of your firm, including its year of inception, ownership structure, affiliated and subsidiary companies and relationships, joint ventures, and/or business partners.
C. Describe any significant developments affecting the firm in the last five years, such as changes in ownership, structure, personnel, or evolution in philosophy. Note any changes in the ownership or management of your firm planned or anticipated during the next two years.
D. Describe your firm's client growth over the last several years and how you have managed this growth (or lack thereof).
E. Is your firm registered with the Securities and Exchange Commission (SEC) under the Investment Advisors Act of 1940? If so, provide a copy of your ADV form.
F. What percentage of your revenue comes from consulting activities? Describe other sources of revenue, and indicate any future plans regarding investment consulting, investment management, or other business activities.

Organizational Structure and Personnel

A. How many employees does your firm have? Indicate the average number of client relationships assigned to each consultant, including any limits to your client/consultant ratio. Provide an organizational chart of your firm.
B. Describe the firm's compensation and incentive programs for consultant, research, and other professionals.
C. Describe your firm's contingency procedures in the event a key consultant assigned to our account becomes incapacitated or unavailable.
D. Describe any current or historical legal or regulatory action against your firm, its principals, or its employees. If applicable, summarize the status of any legal or regulatory proceeding.

Conflicts of Interest

A. Disclose any ownership or financial relationship with any other financial firms, including asset-management firms, brokerage, banking, insurance, or actuarial firms. Has your firm ever received any payment from a money manager you have recommended or considered for recommendation?

B. Explain in detail any other potential sources of actual or perceived conflicts of interest. How does your firm manage these conflicts?

C. Include a copy of your firm's conflict of interest policy.

Client Base and Reference Information

A. What are your firm's total assets under advisement? Provide a current client summary by type (e.g., nonprofit, corporate, individual investors, etc.), including the assets under advisement and number of clients for each type.

B. What is your average nonprofit client portfolio size? What are the portfolio sizes of your ten largest nonprofit clients? Broadly summarize the size range for your nonprofit clients.

C. Describe your firm's experience and expertise with nonprofit organizations.

D. Indicate the number of nonprofit clients lost in each of the past two calendar years, including the reason for each client's loss. Indicate how many nonprofit clients have been added in the past two years?

E. Provide contact information for three client references. The three references should be similar to our nonprofit in terms of size and type. These references will only be contacted if your firm is a finalist.

Scope of Services

A. Provide a summary of the entire range of consulting services your organization provides. Indicate the services you believe are appropriate for this engagement.

B. Describe your consulting philosophy.

C. How often does your firm conduct in-person meetings with clients?

D. Is your firm willing to perform ad hoc projects that may be requested by our nonprofit investment committee?

Broad Investment Strategy

A. Describe your firm's philosophy, process and tools when making broad portfolio recommendations to nonprofit clients. Include specifics about determining appropriate investment objectives, determining portfolio constraints, including various asset classes, formulating investment policy, and developing investment and asset allocation strategies.

B. Describe your philosophy and process for developing and revising investment (or asset allocation) strategy. Include specifics about your approach, including what elements are tactical, strategic or follow some other kind of unique process. Include your firm's most recently revised capital markets assumptions (or forecasts) that drive broad investment (or asset allocation) strategy.

C. Describe your firm's philosophy about the use of non-traditional investment assets such as hedge funds, real assets, and private equity.

D. Summarize the portfolio rebalancing process you typically recommend to clients and why you recommend it.

E. Describe your firm's philosophy about active and passive management.

F. Describe your firm's approach to measuring, evaluating, and managing portfolio risks.

Outsourced Chief Investment Officer (CIO) Services

A. How long have you provided discretionary CIO services?

B. How many of your clients use discretionary CIO services?

C. What services do you provide on a discretionary basis? What discretionary services still require some input from our nonprofit's investment committee?

D. Describe the philosophy, process, and tools your organization uses to establish investment objectives, develop investment policy, and create investment (or asset allocation) strategy. Include your firm's most recently revised capital markets assumptions (or forecasts) that drive investment (or asset allocation) strategy.

E. Describe your process for implementing investment strategy (or asset allocation) changes for nonprofit portfolios. To what extent must our nonprofit board's investment committee be involved in this process?

F. Describe your firm's philosophy about active and passive management.

G. Describe the portfolio rebalancing processes you typically use in your discretionary CIO service. Given the current structure of our portfolio, what process would you recommend?

H. Describe your CIO service's process for monitoring and replacing investment managers.

I. Describe your firm's approach to measuring and managing portfolio risks.

J. Describe your firm's internal risk controls and insurance coverage.

Traditional Investment Manager Research

A. Describe your firm's process to source, research, evaluate, and recommend investment managers.

B. Describe your firm's manager evaluation process that leads to manager retention versus termination recommendations.

C. Describe how you believe your manager research philosophy, process, and/or the capabilities of your investment research professionals differentiate you from other competing firms.

D. Describe the resources you have dedicated to traditional investment manager research, including your investment manager research professionals' names and bios.

Alternative Investment Research

A. Describe your firm's philosophy on alternative investments, including hedge funds, real assets, and private equity.

B. Describe your firm's alternative investments process, capabilities, including hedge funds, real assets, and private equity.

C. What categories within alternative investments do you currently advocate for? Are there any categories you believe are without merit?

D. If your firm has separate individuals and/or departments that are responsible for alternative investment strategy and manager research, describe and provide biographies of key individuals.

Performance Evaluation and Reporting

A. Describe your approach to monitoring and evaluating managers.
B. Describe your process for selecting index benchmarks and peer group universes to evaluate individual manager and aggregate fund performance.
C. Does your firm have the capability to create customized benchmarks for performance measurement?
D. What is the frequency of your performance reports? Provide a sample performance report. Describe your ability to provide customized reporting based on nonprofit client specific preferences or requirements.
E. How quickly after the end of a reporting period are the performance reports made available?

Client Education

A. Does your firm provide clients with research reports on various timely topics outside of quarterly performance reports?
B. Describe any other communications provided to clients. Include samples of newsletters, articles, position papers, reading lists, and so on.
C. Does your firm periodically host educational seminars or conferences for clients?
D. Does your firm make its specialist-experts available to clients on selected topics of importance?

Terms, Fees, and Service Structure

A. Provide a comprehensive fee schedule covering the consulting services you propose to provide.
B. Indicate how travel and other expenses will be handled within the proposed fee. Are there any other services to be provided where fees have not been stated?
C. Does your firm have any minimum fee requirements?
D. What is your policy for the timeliness that either party may terminate the agreement?

Other

A. What sets your firm apart from the competition and what unique value-added services do you expect to provide? What are your firm's key strengths and competitive advantages?
B. Based on the information provided in the cover letter, what observations/suggestions would you make about the investment of our fund?

Send the RFP only to viable candidates. Narrow the list of candidates before sending out the questionnaire. For example, if the committee would not consider the consulting department of a large broker/dealer, don't waste the committee's time or the broker's. This will keep non-candidates out of the process. Describe minimum selection requirements or the so-called "deal killers." This allows the committee to concentrate its valuable time on evaluating and differentiating among the right candidates.

Once the committee has sent out the RFPs and evaluated the answers, it is time to narrow the field. The goal should be to perform face-to-face due diligence on no more than five finalist candidates. If you can winnow the finalists to three, that's even better. It is best to interview all candidates on the same day or at most during a two-day period. If too much time elapses between interviews, distinctions among finalists can blur.

The RFP responses should reveal most of the pertinent information before the face-to-face meeting. Presumably all finalists are at least competent. What, then, is the purpose of the interview? The interview is the time to confirm, or refute, your initial perceptions. Try to understand each firm's *culture, investment philosophy,* and *client service model.* Which candidate best fits your organization's needs and objectives? *Personal compatibility* is important. The committee will work closely with the consultant on important projects with tight deadlines. Don't be too quick to overlook personality quirks that may become irritating. If your organization and the consultant share a similar point of view, other details will fall into place.

In the interview, the committee should ask for demonstrations or specific examples. In each area of service, make the candidates substantiate their claims—make them prove it. Ask each candidate to review fund specifics prior to the meeting and offer observations and suggestions. The investment committee will be able to judge the candidates' level of preparation and expertise.

Often nonprofit investment committees want to skip the "on site visit" step. Don't! Visit the finalists in their shops. Good salespeople can "spin" their firms' capabilities and talent, but it is quite another thing to demonstrate them. Reading biographies is a poor substitute for actually meeting the people who will do the work.

Once the committee has made its decision, get the agreement in writing. What services will be provided? Is there a satisfaction guarantee? What are the remedies if the consultant fails to meet expectations? What is the term of the contract? How do they bill?

Nonprofit institutions should demand language that allows them to end the contract with 30 days written notice and to be obligated only for services rendered up to that point. Your attorney should review the contract. We are not in the business of rendering legal advice, and so have intentionally excluded a sample contract or worksheet. Suffice it to say, legal review is *not* an area to cut corners.

Fees are typically quoted in one of three ways:

1. *Project Basis.* There is a fee for each specific service (e.g., X dollars for an investment policy, Y dollars for a manager search, and so on).
2. *Fixed Retainer.* There is an annual fee to include all services. If the organization's needs are fairly broad, the retainer may be more cost effective than project-based fees. Retainer fees quoted as a set dollar amount are generally more restrictive in terms of the services covered than the asset-based retainer.
3. *Asset-Based Retainer.* The annual fee is quoted as a percentage of assets. This is generally the broadest contract in terms of services ("all services, when needed"). The asset-based retainer has the advantage that your committee will make full use of the consultant without worrying about "starting the meter." Also, during down markets the consultant "shares your pain."

Effective Use of a Consultant

How does the organization get its money's worth after it has hired a consulting firm? First, think of the consulting firm as an extension of your staff; tell them what is expected. Also, someone on the committee, a "point person," should help them understand the organization, including the personalities and perspectives of the players.

Next, give them as much of the work as possible. They'll make it obvious if they don't consider a certain task to be a part of their assignment. If the committee is unsure of which way to go at key turning points, let the consultant research the alternatives. Instruct them to succinctly present pros and cons and provide detailed backup.

Ask them to explain their processes. How do they reach their conclusions? For example, if conducting an investment manager search, get the details. How are candidates to be screened? The committee may want to add or subtract certain criteria.

Use their experience. They probably know what works and what doesn't. Trust them. Obviously, the nonprofit investment committee controls the decision, but it pays to be open-minded. If committee members don't understand something, they should make the consultant explain it. It is the consultant's job to educate committee members so they can be better stewards. See Chapter 10 on *outsourced CIO services* for another way to effectively use a consulting firm.

Conclusion

An effective investment-consulting firm should add value many times its fee. The effective firm helps the committee determine proper objectives, and channels the sometimes inevitable debate caused by conflicting priorities. The firm should arm the investment committee with sage advice when difficult fiduciary decisions must be made and provide valuable context and continuity as members rotate on and off the committee. An effective consulting firm can often cut costs significantly by aggressively negotiating on the committee's behalf. Lastly, an effective consulting firm should bring fresh ideas that lead to better investment strategy, execution, and improved risk-adjusted performance.

CHAPTER 14

Behavioral Finance

E very Wall Street trader knows that fear and greed move markets. This stark admission, that human emotions are a major driver of markets, flies in the face of the "rational investor" assumptions rooted in Modern Portfolio Theory (MPT). Based on the *Efficient Market Hypothesis*, academic researchers have built mathematical models to describe financial markets. William Sharpe developed the *Capital Asset Pricing Model* to explain security and portfolio price movements. Other models such as *Arbitrage Pricing Theory* attempt to further refine the theories. For years the *Efficient Market Hypothesis* ruled academia. Its basic tenet is that all known information is already reflected in security prices. The implication is that it is impossible for an investor to "beat the market" over time. The entire index fund industry is built on that premise.

But there have always been nagging questions. There is evidence that value stocks tend to outperform over long periods. Can this be reconciled in an intellectually honest manner with the efficient market hypothesis? There seems to be a measurable "January effect." What causes it? What leads to market bubbles . . . and crashes?

Ardent believers in the efficient market hypothesis have claimed that successful long-term investors like Warren Buffett and Bill Gross must merely be the *lucky survivors*. But others have had their doubts. One can identify superior surgeons, lawyers, athletes, dancers, singers, actors, business people, and even politicians. Why should investing be the only human activity where it's impossible to be skillful?

Over the past few decades, a new line of research has developed a theory that is 180 degrees opposite to the Efficient Market Hypothesis. *Behavioral finance* takes a psychological view of market behavior. Professors Richard Thaler at the University of Chicago, Terrance Odean at the University of California, Berkeley, Hersh Shefrin at Santa Clara University, and others have developed a body of work that has gradually come to ascendancy. Their basic premise is that humans are *not* rational when it comes to investing. Furthermore, investors are not only irrational, but they are irrational in predictable ways.

In this chapter we identify some of these human tendencies. Over millennia people have evolved mental short-cuts called *heuristics* to deal with the complexities of existence. These heuristics, while generally helpful, sometimes result in conceptual flaws. Think of these flaws as "bugs" in a computer program. Hopefully this overview will help your nonprofit fund's investment committee avoid some of the all-too-human tendencies to shoot ourselves in the foot.

Trying to Break Even

As an addicted gambler can attest, people often prefer large uncertain losses to smaller certain ones. This is clearly not logical, either for a gambler or an investor. Yet investors often behave like desperate gamblers, trying to quickly break even after sour bets by increasing portfolio risk. A rational investor would be guided by portfolio objectives and constraints that do not change based on short-term portfolio fluctuations.

Snake Bitten

An investor may become "snake bitten" after suffering portfolio losses. The opposite of trying to break even, a snake-bitten investor may suddenly reduce or eliminate portfolio risk in order to avoid making the same mistake twice. We've all heard the phrase "locking the barn door after the horse is gone." Before the 2008 financial crisis, many investors overestimated their risk tolerance. Only after they experienced the loss did they adopt a more conservative posture, thereby guaranteeing that they wouldn't participate in the rebound. They experienced the entire downside consequence of risk-taking activities while missing the longer-term upside potential.

Biased Expectations and Overconfidence

Many investors have too much confidence in their ability to forecast the future believing their expectations are more likely to be realized than those of others. Overconfident investors tend to discount any information that doesn't support their opinions. For example, in February 2009, one investment committee member asserted, "Since the global economy and stock market will remain weak for the rest of the year, we should disregard our investment policy and dump all of the equities in our endowment portfolio and invest in T-bills." In spite of the fact that the S&P 500 had already fallen about 51 percent from its peak (between November 2007 and February 2009) and that (short-term) stock market forecasting, especially inflection points, is notoriously difficult; the committee member was absolutely certain about his expectations. Overconfident investors often put too many eggs in the wrong basket and usually at the worst possible time. In this particular example, this overconfident investment committee member was able to convince others on the investment committee to move the portfolio from an 80 percent equity allocation mix to a 75 percent fixed income mix, heavily skewed to cash, in late February 2009. From February 28 to December 31 of 2009, the S&P 500 Index returned 54.56 percent while T-bills effectively returned zero. He was correct that the economy would be relatively weak for most of 2009, but the market had already discounted that information.

Herd Mentality

Investors sometimes blindly follow the majority position or the "loudest" high-conviction idea. They fall prey to the *herd mentality*. The loudest idea is often the absolutely worst idea. Psychological studies show that people have a difficult time dissenting within a group. In a committee-driven investment process, groupthink can be damaging. Such portfolios tend to have poor risk controls and to be poorly diversified.

Asset Segregation or Mental Accounting

Instead of evaluating the return-and-risk impact of a particular asset class or investment on the aggregate portfolio, investors often fixate on individual assets as if they were owned in a vacuum. This can lead to a breakdown in effective portfolio construction principles. For example, one might fixate on the risks of *commodity futures* while ignoring that the addition of that asset class actually *reduces* the expected volatility of a portfolio because of the low correlation coefficient.

Investors apply the mental accounting heuristic to returns as well. An investment committee member once stated, "Since the target return of our portfolio is 8 percent per year, we should eliminate all asset classes that won't get at least 8 percent, including all of our investment-grade bonds." In this example of naïve mental accounting the committee member had fixated on individual assets when the objective return of 8 percent is for the entire portfolio. As described in Chapter 2, by blending non-correlating assets, one produces portfolios with higher expected returns at each risk level.

A common example of mental accounting is "playing with the house's money." Gamblers are willing to take greater risk with winnings than with their principal. They don't view a dollar of winnings as equal to a dollar of principal. Like the gambler, investors are often more willing to lose what they view as the "gain" rather than what they view as "principal." Asset segregation like this results in suboptimal total portfolio risk-adjusted returns. There's a reason casinos thrive.

Cognitive Dissonance

Cognitive Dissonance Theory was developed in 1957 by social scientist Leon Festinger. Cognitive dissonance is an uncomfortable feeling caused by holding conflicting ideas simultaneously. Since people are driven to be consistent they either alter the behavior or, more commonly, they alter their beliefs. Festinger's thesis is that people often conveniently avoid or ignore information that might cause cognitive dissonance. Cognitive dissonance theory can explain irrational human behavior in its many forms, including how we make investment decisions.

Take, for example, a nonprofit investment committee that disregarded expert advice, dumped stocks, and allocated heavily to cash near the March 2009 market bottom. The members later refused to acknowledge that their costly action was a mistake. It was easier for them to rationalize their decision and maintain their beliefs rather than to admit they made a multi-million-dollar blunder. If not held in check, cognitive dissonance can be a major barrier to accountability and can be very expensive!

Anchors

An *anchor* is a reference point that shapes thought. Professor Thaler demonstrates anchoring during group lectures. He asks audience members to write down their birthday as a number. If someone was born on December 20, they would write down 1220. He then asks the audience to estimate Charlemagne's year of birth. Since most people don't study history, they are relegated to guessing. An interesting phenomenon occurs; people tend to make their estimates as a function of their own birthday. In other words, an audience member who was born on May 19 would be likely to guess Charlemagne lived in the sixth century. Someone who was born in November might guess the 12th century!

Quantitative and *moral anchors* often end up overwhelming the investment decision-making process. Quantitative anchors measure an investment relative to some arbitrary reference price. For example, an investor buys a stock at $100 and watches it decline to $50. In the investor's mind, the stock remains a $100 stock. The investor is anchored to $100 and is unwilling to sell at $50 regardless of the fundamental outlook for the stock.

Moral anchors center around qualitative factors such as narratives, stories shared with others, and rationalizations. In 1999, "pie in the sky" stories about the Internet kept hyperventilating investors buying, even though some of their purchases were trading at multiples of 100 or 200 times earnings. (In fact, companies with no earnings whatsoever did best.) The moral anchor overwhelmed fundamental considerations and even common sense.

Fear of Regret and Seeking Pride

Fear of regret refers to the pain felt after making a bad investment decision. It causes investors to hold on to losers too long. "If I haven't sold, I haven't taken a loss." Conversely, investors *seek pride*. They want to experience the joy of making a wise investment decision. Seeking pride can lead investors to sell too quickly so they can boast about the associated profit.

Representativeness

Investors often rely on certain characteristics to be representative of future investment success. For example, the *value-expressive* investor might view a good company as a good investment. However, good companies are often bad investments if the market's optimistic expectations are already factored into the current stock price. You may be better off buying an underpriced "bad" company than an overvalued "good" one. But to the value-expressive investor, the good company is always preferred over the bad company, no matter what the valuation.

Familiarity

Investors often choose investments with which they are most familiar, or "the devil they know." This tendency can lead to poorly diversified portfolios that are overly concentrated in domestic blue chip stocks and investment-grade bonds. Committees tend to under allocate to small-cap stocks, foreign stocks, high-yield bonds, real estate, foreign bonds, inflation-indexed bonds, emerging-market stocks or bonds, or alternative asset classes or investment strategies. One well-documented example is the unfortunate habit 401(k) participants have of overallocating to their employer's company stock. If the company fails they not only lose their jobs, they also lose their retirement savings.

Investor Personality Types

One can categorize investors by broad personality types. This can be helpful in understanding the way individuals make investment decisions. Granted, there may be subtle variations, but there seems to be four broad investor personality types:

1. *The Suspicious Investor.* Suspicious investors are very cautious and exhibit a strong desire for financial security. They are the most risk averse. They focus on very safe investment vehicles with little potential for loss. Individuals in this category tend to overanalyze investment opportunities, but once they make investment decisions, their portfolios exhibit relatively low turnover and low volatility.
2. *The Process-Oriented Investor.* Process-oriented investors are methodical and maintain a keen eye on risk. They perform their own research and rarely make emotional investment decisions. Their investment decisions tend to be conservative or risk averse. Working with these investors on investment committees can be difficult due to the confidence they place in their own investment processes.
3. *The Structured Investor.* Structured investors are the most individualistic. They do their own homework and are confident in their abilities. They are capable of questioning inconsistencies in analyst or consultant recommendations or conclusions. They are unlikely to get caught up in a herd mentality. Structure investors are less risk averse than process-oriented investors.
4. *The Unstructured Investor.* Unstructured investors are spontaneous. They often chase the latest hot investments. They are often *risk seeking* rather than *risk averse.* Their portfolios typically exhibit high turnover, and winning investment decisions are often negated by high transaction costs. Risk considerations are often secondary to their investment decision-making process. Investment decisions are often based on "gut instinct."

Risk-Seeking Behavior

A fundamental tenet of MPT is that all investors are rational, preferring less risk. In reality, investors are often risk-seeking as they search for short-term lottery-type payoffs rather than sustainable long-term superior risk-adjusted returns. Risk seekers often get caught up in the hype of the latest hot investment. The gambling culture in the United States or a powerful adrenaline rush might explain why investors frequently seek risk rather than work to minimize it. "Get rich quick" stories told by successful risk seekers (e.g., dot-com millionaires in the late 1990s or home flippers during the first decade of the twenty-first century) can cause others to seek out similar low-probability, but high-payoff investment opportunities.

Naturally Occurring Ponzi Schemes and Market Bubbles

According to the Merriam-Webster Online Dictionary, a Ponzi scheme is "an investment swindle in which some early investors are paid off with money put up by later ones in order to encourage more and bigger risks." Charles Ponzi concocted a scheme in 1909 to sell notes promising a 40 percent profit in 90 days. Instead of actually investing the money, Ponzi used new investor dollars to buy out prior investors. As the number of new investors grew, it eventually became impossible to continue the scheme. The highly publicized collapse led to the term *Ponzi scheme.*

While different than "actual" Ponzi schemes like the Bernie Madoff fraud, speculative bubbles follow a similar naturally occurring Ponzi dynamic. Later investors hear success stories from early-stage investors and eagerly jump into the market. As share prices or asset values keep rising, the accelerating prices themselves create a positive feedback loop. When the world runs out of new investors, the market collapses. Once the collapse begins, a negative feedback loop is created and prices fall faster and faster. According to one story, Joseph Kennedy got a stock tip from his shoeshine boy in 1928, and decided to sell all his holdings. He figured that if the shoeshine boy was in stocks, there must be nobody left to keep the Ponzi process going.

Bubbles in specific sectors (e.g., technology stocks in the late 1990s) or within a whole market (e.g., the stock market in 1929) can take years to form. Value-conscious investors who remain on the sidelines during the early stages of the positive feedback loop are often criticized by clients and peers for missing the boat. They feel compelled to join the party in later stages to save their investment jobs or just to save face. The most recent naturally occurring Ponzi process was in the residential real estate market. Early-stage investors saw their home values increase precipitously. As a result, many decided to engage in the highly speculative activity of flipping homes, and banks facilitated such activity by adopting lax lending standards. Since nationwide home prices had not declined year-over-year for the prior 75 years, few paid attention to the risk.

Virtually all naturally occurring Ponzi schemes or market bubbles share several common characteristics. First, the risk of the investment or activity is overly discounted (or completely ignored) by a large group of market participants. For example, technology and the Internet were perceived as the wave of the future in 1999, so investors discounted risk and ignored the need for rational money-making business models and valuations. The compelling narrative overwhelmed other commonsense considerations.

A second shared characteristic of naturally occurring Ponzi schemes is an implicit belief in the "greater fool theory." One rationalizes buying over-valued assets because she believes that she will be able to sell it to someone else ("a greater fool") at an even higher price in the future.

A third characteristic that is involved in the most damaging market bubbles is the use of excessive leverage or borrowing. Excessively leveraging an investment idea whose risk is ignored combined with the greater fool thesis often leads to a powder keg of future pain, not only for the investor, but also other market participants who may be innocent bystanders.

Conclusion

It is important to balance the logic-driven tenets of MPT with the irrational human tendencies documented by Behavioral Finance Theory. After all, the human beings that drive global financial markets are not robots driven by pure logic. Harry Marko-witz, the father of Modern MPT, described his own investment strategy: "I should have computed the historical covariances of the asset classes and drawn an efficient frontier. Instead, I visualized my grief if the stock market went way up and I wasn't in it—or if it went way down and I was completely in it. My intention was to minimize my future regret. So I split my contributions fifty-fifty between bonds and equities."[1] If the father of MPT can fall prey to fear of regret, your investment committee should be careful as well.

Note

1. Zweig, Jason. "Five Investing Lessons from America's Top Pension Fund." *Money.* January, 1998.

CHAPTER 15

Legal Aspects of Investing Charitable Endowment, Restricted, and Other Donor Funds

I t is difficult to generalize about the legal issues involving every aspect of investing charitable endowment, restricted, and other donor funds. However, fiduciaries involved in such activities should be aware of several legal parameters and guidelines. Factors that may influence legal consequences include the following:

- Whether the investing is being done by a corporation or trust;
- Whether the donor of gifted funds has effectively restricted the nature of the investments;
- Whether the gift is for "endowment," restricted, or unrestricted purposes;
- The applicability of a wide variety of common and statutory laws, including the "prudent man" rule, the Uniform Prudent Investor Act (UPIA), the Uniform Prudent Management of Institutional Funds Act (UPMIFA) (or some state's variant or predecessor), and the "Private Foundation" restrictions imposed by Chapter 42 of the United States Internal Revenue Code of 1986 and equivalent state statute; and
- Generally Accepted Accounting Principles (GAAP) accounting treatment.

We will not go in-depth into legal "standing," or who has the right to enforce investing rules by fiduciaries of charitable and similar endowment or restricted funds. However, depending on the laws of a particular state, attempts to enforce the rules may be brought by a state's Attorney General or another public official. Enforcement may also be brought by the institution as a beneficiary or by its Board of Trustees. Clients of the institution (e.g., students or patients), donors or their heirs, or other legally interested parties may have standing as well.

Nature of Endowment or Restricted Funds

When a donor writes an unrestricted check to an institution, the institution typically segregates and spends those funds for ordinary operating purposes. If a donor writes a check for *restricted* capital purposes, the institution typically segregates and spends those funds for the intended capital purposes. In both cases, the institution typically invests the funds in such a manner to minimize market risk so the funds remain available for the intended purposes.

However, when a donor makes a contribution for *endowment* or custom designed *restricted* purposes, particularly if there is restriction on investment, a variety of legal issues may arise. The word "endowment" is often used loosely, but the legal nature of an "endowment" reflects a variety of circumstances.

Endowments Created by the Board

One of the most common types of funds called an endowment is one created by resolution of the governing board of the organization (*Board of Directors* or *Trustees* or some other designation). Sometimes the resolutions are quite broad, and often they are quite old. In some cases, the original resolution and its several amendments may be difficult to locate. Sometimes they are created as a special purpose fund for which funds are specifically solicited. Several such funds might be created over a period of years.

The original resolution is an important document, but so are the fund-raising letters and materials submitted to potential donors over the years. All of these help define how the endowment has been presented to donors and what board-imposed restrictions on use or investment exist.

For instance, an endowment may have been created that said "income" shall be used for the benefit of the institution (or departments or programs) and "principal" shall not be used.

The endowment may also have been created as a separate "trust" (complete with a mechanism for naming trustees or implying that the institution's Board acts as trustee), or, more commonly, it may simply be a component part of the institution's asset base.

Donor-Created Endowment Funds

Sometimes donors create their own endowment funds for particular purposes, such as a named scholarship or support of a department or program. These donor-created endowment funds typically have a separate gift instrument, which may be very specific as to distributions of income and principal, investment restrictions, and so forth. However, they may at times be simple one-paragraph letters or provisions in wills or other estate-planning documents. For example, "I bequeath $100,000 to Great State University for endowment in support of the fine arts department."

The endowment may be created as, or purport to be, a separate trust using general language. For example, "I bequeath $100,000 in trust to Great State University for endowment purposes." On the other hand, it may use specific language naming trustees. For example, "I bequeath $100,000 to my friends Bill and George as trustees of a trust to be used in support of Great State University."

Donor-Created Restricted Gifts or Funds

A donor may make a gift to a charitable institution with program restrictions ("to fund a chair of capitalism and economic freedom") that may not constitute a trust and that may or may not be regarded as an "endowment." For instance, gifts with time restrictions ("to be used to build a new gymnasium within 10 years") are rarely treated as "endowment" but rather as "restricted" gifts, all of whose funds and earnings can be expended at the free discretion of the institution for the stated purposes. It is often difficult to tell what the legal nature of the gift is at all!

GAAP Accounting Treatment

The GAAP accounting treatment of gifts required by Financial Account Standards Board statement 117 (FASB 117) and an accompanying FASB staff position called FSP 117-1 is important to those investing endowment funds because of the classification of gifts and the impact of allocating investment losses among the different accounting classifications.

Generally speaking, board-restricted endowments are treated by FASB 117 as "unrestricted" even though everyone understands the intent was for them to be restricted. To the frustration of donors and confusion of later Boards, absent a strong showing of donor intent that gifted funds may not be spent by the Board, the institution's accountants often lump such funds into the "unrestricted" category. As noted later, there may be inconsistencies between this accounting treatment and the obligations of the Board under the state's *Uniform Prudent Management of Institutional Funds Act* (UPMIFA). There may also be inconsistencies between this accounting treatment and attempts to protect (what the Board and donors thought were) restricted funds from the claims of unsecured creditors in the event of bankruptcy.

FASB 117 classifies gifts that are intended for specific use within a reasonably definable time frame as "temporarily restricted" during the period of time it takes to accomplish the specific use. For example, a gift to "renovate Old Main" would be treated as temporarily restricted until it has been expended for the renovation of Old Main.

FASB 117 generally permits gifts to be treated as restricted for "endowment" purposes only when there is clear evidence that the donor intended that the Board would not have the authority to spend all the gift funds or there is a separate "trust" created by the donor. "Income only" may be an adequate restriction, but the definition of "income" is modified by the application of UPMIFA (and its predecessor Uniform Management of Institutional Funds Act [UMIFA]). "Restrictions to particular purposes" is generally not adequate for GAAP purposes in the minds of many accountants unless the gift instrument limits the ability of the Board to spend all the gift funds for that purpose.

General Statement about Investing Endowment

Although the legal rules applicable to investment of endowment or similar funds may be influenced by whether the fund is a separate "trust," the standards no longer differ materially between the two.

Context: The Historical Prudent Man Rule

The classic Massachusetts Supreme Court case of *Harvard v. Amory* established in 1830 a standard that trustees "should observe how men of prudence, discretion, and intelligence manage their own affairs, not in regard to speculation, but in regard to the permanent disposition of their funds, considering the probable income, as well as the probable safety of capital to be invested."

In its time this was a radical extension of the trustee's duties. Trusts were created in England to avoid the rule that the eldest son would inherit the family property. For several centuries the primary role of the trustee (usually a friend burdened by the responsibility since corporate trustees were not permitted until the late eighteenth and early nineteenth centuries) was to maintain the family farm and deliver it after a period of years to one or more named beneficiaries. This system for escaping the reins of feudalism has developed into a vehicle for the investment of vast sums of personal wealth.

This so-called "prudent man" rule became part of American common law and was enacted as legislation in the several states. Some state laws went further and prohibited investments in common stocks unless they were on a permitted list and/or did not exceed certain percentages. The prudent man rule has been supplanted over time in nearly every state by the "prudent investor" rule.

Trusts: The Prudent Investor Act

Nearly every state has adopted the prudent investor rule by enacting some version of what is called the *Uniform Prudent Investor Act* (UPIA) developed in 1994 by the National Conference of Commissioners on Uniform State Laws. Of course, as various states adopt slight variations to this "uniform" act, the uniformity disappears. Thus, the general statements in this chapter need to be evaluated by reference to the specifics of each state's laws.

As with the historic prudent man rule, the application of the UPIA is technically to fiduciaries of trusts, including charitable trusts. However, as noted below, essentially the same standards have been applied by virtually all states to non-trust endowments by UPMIFA.

The prudent investor rule will give investment managers comfort since it speaks in terms that are familiar to them. Although it may be varied by the terms of particular instruments, the UPIA generally makes five fundamental alterations in the former criteria for prudent investing:

1. The standard of prudence is applied to any investment as part of the *total portfolio*, rather than to individual investments. In the trust setting, the term portfolio embraces all the trust's assets.
2. The trade-off in all investing between risk and return is identified as the fiduciary's central consideration.
3. All categorical restrictions on types of investments have been abrogated. The trustee can invest in anything that plays an appropriate role in achieving the risk/return objectives of the trust and that meets the other requirements of prudent investing.

4. The requirement that fiduciaries diversify their investments has been integrated into the definition of prudent investing.
5. The much criticized former rule of trust law forbidding the trustee to delegate investment and management functions has been reversed. Delegation in many states' version of the Prudent Investor Act is now permitted, subject to safeguards. In fact, in some circumstances, trustees may be able to absolve themselves of personal liability for investing if the responsibility is delegated to and accepted by an investment manager. However, trustees still have the responsibility for monitoring investments in light of trust goals and guidelines established by the trustees.

The comments to the UPIA state that the Act is centrally concerned with the investment responsibilities arising under a private trust, but that the prudent investor rule also bears on charitable and pension trusts. Furthermore, although the UPIA by its terms applies to trusts and not to charitable corporations, the comments state that the standards of the Act can be expected to inform the investment responsibilities of directors and officers of charitable corporations.

Uniform Prudent Management of Institutional Funds Act

Some variation of the UPMIFA has been enacted in nearly every state (the only current exceptions are Mississippi and Pennsylvania, which have equivalent provisions as part of its Uniform Trust Act).

UPMIFA replaces the previous UMIFA. The major differences are that UPMIFA adopts a standard of investing much like the Prudent Investor Act, and it provides considerable flexibility whereby an institution can access principal in contravention of a donor's restriction of use only to "income."

Application

UPMIFA applies to an "institutional fund," which means a fund held by an institution organized and operated exclusively for charitable purposes for its exclusive use, benefit, or purposes. It does not generally apply to a "trust" held by a third-party trustee such as a bank or trust company or individual for such an institution or to a fund in which any beneficiary that is not such an institution has an interest. UPMIFA as enacted by any particular state (e.g., New York) may apply to an endowment fund whose trustee is a not-for-profit corporation whether or not it is a charitable-purpose corporation.

It is important to recognize that the prudent investment standards apply to all institutional funds. They do not just apply to those institutional funds that are classified as "endowment funds" or "restricted" funds.

This means that a board-created endowment fund can become an endowment fund subject to UPMIFA if a donor makes a gift to the board created endowment fund, and the terms of the endowment fund are then discerned not only by reference to the original board resolution but also by reference to agreements, memoranda, or fund-raising materials used to solicit gifts to the endowment fund. It should be no surprise that these are not always consistent!

Standard of Care Applicable to All Institutional Funds

UPMIFA provides that an institution shall exercise the standard of care consistent with the applicable state law governing its form of organization as a corporation or trust, thus ducking an age-old question of whether different standards of prudent conduct apply to these two different forms of entity. Without regard to the form of entity, an institution must invest and manage an institutional fund as a prudent investor would and shall consider the following:

- The terms of the gift instrument;
- The purposes of the institution;
- The purposes of the institutional fund;
- The expenditure requirements of the fund;
- The long-term and short-term needs of the institution in carrying out its purposes;
- Present and future financial resources of the institution;
- General economic conditions;
- The possible effect of inflation or deflation;
- The expected tax consequences, if any, of investment decisions or strategies;
- The role that each investment or course of action plays within the overall investment portion of the institutional fund;
- The expected total return from income and appreciation of investments;
- Other resources of the institution;
- The needs of the institution and the institutional fund to make distributions and to preserve capital;
- An asset's special relationship or special value, if any, to the purposes of any gift instrument, or to the institution;
- The expected costs of investment and management decisions or strategies; and
- Any other relevant circumstances.

In addition, an institution's investment and management decisions about an individual asset must be made not in isolation but in the context of the institutional fund's portfolio of investments as a whole and as part of an overall investment strategy having risk and return objectives reasonably suited to the fund and to the institution. An institution must also make a reasonable effort to verify the facts relevant to the investment and management of institutional fund assets.

In terms of diversification, UPMIFA requires that an institution shall diversify the investments of an institutional fund unless the institution reasonably determines that, because of special circumstances, the purposes of the fund are better served without diversifying.

Investment Authority; Delegation of Investment Management

In addition to an investment authorized by a gift instrument or by a law other than UPMIFA, and subject to any specific limitations set forth in a gift instrument or in a law other than UPMIFA, UPMIFA provides that an institution:

- Within a reasonable time after receiving property, shall review the property and make and implement decisions concerning the retention and disposition of the assets, in order to bring the institutional fund into compliance with the purposes, terms, distribution requirements, and other circumstances of the institution, and the requirements of UPMIFA;
- May invest in any kind of property or type of investment consistent with the standards of UPMIFA;
- May make programmatic investments;
- May include all or any part of an institutional fund in any pooled or common fund maintained by an institution; and
- May invest all or any part of the institutional fund available for investment, including shares or interests in regulated investment companies, mutual funds, common trust funds, investment partnerships, real estate investment trusts, or similar investments by which funds are commingled.

Subject to any specific limitations set forth in a gift instrument or in law other than UPMIFA, any institution may delegate to agents *outside the institution* investment and management functions that a prudent institution could properly delegate under the circumstances. Members of the governing board of an institution are not liable to the institution for the decisions or actions of the agent to whom the function was delegated if the members of the governing board comply with the following:

- Select an agent;
- Establish the scope and terms of the delegation, consistent with the purposes of the institutional fund; and
- Periodically review the agent's actions in order to monitor the agent's performance and compliance with the terms of the delegation.

By accepting the delegation of an investment or management function from an institution, the agent incurs an obligation to the institution to exercise reasonable care, skill, and caution to comply with the terms of the delegation and submits to the jurisdiction of the courts of the state to which the institution is subject.

Appropriation of Assets in the Institutional Fund

Generally speaking, the definitions of and restrictions on the use of "income" or "principal" in private trusts (including charitable trusts) are governed by the terms of the governing instrument (e.g., a will) and the applicable state's Principal and Income Act. In private trusts, "principal" ordinarily includes not just the value of the original funding but also realized and unrealized investment growth in that value. However, even that concept is being eroded in the case of private trusts (through the enactment of a more modern version of the *Uniform Principal and Income Act* that permit more flexible definitions of "income").

One of the most important aspects of UPMIFA is its sanction of the use of assets in an "endowment" fund by the governing board notwithstanding a limitation in the gift instrument that only "income," "interest," "dividends," or "rents, issues or profits" may be used, or that "principal" should be preserved or may not be invaded.

The prior UPMIFA attempted to accomplish this by permitting the appropriation of the value of an endowment fund over its "historic dollar value," which generally meant the value at the time of each gift to the fund. (Funds wholly expendable by the institution are not affected by this limitation.) However the historic-dollar-value provision created serious problems for institutions whose endowment values had eroded with market downturns.

UPMIFA provides that an institution may expend so much of an endowment fund as the institution determines to be prudent for the uses, benefits, and purposes for which the endowment is established. In making its determination, the institution is required to exercise "reasonable care, skill, and caution," and shall consider:

- The terms of the gift instrument;
- The purposes of the institution;
- The purposes of the endowment fund;
- The long-term and short-term needs of the institution;
- Other resources of the institution;
- General economic conditions;
- The possible effects of inflation or deflation;
- The preservation of the purchasing power of the endowment fund;
- The investment policy of the institution;
- The duration of the endowment fund; and
- Any other relevant circumstances.

Some states have provided safe harbors for spending within a range based on percentages of the assets of the fund, and some institutions have adopted such ranges as matters of internal policy and discipline. For instance, New York's version of UPMIFA assumes imprudence if the distribution is greater than 7 percent of asset value.

Notwithstanding this statutory flexibility, institutions should always review the underlying gift instrument. UPMIFA is intended to provide rules of construction, but the institution may not ignore the donor's intent that a fund be maintained as an endowment or other clear expression of a donor's intent that does not require further construction.

Some states, like New York, have extended the application of UPMIFA to endowment funds *existing* at the time of enactment but require some form of notice to available donors prior to appropriating funds under the UPMIFA rules.

Private Foundation Rules

For federal tax purposes, all charitable and other organizations classified as tax exempt under Section 501(c)(3) of the U.S. Internal Revenue Code are classified either as a "private foundation" or an organization that is not a "private foundation."

Organizations that are not private foundations include churches, schools, hospitals, and public fund-raising and membership organizations (such as the United Way, the Boy and Girl Scouts, and organizations such as symphony orchestras) that meet arithmetic fund-raising tests described in regulations under Internal Revenue Code Section 509(a)(1). All other "Section 501(c)(3)" organizations are private foundations.

The fact that the word foundation is included in the organization's name is irrelevant. A typical "community foundation," for instance, is not a "private" foundation. However, the typical family foundation or privately funded charitable trust is a private foundation.

An organization that is a private foundation is subject to Chapter 42 of the Internal Revenue Code (and equivalent state law), which, among other things, contains investment restrictions.

Section 4944 of the Internal Revenue Code (and equivalent state law) provides that a private foundation may not make investments that "jeopardize" the organization's tax-exempt purpose, a provision that is interpreted by the Treasury Regulations as imposing what is effectively a prudent man rule within the tax code. Since these regulations were adopted in 1972, they have not kept up with modern investment strategies such as total-return investing and modern portfolio theory (e.g., puts, calls, and straddles are supposed to be given "special scrutiny"). Excise tax penalties may be imposed on the organization and its officers, directors, and managers for violation of the rules.

Section 4943 of the Internal Revenue Code (and equivalent state law) generally provides that a private foundation may not hold any voting or equity interest in a particular business enterprise to the extent it exceeds 20 percent or less of the amount held by so-called disqualified persons (essentially the trustees, officers, managers, and substantial contributors to the foundation and members of their families and trusts or other entities in which they hold a requisite interest). Substantial excise tax penalties may be imposed on the organization and its officers, directors, and managers for violation of the rules.

Conclusion

The legal aspects of investing charitable endowment, restricted, and other donor funds can get quite complicated. The applicable investment rules depend on a number of detailed questions about the nature of the fund and the institution for which it is being invested. If you are unclear about these rules, seek clarification from your legal counsel.

Final Thoughts

We have explored many topics that have hopefully given you some useful ideas for enhancing the investment strategy and improving the oversight procedures for your nonprofit fund.

In the preface, we discussed the many *challenges* that society and nonprofit organizations are likely to face in the twenty-first century. These challenges include increased demand for the services provided by nonprofit organizations resulting from economic headwinds and geopolitical realities.

In Chapter 1, we summarized the critical *three levers* exercise that should drive overall investment objectives and constraints. We also discussed how a fund's *three levers (inflows, outflows,* and *required returns)* should drive the *investment policy statement.*

In Chapter 2, we outlined various *asset allocation* frameworks, and why asset allocation is the greatest determinant of a portfolio's performance (both return and risk). We explored *modern portfolio theory* and *capital market assumptions* and how to overcome their various shortcomings with a modified framework that accommodates *non-normal returns* and inevitable *forecasting error.* We reviewed *strategic, tactical,* and *integrated asset allocation steering frameworks,* including the potential benefits and drawbacks of each. We also explored the many lessons learned during historical crises, especially the one in 2008.

In Chapters 4 and 8, we laid out a robust framework for *traditional asset class manager selection* as well as effective methods *for monitoring and evaluating managers* on an ongoing basis. We also included a framework for making the difficult *manager termination and retention* decisions when managers inevitably fall from grace.

In Chapters 3, 5, 6, and 7, we explored *traditional global financial asset classes* (e.g., global stocks and bonds) and *alternative investments (e.g., hedge funds, private equity,* and *real assets).* We discussed the role each asset class (or trading strategy) can play within a broad investment strategy.

In Chapters 9, 10, 12, 13, and 14, we explored the best practices of *effective investment committees,* including how to select outside vendors and services (e.g., *custodians, transition managers, brokers, administrators, record keepers, investment consultants,* and *outsourced CIO services).* We also discussed *behavioral finance* and how effective investment committees avoid the disastrous mistakes that human beings seem hardwired to make.

In Chapters 11 and 15, we discussed important considerations for nonprofits that wish to reflect their values through their investment decisions (*environmental, social, and corporate governance-focused investing*) as well as how to navigate the complex nonprofit legal and regulatory frameworks (*legal aspects of investing charitable endowment, restricted, and other donor funds*).

Takeaways

If you take away only three ideas from this book, they should be:

1. The *three levers exercise* is the crucial step in order to properly align the nonprofit fund's mission with the appropriate investment objective.
2. The *asset allocation strategy* will be the most important long-term performance factor; get this right *before* you dedicate valuable time and resources to selecting investment managers.
3. *Quality help is available* if your nonprofit organization does not have the time, experience, or resources to effectively oversee fund assets. The stakes are too high to avoid seeking outside assistance when it can help!

Conclusion

Your role in overseeing nonprofit investments is both noble and material. Like most fiduciaries, you do what you do to make a difference. Maybe you're a volunteer board member, or a donor who has created a private foundation. In any case, you recognize you have a responsibility and are likely reading this book because you care deeply about your mission. You want to give your organization every opportunity to succeed. Hopefully the information in this book will help you to reach that worthy goal.

Case Study: Developing Capital Market Assumptions

The following case study has excerpts from DiMeo Schneider & Associates, L.L.C.'s 10-year return, standard deviation, correlation, and tail (non normal) forecast white paper (for 2011 to 2020).

DiMeo Schneider & Associates, L.L.C. reviews and updates asset class assumptions at least annually to reflect 10-year *ex ante* estimates for asset class returns, standard deviations, skewness, kurtosis, and correlations. The following is a summary of our January 2011 to December 2020 capital market forecasts.

Definitions

DiMeo Schneider & Associates, LLC's Frontier Engineer™ portfolio optimization requires 10-year forecasts of the following metrics:

- **Expected Median Annual Return**[1] of each asset class
- **Expected Annual Geometric Return**[2] of each asset class
- **Expected Annual Standard Deviation** of each asset class
- **Expected Correlation** among all asset classes
- **Expected Skewness** of each asset class (correct for asymmetry)
- **Expected Kurtosis** of each asset class (correct for tails)

10-Year Median Annual Return Forecast

The annual median return forecast represents the expected midpoint of all possible future 10-year median returns for an asset class. These *ex ante* return estimates (or expected returns) will not be realized over the 10-year time horizon. We expect the median (10-year return) to have a 50 percent probability of being higher or lower than the forecast.

10-Year Geometric Annual Return[3] Forecast

The geometric return forecast represents the expected midpoint of all possible future 10-year outcomes for an asset class. These *ex ante* return estimates (or expected returns) will not be realized over the 10-year time horizon. We expect the geometric return to have a 50 percent probability of being higher or lower than the forecast.

10-Year Annual Standard Deviation Forecast

The 10-year standard deviation forecast expresses the median expected (normally distributed) variability of annual returns about the mean. The higher the standard deviation, the more uncertain is the outcome.

Expected Correlation among All Asset Classes

The 10-year forecast of asset class correlation coefficients quantifies the degree to which two assets are expected to move together. The correlation coefficient can range from -1 (perfect negative correlation) to $+1$ (perfect positive correlation).

Expected Skewness of Each Asset Class

The 10-year skewness forecast quantifies the degree of expected asymmetry of the return distribution. If the left tail is more pronounced than the right tail, the asset has negative skewness. If the reverse is true, it has positive skewness. If the two are equal, it has zero skewness (normally distributed).

Expected Kurtosis of Each Asset Class

The 10-year kurtosis forecast of each asset class quantifies the degree of expected peakedness (or flatness) of a distribution. If excess kurtosis is positive, the distribution is more peaked (with extreme events). If excess kurtosis is negative, the distribution is flatter (with fewer extreme events).

Forecasting Methods

Returns

Ten-year asset class return forecasts were developed using various methodologies including:

1. Risk premium method
2. Equity returns decomposition method
3. Black-Litterman (for global equity)
4. Fixed income returns decomposition method
5. Commodity futures returns decomposition method
6. Corrections for extreme asset class over/under valuation (or other disequilibrium in capital market assumptions)

1. The Risk Premium Method adds a risk premium to a referenced asset's return forecast.

$$\textbf{Return} = (\textbf{RA}) + / - (\textbf{RP})$$

RA = Forecasted Return of "Reference Asset"
RP = Appropriate "Risk Premium" Added to Referenced Asset's forecast.

2. The Equity Returns Decomposition Method breaks out the components of equity returns.

$$\textbf{Return} = [(1 + \textbf{DIV}) \times (1 + \textbf{P/E}) \times (1 + \textbf{REG}) \times (1 + \textbf{CPI})] - 1$$

DIV = Dividend Yield
P/E = Price/Earnings Expansion/Contraction
REG = Real Earnings Growth = [Return on Equity] × [Earnings Retention Ratio]
CPI = Inflation (Consumer Price Index)

The following is the Modified Equity Returns Decomposition Method for REITs and MLPs:

$$\textbf{Return} = [(\textbf{DY}) + (\textbf{RPR}) +/- (\textbf{YLD C}) + (\textbf{CPI})]$$

DY = Dividend/Distribution yield
RPR = Real price return excluding yield compression
YLD C = Price return resulting from yield compression
CPI = Inflation

3. The Black-Litterman Method uses reverse mean-variance optimization to arrive at unbiased asset class return forecasts by inputting correlation, volatility, and market cap weights, then solving for (equilibrium) expected returns (or risk premiums).
   - Market capitalization weights for each asset
   - Correlation between the assets
   - Volatility (or standard deviation) of assets
   - Risk-free rate
   - The risk-aversion coefficient of the reference market portfolio

4. The Fixed Income Returns Decomposition Method forecasts the components of fixed income index returns (Yield Δ and Price Δ) and combines them for a total return forecast.

$$\textbf{Returns} = (\textbf{YLD}) +/- (\textbf{CUR}) +/- (\textbf{PE})$$

YLD = Bond Index YTM
CUR = Expected currency affect derived from interest rate parity
PE = Bond Index "Price Effect"

5. The Commodity Futures Index Returns Decomposition Method forecasts and aggregates the components of a commodity futures index's total return.

$$\textbf{Returns} = (\textbf{Spot}) +/- (\textbf{Roll}) +/- (\textbf{CR})$$

Spot = Spot price return, which is assumed to be consistent with CPI forecast
Roll = Roll return expected to be earned from holding a futures contracts to (near) maturity
CR = Collateral Return, which is earned by the return of the asset used to collateralize futures/swaps (i.e., TIPS, T-Bills, etc.)

6. DiMeo Schneider & Associates, LLC. reserves the right to make corrections for extreme over or undervaluation of asset classes (or capital markets disequilibrium) when developing forecasts. An example of such a correction would be if an asset class is over or undervalued by two or more standard deviations relative to historical valuation metrics (i.e., S&P 500 earnings yield relative to the 10-year Treasury yield). Another example would be if the 10-year nominal U.S. Treasury versus the 10-year U.S. TIPS spread was skewing implied inflation expectations due to an unusually large TIPS illiquidity risk premium during a period of market stress (and flight to liquidity). An expectation of mean-reversion in relative valuations (convergence of spread relationship) may be used when developing 10-year capital market assumptions.

Standard Deviation

Standard deviation is derived by calculating the rolling annual standard deviation of all historical 12-month periods. For asset classes with short track records, adjustments to historical standard deviations may be made where appropriate. Such adjustments may be made using the following methodology:

Standard Deviation (σ) of Asset =

$$\frac{[\text{Short-term } \sigma \text{ of asset}] \times [\text{Long-term } \sigma \text{ of comparable asset}]}{[\text{Short-term } \sigma \text{ of comparable asset}]}$$

Correlation

Correlation is calculated using long-term historical monthly data over common time periods with the exception of the risk-free asset, or cash, which is assumed to have a zero correlation to all asset classes (except short-term bonds).

Skewness and Kurtosis

We observe (monthly) skewness and kurtosis for each asset class over a uniform period of time (1997 to 2010). Failing to observe skewness and kurtosis over a uniform period of time for each asset class, especially during periods of stress (i.e., no emerging markets data for October of 1987), will likely understate the impact of extreme events for asset classes with shorter return streams relative to those with longer return streams. Adjustments may be made to skewness and kurtosis from historical measures if warranted (i.e., qualitatively adjust for hedge fund survivorship bias, etc.)

10-Year Return Forecasts by Asset Class

1. **INFLATION (CPI):** CPI is used as a building block of total return for several asset classes. The unbiased forecast of CPI is the difference between the 10-year nominal U.S. Treasury yield and the 10-year TIPS real yield. As of December 31, 2010, this difference was 2.3 percent (i.e., 3.30 percent −1.00 percent).

The following are the implied break-even and forward CPI rates based on the break-even inflation rates priced into nominal and inflation-protected U.S. Treasuries.

Implied Break-Even CPI (12/31/10)

Maturity	Nominal	TIPS	Implied CPI
5 Years	2.0%	0.2%	1.8%
7 Years	2.7%	0.7%	2.1%
10 Years	3.3%	1.0%	2.3%
20 Years	4.1%	1.6%	2.5%
30 Years	4.3%	1.9%	2.5%

Implied Forward CPI (12/31/10)

Forward CPI	Implied CPI
1-5 Years	1.8%
5-10 Years	2.8%
10-20 Years	2.8%
20-30 Years	2.4%

While the annualized 10-year CPI forecast is 2.3 percent, the expectation is for lower inflation in the first five years (i.e., 1.8 percent) and higher inflation in the last five years (i.e., 2.8 percent).

10-Year Forecast of Annual CPI: 2.3 percent

2. **U.S. INVESTMENT-GRADE FIXED INCOME:** As of December 31, 2010, the Barclays Capital U.S. Aggregate Bond Index had 7,999 issues with an average maturity of 6.67 years and an average duration of 4.8 years. The average credit quality of the index was AAA. The unbiased return forecast for the Barclays Capital U.S. Aggregate Bond Index is its current yield-to-maturity (i.e., 2.85 percent as of December 31, 2010).

Barclays Capital U.S. Aggregate Bond Index Metrics (12/31/2010)

Sector	%	Maturity	%	Credit	%	Holdings	Value
U.S. Govts/ Agencies	43.5	1-3 Years	24.0	AAA	77.1	Number of Issues	7,999
U.S. Inv Grade Corporates	19.5	3-5 Years	28.7	AA	4.5	Average Quality	AAA
U.S. MBS/ABS	2.8	5-7 Years	22.9	A	9.9	Average Maturity	6.67
Mortgage Passthrus	31.7	7-10 Years	13.2	BBB	8.5	Average Duration	4.80
Other	2.5	10-20 Years	3.7	BB or lower	0.0	Average Coupon	4.25
		> 20 Years	7.5			Average YTM	2.85

10-Year Forecast of Geometric Return: 2.9 percent

3. **TIPS:** The Barclays Capital U.S. Treasury Inflation Protected Securities Index includes all publicly issued U.S. Treasury inflation-protected securities that have at least one year remaining to maturity, are rated investment grade and have $250 million or more of outstanding face value. As of December 31, 2010, the

Barclays Capital U.S. Treasury Inflation Protected Securities Index had 30 issues (all AAA U.S. Sovereign) with an average real yield of 0.58 percent and an average maturity of approximately nine years.

Barclays Capital U.S. TIPS Index Maturity Spectrum (12/31/2010)

Maturity (yrs)	Percent
1-5	37.7%
5-10	31.2%
10-15	5.5%
15-20	21.4%
20-25	1.4%
>25	2.9%

Combining the real yield to maturity of the Barclays Capital U.S. Treasury Inflation Protected Securities Index (0.58 percent) with the forecasted inflation rate (2.3 percent) leads to an expected total return of 2.88 percent (i.e., 0.58 percent + 2.3 percent).

10-Year Forecast of Geometric Return: 2.9 percent

4. **HIGH-YIELD BONDS:** As of December 31, 2010, the Citigroup U.S. High Yield Index had 1,540 issues (all BB rated or lower) representing $781 billion in market value. The average YTM was 7.89 percent with an average life of 6.75 years (and a 4.43-year average duration). The following chart reflects additional high-yield bond market metrics as of December 31, 2010:

Citigroup U.S. HY Index (December 31, 2010)

Market Value ($B)	Par Value ($B)	MV/PV	Average Coupon (per $100 Par)	Coupon/ MV Yield	Current YTM
$781	$755	104%	$8.41	8.13%	7.89%

BB Corporate Spreads vs. 7-year U.S. Treasuries (1991-2010)

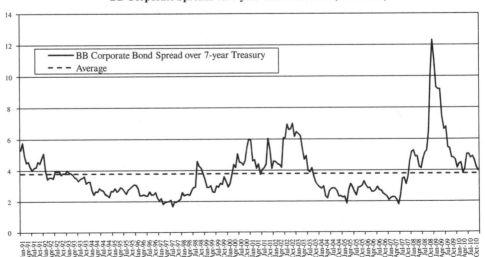

- As of December 31, 2010, the BB-rated Corporate Bond spread versus the seven-year U.S. Treasury Note was +3.95 percent, which is 0.17 percent above the long-term historical average (of +3.78 percent) between 1991 and 2010.
- From November 1984 to December 2010, the ML High Yield Master Index returned 9.70 percent versus 8.07 percent for the Barclays Capital U.S. Aggregate Bond Index, representing a historical risk premium of 1.63 percent of high-yield bonds (over investment-grade intermediate bonds).
- Unprecedented (wide) credit spreads during late 2008 and early 2009 predicted unprecedented default rates (and low recovery rates). Actual 2009 and 2010 default rates proved significantly lower than expectations.
- On a trailing 12-month basis through September 2010, the U.S. high-yield default rate fell to 3.5 percent, down from 4.5 percent at the end of June 2010 and 13.7 percent at the end of 2009. According to Fitch, the high-yield default rate has posted its biggest post recession decline on record in 2010.
- According to Fitch, the 2010 high yield market default rates will finish near 1 percent (on a par-based rate).
- We believe the historically observed 1.63 percent excess return of high-yield bonds over investment-grade intermediate bonds (i.e., from 1984 to 2010) understates the return potential for the next 10 years. Current yield spreads are wide given the currently low level of default rates and relatively high recovery rates.
- According to Fitch, the weighted average recovery rate on all defaults through September 2010 was 54 percent of par, above 2009's 34.1 percent. The 2010 loss rates associated with bond defaults has therefore declined significantly to 0.23 percent when combining the year-to-date (through September 30, 2010) default rate of 0.5 percent with a recovery rate of 54 percent of par on the defaulted issues.
- Based on the Altman methodology, the market is pricing in an approximate 1.9 percent annual loss rate (3.1 percent default and 38.4 percent recovery) as of December 31, 2010. This implies a 6.0 percent expected return (i.e., 7.89 percent YTM minus a 1.9 percent loss rate). We believe that current fundamentals support a lower-than-predicted default rate and a higher-than-predicted recovery rate for 2011 than represented by current valuations. However, we believe the Altman methodology reflects a more fair view of risk over a full market cycle (beyond 2011). A 6.0 percent expected return reflects a 3.1 percent risk premium for high-yield bonds versus the aggregate U.S. investment-grade bond market (i.e., the Barclays Capital U.S. Aggregate Bond Index), which is a ~1.5 percent higher risk premium than what was observed during the last 26 years (i.e., 1984 to 2010).

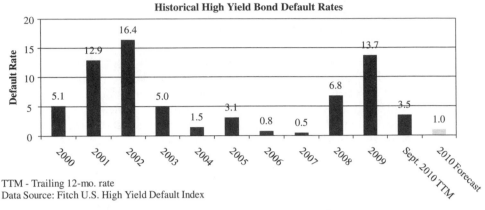

Historical High Yield Bond Default Rates

TTM - Trailing 12-mo. rate
Data Source: Fitch U.S. High Yield Default Index

Historical High-Yield Bond Recovery Rates[4]

Year	Weighted Average Recovery Rate	Median Recovery Rate
2000	24.9%	20.0%
2001	29.8%	15.8%
2002	22.5%	21.9%
2003	44.4%	36.6%
2004	62.1%	51.6%
2005	57.6%	61.3%
2006	64.3%	60.0%
2007	66.4%	69.1%
2008	45.8%	19.6%
2009	34.1%	24.9%
Sept. 2010	54.0%	50.0%

Altman Methodology Applied as of December 31, 2010[5,6]

	Market Value ($B)	Par Value ($B)	MV/PV	Average Coupon (per $100 Par)	Coupon/ MV Yield	Current YTM	
	$781	$755	104%	$8.41	8.13%	7.89%	
10-Year Treasury	Current YTM	Current Spread	Coupon/ MV Yield	Coupon/ Par Yield	Assumed Annual Default Rate	Assumed Annual Recovery Rate	Assumed Annual Loss Rate
3.30%	7.89%	4.6%	8.13%	8.41%	3.1%	38.4%	−1.9%

10-Year Forecast of Geometric Return: 6.0 percent

5. **FOREIGN FIXED INCOME (JPM Global Non-U.S. Index):** Interest Rate Parity is used to calculate the expected hedged currency return of the non-U.S. bond markets (in U.S.-dollar terms). The difference in risk-free rates across borders must be explained by the currency Spot-Futures exchange rate relationship.

If not, it would be possible to borrow in one currency, lend in the other, and lock in an arbitrage profit.

Global Bond Market Yields & Risk Free Rates (December 31, 2010)[7]

Country	3 Mo. T-Bill	Index YTM	Global Weight X-U.S.
Australia	4.8	5.4	1.1
Belgium	0.5	3.7	2.7
Canada	1.0	3.1	2.8
Denmark	4.3	2.9	0.9
France	0.4	3.1	9.7
Germany	0.3	2.8	9.4
Italy	1.3	4.7	10.2
Japan	0.1	1.2	46.6
Netherlands	0.4	2.9	2.6
Spain	1.2	5.2	4.1
Sweden	1.4	3.2	0.7
United Kingdom	0.6	3.7	9.1
Weighted-Average	0.51	2.50	

United States   0.12

Interest Rate Parity (90 days)   **Current Spot-Futures Relationship:**

$$F_{d/f} = S_{d/f} \times (1 + I_d)/(1 + I_f)^{1/4}$$

$\text{Futures}_{d/f} = \$0.999017621/\text{€}^8 1.00$

$\text{Spot}_{d/f} = \$1.00/\text{€}1.00$

The weighted-average risk free rate in the JPM Global Non-U.S. Bond Index was 0.51 percent on December 31, 2010 compared to 0.12 percent for the 90-day U.S. T-bill. Interest rate parity and a zero arbitrage assumption suggest that the U.S. Dollar/Foreign Currency Basket Spot-Futures spread is approximately −0.39 percent (0.12 percent −0.51 percent). If one were long €1.00 worth of foreign denominated 90-day T-bills, they could short €1.00 worth of foreign currency (hedging foreign currency risk) and receive $0.999017621 in 90 days (Currency Effect = −0.098 percent per quarter return; annualized −0.39 percent).

- As of December 31, 2010, the JPM Global Non-U.S. (Hedged) Bond Index was yielding +**2.50 percent.**
- Hedged annualized currency return −**0.39 percent**
- The foreign bond yield (2.50 percent) + the foreign currency appreciation (−0.39 percent) = **2.11 percent**
  10-Year Forecast of Geometric Return: 2.1 percent

6. **REAL ESTATE (REITs):** From 1971 to 2010, the NAREIT Equity REIT Index had a total annualized return of 12.01 percent. The price component of return was 3.79 percent. 1.45 percent (annualized) of this price return came from yield compression (*as the dividend yield fell from 6.13 percent in 1972 to 3.54 percent in 2010),* and that CPI averaged 4.42 percent annually, so the real price return (excluding yield expansion/compression) was −2.08 percent annually. At 8.22 percent annually, the dividend was the largest component of return. The following returns decomposition model is used to forecast returns where total return is a function of dividend yields, real price return (excluding yield compression), yield compression, and CPI (inflation).

Returns Decomposition Method: $[(\textbf{DY}) + (\textbf{RPR}^9) + (\textbf{YLD C}) + (\textbf{CPI})]$

$$(1972 \text{ to } 2010) : [(8.22 \text{ percent}) + (-2.08 \text{ percent}) + (1.45 \text{ percent}) + (4.42 \text{ percent})] = 12.01 \text{ percent}$$

$$\text{Forecast } (2011 \text{ to } 2020) : [(3.54 \text{ percent}) + (0 \text{ percent}) + (0 \text{ percent}) + (2.30 \text{ percent})] = 5.84 \text{ percent}$$

DY = Dividend yield (8.22 percent from 1972 to 2010)
RPR = Real price return excluding yield compression (2.08 percent from 1972 to 2010)
YLD C = Price return resulting from yield compression (+1.45 percent from 1972 to 2010). Dividend yield fell from 6.13 percent in 1972 to 3.54 percent in 2010
CPI = Inflation (4.42 percent from 1972 to 2010)

10-Year Forecast of Geometric Return: 5.8 percent

7. **LARGE-CAP U.S. EQUITIES:** The 10-year geometric return forecast for large-cap U.S. equities (S&P 500) is derived by averaging the following two methods (i.e., Returns Decomposition & Risk Premium methods).

Returns Decomposition Method: $[(\textbf{1} + \textbf{DIV}) \times (\textbf{1} + \textbf{P/E}) \times (\textbf{1} + \textbf{REG}) \times (\textbf{1} + \textbf{CPI})] - \textbf{1}$

$$\text{Forecast } (2011 - 2020) : [(1 + 1.8 \text{ percent}) \times (1 + 0 \text{ percent}) \times (1 + 3.1 \text{ percent}) \times (1 + 2.3 \text{ percent})] - 1 = 7.4 \text{ percent}$$

DIV = Dividend Yield
P/E = P/E Expansion/Contraction
REG = Real Earnings Growth = [Return on Equity] × [Earnings Retention Ratio]
CPI = Inflation (Consumer Price Index)

10-Year Forecast (as of 12/31/2010)[10,11,12,13]

	Current P/E (S&P 500)		14.5	
	Current E/P (S&P 500)		6.9%	
DIV	Current Dividend Yield (S&P 500)	×	1.8%	+1
ERR	Current Earnings Retention Ratio (S&P 500)		74%	
	Current Dividend Payout Ratio (S&P 500)		26%	
ROE[3]	Historical Real Return on Equity (ROE)		4.3%	
REG[4]	Expected Real Earnings Growth	×	3.1%	+1
CPI	Expected Inflation	×	2.3%	+1
	Expected Nominal Earnings Growth		5.4%	
P/E	P/E	×	0%	+1
	Total Forecasted Return		**7.4%**	

Risk Premium Method: $[(\text{LTB})+(\text{HRP})]$

1926 to 2010 : [(5.54 percent) + (4.32 percent)] = 9.87 percent

Forecast (2011 to 2020) : [(4.4 percent) + (4.3 percent)] = 8.70 percent

LTB = Long-Term Government Bond index return / yield (30-Year Treasury)
HRP = Historical Risk Premium (Equity Premium over long-term government
     bond index from 1926 to the present.

	Historical: 1926 to 2010			**10-Year Forecast (12/31/10)**	
LTB	Historical Long-Term Gov Bond Return	5.54%	LTB	Current Long-Term Gov Bond Yield (30-Year Treasury)	4.4%
HRP	Historical Equity Return – Long-term Gov Bond Return	4.32%	HRP	Historical Equity Return – Long-term Gov Bond Yield	4.3%
	S&P 500 Total Return	9.87%		Total Forecasted Return	8.7%

- Returns Decomposition Method: 7.4 percent
- Risk Premium Method: 8.7 percent
- Average of Two Methods: 8.1 percent
  10-Year Forecast of Geometric Return: 8.1 percent

8. **MID-CAP U.S. EQUITIES:** Using historical correlations and volatility for Large-, Mid-, and Small-Cap U.S. Equity (from 1979 to 2010) and U.S. market-cap weights, the (unbiased) Black-Litterman arithmetic return forecast for Mid Cap is 10.6 percent (versus 9.7 percent for large cap). Adjusting for forecasted volatility (19.4 percent Annual Standard Deviation), the expected geometric return is 8.7 percent.
   10-Year Forecast of Geometric Return: 8.7 percent

9. **SMALL-CAP U.S. EQUITIES:** Using historical correlations and volatility for Large-, Mid-, and Small-Cap U.S. Equity from 1979 to 2010, and their U.S. market-cap weights, the (unbiased) Black-Litterman arithmetic return forecast for Small Cap is 11.3 percent (versus 9.7 percent for large cap). Adjusting for forecasted volatility (21.9 percent Annual Standard Deviation), the expected geometric return is 8.9 percent.

10-Year Forecast of Geometric Return: 8.9 percent

Black-Litterman (Mid & Small Cap U.S. Equity)

Market Caps			Volatility			Correlation Matrix				Covariance Matrix			
Segment	% MC		Segment	St. Dev.			Large Cap	Mid Cap	Small Cap		Large Cap	Mid Cap	Small Cap
Large Cap	71.7%		S&P 500	15.5%		Large Cap	1.00	0.94	0.83	S&P 500	2.42%	2.51%	2.58%
Mid Cap	19.6%		RMID	17.3%		Mid Cap	0.94	1.00	0.94	RMID	2.51%	2.98%	3.25%
Small Cap	8.7%		R2000	20.0%		Small Cap	0.83	0.94	1.00	R2000	2.58%	3.25%	4.01%
11/30/10 MC			*1979-2010*			*1979-2010*				*1979-2010*			

Mkt St. Dev	15.85%
Mkt Varianc	2.51%
Mkt RP	9.88%
RA Coeffici	3.93
RFR	0.12%

[MC1%*COV1+MC2%*COV2+MC3*COV3] X RA Coeff. + RFR

Solve for Mkt RP w/ Large Cap = 8.1%

	Large Cap	Mid Cap	Small Cap
Arith Ret.	9.7%	10.6%	11.3%
St. Dev.	18.2%	19.4%	21.9%
Ge. Ret	8.1%	8.7%	8.9%

Risk Aversion Coefficient = MRP/VAR

10-Yr Forecast St. Dev.different from 1979-2010

RA Coefficient (i.e., Risk Aversion Coefficient) = Mark Risk Premium / Market Variance
Ten-year forecast standard deviation different from 1979-2010 historical standard deviation

10. **FOREIGN-DEVELOPED EQUITIES:** Using historical correlation and volatility for U.S. Equity, Foreign-Developed, and Emerging-Markets from 1988 to 2010, the (unbiased) Black-Litterman arithmetic return forecast for Foreign Developed Equity is 11.8 percent. Adjusting for forecasted volatility (23.9 percent Annual Standard Deviation), the expected geometric return is 8.9 percent.

10-Year Forecast of Geometric Return: 8.9 percent

11. **EMERGING-MARKETS EQUITIES:** Using historical correlation and volatility for U.S. Equity, Foreign-Developed, and Emerging-Markets from 1988 to 2010, the (unbiased) Black-Litterman arithmetic return forecast for Emerging Markets Equity is 14.3 percent. Adjusting for forecasted volatility (31.4 percent Annual Standard Deviation), the expected geometric return is 9.4 percent.

10-Year Forecast of Geometric Return: 9.4 percent

Black-Litterman (Foreign Developed & Emerging Markets)

Market Caps			Volatility			Correlation Matrix				Covariance Matrix			
Segment	% MC		Segment	St. Dev.			US	For. Dev.	Em. Mkt		US	For. Dev.	Em. Mkt
U.S. Equity (R3000)	43.0%		U.S. Equity (R3000)	15.1%		U.S. Equity	1.00	0.71	0.68	U.S. Equity (R3000)	2.29%	1.90%	2.49%
Foreign Dev. Equity	43.5%		Foreign Dev. Equity	17.6%		Foreign Dev.	0.71	1.00	0.68	Foreign Dev. Equity	1.90%	3.11%	2.90%
Emerging Mkt	13.5%		Emerging Mkt	24.2%		Emerging Mkt	0.68	0.68	1.00	Emerging Mkt	2.49%	2.90%	5.84%
11/30/10 MC			*1988-2010*			*1988-2010*				*1988-2010*			

Mkt St. Dev.	15.62%
Mkt Variance	2.44%
Mkt RP	11.10%
*RA Coefficient	4.55
RFR	0.12%

[MC1%*COV1+MC2%*COV2+MC3*COV3] X RA Coeff. + RFR

Solve for Mkt RP w/ U.S. Equity Arith = 9.88% (US B-L)

	US	For. Dev.	Em. Mkt
Arith Ret.	9.88%	11.8%	14.3%
St. Dev.*	18.4%	23.9%	31.4%
Ge. Ret	8.2%	8.9%	9.4%

Risk Aversion Coefficient = MRP/VAR

*10-Yr Forecast St. Dev.different from 1988-2010

RA Coefficient (i.e., Risk Aversion Coefficient) = Mark Risk Premium / Market Variance
Ten-year forecast standard deviation different from 1988-2010 standard deviation.

12. **COMMODITY FUTURES INDEX:** The long-term historical risk premium for Commodity Futures has matched the equity risk premium (1959 to 2004).[14] The expected return of a Commodity Futures index is comprised of an expected spot price appreciation of the underlying commodities (expected to match inflation/CPI over a full market cycle), the expected excess return generated from the roll return in a forward contract and the return generated from holding T-bills (or TIPS) as collateral for the futures contracts. From January 1970 to September 2008, the components of total return for the Goldman Sachs Commodity Futures Index were as follows:

January 1970 to September 2008 Total Return[15] = Spot Return (4.8 percent[16]) + Roll Return (0.5 percent) + T-Bill Return (5.6 percent) = Total Return (11.8 percent)

2011 to 2020 Forecast (w/T-bills) = Spot Return (2.3 percent[17]) + Roll Return (0 percent[18]) + T-bill Return (2.3 percent[19]) = Total Return (4.6 percent)

2011 to 2020 Forecast (w/T-TIPS) = Spot Return (2.3 percent)+ Roll Return (0 percent) + TIPS Return (2.9 percent[20]) = Total Return (5.2 percent)

10-Year Forecast of Geometric Return: 5.2 percent

13. **HEDGE FUNDS (DIVERSIFIED MULTI-STRATEGY PORTFOLIO):** Hedge funds are not an asset class, but an amalgam of trading strategies with exposures (often leveraged) to many different esoteric risk factors. The return stream for hedge funds is also unique and less comparable to true asset classes. Historical (aggregated) hedge fund return streams frequently have properties that make the payoff structure more non-normal than most other assets (i.e., a payoff structure similar to underwriting flood insurance). That is, volatility will often be low from month to month, but with lower probability, usually left tail events occur with much higher consequence. The hedge fund return forecast is also unique in that it is the only investment category with a net positive manager alpha assumption. That is, the hedge fund return forecast is not meant to represent a return expectation for the aggregate hedge fund market, but rather a skillful portfolio of hedge funds. For purposes of measuring historical risk exposures (correlations to other asset classes) of hedge funds, the HFRI Fund of Funds Index is used as the proxy. The return, risk, correlation, skewness, and kurtosis assumptions are subject to change on a product-by-product or strategy-by-strategy basis.

The current 10-year standard deviation (or volatility) forecast for a 60 percent investment-grade U.S. fixed-income and 40 percent U.S. equity mix is 9.3 percent, which matches the current 10-year standard deviation forecast for a diversified multi-strategy portfolio of hedge funds. This 60 percent fixed and 40 percent equity mix has approximately a 5.5 percent 10-year return forecast.

Our expectation is for a skillful and diversified pool of hedge fund managers to add 3 percent of excess return (i.e., 5.5 percent + 3 percent = 8.5 percent) at approximately the same volatility level.

10-Year Forecast of Return: 8.5 percent[21]

14. **Energy Infrastructure MLPs (Master Limited Partnerships):** As of December 31, 2010, the Alerian MLP Index Yield was 6.2 percent. For most MLPs, the ability to increase distributions is a function of inflation (i.e., many midstream MLPs have inflation adjustors), demand growth for energy (i.e., oil, natural gas, etc.), and accretive acquisition growth.

Returns Decomposition Method: $[(\mathbf{DY}) + (\mathbf{RPR}^{22}) + (\mathbf{YLD\ C}^{23}) + (\mathbf{CP}I^{24})]$

$$(1996-2010): [(7.81 \text{ percent}) + (4.41 \text{ percent}) + (2.17 \text{ percent}) + (2.41 \text{ percent})] = 16.79 \text{ percent}$$

$$10\text{-Year Forecast}: [(6.2 \text{ percent}) + (1.25 \text{ percent}) + (0.0 \text{ percent}) + (2.3 \text{ percent})] = 9.75 \text{ percent}$$

DY = Distribution yield (7.81 percent from 1996 to 2010)

RPR = Real price return excluding yield compression (4.41 percent from 1996 to 2010)

YLD C = Price return resulting from yield compression (+2.17 percent from 1996 to 2010). Distribution yield fell from 8.98 percent in December 1995 to 6.2 percent in December 2010).

CPI = Inflation (2.41 percent from 1996 to 2010).

10-Year Forecast of Geometric Return: 9.8 percent

15. **Private Equity:** We assume investors demand a 3 percent risk premium over large-cap U.S. equities (after fees and expenses) to justify the risk and illiquidity of investing in private equity. The private equity return forecast is not meant to represent a return expectation for the aggregate private equity market, but rather a portfolio of skillful private equity funds. This return forecast is subject to change depending upon the unique properties of the private equity investment product (i.e., buyout, venture, etc.).

10-Year Forecast of Geometric Return: 11.1 percent

Standard Deviation Forecasts

Annualizing a historical monthly standard deviation by multiplying by the square root of 12 understates true annual volatility (because of monthly serial correlation). Therefore, standard deviation is derived (for all asset classes) by calculating the annual standard deviation of all historical 12-month periods.

An adjustment will be made to asset classes with shorter return streams that will attempt to normalize volatility between asset classes. The methodology is used for the following asset classes:

Asset Classes

- High-Yield Bonds (November 1984)
- Inflation-Indexed Bonds (March 1997)
- Foreign Bonds/50 percent hedged (January 1985)
- Emerging Markets (January 1988)
- Hedge Funds (January 1990)
- MLPs (January 1990)

Methodology

Standard Deviation (σ) of Asset =

$$\frac{[\textbf{Short term } \sigma \textbf{ of asset}] \times [\textbf{Long term } \sigma \textbf{ of comparable asset}]}{[\textbf{Short term } \sigma \textbf{ of comparable asset}]}$$

Private Equity

There is no observable monthly return stream for a private equity index. Private Equity has an assumed 11.1 percent return (or a 3 percent risk premium over large-cap U.S. equities). Using the CAPM, the 3 percent risk premium requires a 1.58 beta (relative to large-cap U.S. equities). As a practical matter, private equity will be constrained based on the liquidity constraints.

    10-Year Forecasted Annual Standard Deviation: 28.7 percent = 1.58 (β) × 18.2 percent (large cap U.S. σ)

Differentiating Arithmetic and Geometric Assumptions

1. Arithmetic Return versus Geometric Returns

The arithmetic average annual return is always equal to or greater than a geometric (or compounded) annualized return. Since the CAPM and the Black-Litterman are single-time-period models, they forecast an arithmetic return (i.e., one-year). On the other hand, geometric returns are more appropriate for quantifying expected holding period returns (i.e., 10 years).

Geometric Return = [**Arithmetic Return**] − [(**Standard Deviation**)^2]/**2**

    The Frontier Engineer asset allocation modeling seeks to optimize (the median expected) aggregate portfolio geometric returns (per unit risk) rather than arithmetic returns (per unit risk).

2. Conclusion

Two low correlating assets with the same arithmetic return have a higher geometric return when combined within a portfolio (and rebalanced) than either has on a stand-alone basis.

Return and Risk Assumptions[25,26]

Asset Class	Expected Median Annual Return	Expected Geometric Annual Return	Expected Risk (σ)	Skew	Kurt
Cash	0.1%	0.1%	0.0%	—	—
TIPS	3.4%	2.9%	10.5%	−0.86	5.37
U.S. Bonds	3.2%	2.9%	7.2%	−0.38	1.21
Int'l Bond	2.7%	2.1%	11.2%	0.06	0.38
HY Bond	7.4%	6.0%	16.6%	−1.31	9.25
Large Cap U.S.	9.7%	8.1%	18.2%	−0.63	0.64
Mid Cap U.S.	10.6%	8.7%	19.4%	−0.80	1.84
Small Cap U.S.	11.3%	8.9%	21.9%	−0.51	0.71
REITs	8.5%	5.8%	23.1%	−0.75	7.48
Int'l Equity	11.8%	8.9%	23.9%	−0.69	1.36
Em. Mkts. Equity	14.3%	9.4%	31.4%	−0.84	1.75
Commodity Futures	7.1%	5.2%	19.6%	−0.95	4.48
Hedge Funds Portfolio	8.9%	8.5%	9.3%	−2.00	8.00
Private Equity	15.2%	11.1%	28.7%	−0.51	0.71
MLPs	11.9%	9.8%	20.6%	−0.51	2.20
Muni (3-7)	4.0%	3.9%	5.0%	−0.33	0.94

Expected returns, risks, and correlations for esoteric investments including the following categories will be determined (or edited) based on product-specific factors:[27]

- Absolute Return Investment Strategies (Hedge Funds and CTAs)
- Energy Infrastructure Master Limited Partnerships (MLPs)
- Private Equity
- Timberland
- Other Natural Resources Investments
- Infrastructure Investments
- Structured Products
- Custom Liability-Driven Fixed Income Portfolios
- Custom Municipal Bond Portfolios
- Others as Circumstances Warrant

Correlation Matrix

	Cash	TIPS	U.S. Bonds	Int'l Bond	HY Bond	LC U.S.	MC U.S.	SC U.S.	RE	Int'l Eq	EM	CF	HFs	PE	MLP	Muni
Cash	1.00	0.00	0.00	0.00	0.00	0.00	0.00	0.00	0.00	0.00	0.00	0.00	0.00	0.00	0.00	0.00
TIPS	0.00	1.00	0.75	0.56	0.28	0.03	0.07	0.00	0.19	0.09	0.10	0.56	0.10	0.00	0.10	0.55
U.S. Bonds	0.00	0.75	1.00	0.51	0.28	0.22	0.22	0.13	0.20	0.17	0.01	0.32	0.08	0.13	0.13	0.72
Int'l Bond	0.00	0.56	0.51	1.00	0.09	0.04	0.00	-0.05	0.06	0.40	0.06	0.24	-0.02	-0.05	0.03	0.45
HY Bond	0.00	0.28	0.28	0.09	1.00	0.57	0.63	0.59	0.60	0.51	0.55	0.26	0.46	0.59	0.53	0.22
Large Cap U.S.	0.00	0.03	0.22	0.04	0.57	1.00	0.94	0.83	0.61	0.65	0.66	0.24	0.52	0.83	0.34	0.10
Mid Cap U.S.	0.00	0.07	0.22	0.00	0.63	0.94	1.00	0.94	0.70	0.63	0.69	0.27	0.58	0.94	0.40	0.10
Small Cap U.S.	0.00	0.00	0.13	-0.05	0.59	0.83	0.94	1.00	0.71	0.58	0.67	0.21	0.56	1.00	0.36	0.04
REITs	0.00	0.19	0.20	0.06	0.60	0.61	0.70	0.71	1.00	0.48	0.45	0.24	0.28	0.71	0.32	0.11
Int'l Equity	0.00	0.09	0.17	0.40	0.51	0.65	0.63	0.58	0.48	1.00	0.68	0.30	0.51	0.58	0.33	0.09
Em. Mkts. Equity	0.00	0.10	0.01	0.06	0.55	0.66	0.69	0.67	0.45	0.68	1.00	0.29	0.66	0.67	0.37	0.01
Commodity Futures	0.00	0.56	0.32	0.24	0.26	0.24	0.27	0.21	0.24	0.30	0.29	1.00	0.39	0.21	0.29	0.05
Hedge Funds	0.00	0.10	0.08	-0.02	0.46	0.52	0.58	0.55	0.28	0.51	0.66	0.39	1.00	0.56	0.31	0.10
Private Equity	0.00	0.00	0.13	-0.05	0.59	0.83	0.94	1.00	0.71	0.58	0.67	0.21	0.56	1.00	0.36	0.04
MLPs	0.00	0.10	0.13	0.03	0.53	0.34	0.40	0.36	0.32	0.33	0.37	0.29	0.31	0.36	1.00	0.21
Muni (3-7)	0.00	0.55	0.72	0.45	0.22	0.10	0.10	0.04	0.11	0.09	0.01	0.05	0.10	0.04	0.21	1.00

Notes

1. Median return is used because it does not require a normal return distribution assumption.

2. The expression of the expected geometric return forecast (from median returns) requires a normal return distribution assumption (i.e., that mean is equal to median). This is for illustrative purposes (only). The geometric return forecasts will be expressed as if returns were normal (i.e., median is equal to mean). For Frontier Engineer optimization, asset class return distributions do not have to be normally (Gaussian) distributed.

3. Geometric Return = Arithmetic Mean or Median Return $- \sigma^2/2$.

4. Source: Fitch U.S. High Yield Default Index.

5. Source: Altman Mortality Rate Default and Recovery Forecast: Default Rate $= -3.25$ percent $+ 1.25$X HY Spread versus 10-year Treasury (3.30 percent on December 31, 2010). $R^2 = 0.694$.

6. Source: Altman Recovery Rate Algorithm. Recovery Rate $= 0.1457 \times$ (Default Rate) -0.2801. Historical $R^2 = 0.6531$.

7. Source: Bloomberg.

8. €= Basket of Foreign Currencies

9. Unlike traditional stocks, REITs pay out virtually all their earnings (or FFO) in dividends and rely on the issuance of new equity (and debt) to grow earnings (or FFO). Therefore, the expected long-term RPR is capped at zero.

10. P/E derived from S&P top-own 2011 reported earnings estimates and December 31, 2010 S&P 500 index price. Source: Standards and Poor's.

11. Dividend yield based on December 31, 2010 S&P 500 price and dividends over prior 12 months (through December 31, 2010).

12. ROE = REG / ERR

13. REG = ERR $\times$ ROE. The expected real earnings growth rate (REG) is a function of (Return on Equity) $\times$ (Earnings Retention Ratio). From 1926 to 2000, real earnings grew at a 1.75 percent annual rate. Over the same time, the implied earnings retention ratio averaged 41 percent, which implies an average return on equity of 4.3 percent (1.75 percent/ 41 percent). Using the historical implied return on equity (4.3 percent) and the current earnings retention ratio (74 percent), the expected real earnings growth rate is 3.1 percent (74 percent $\times$ 4.3 percent).

14. Source: Gorton, Gary B., and K. Geert Rouwenhorst, 2005. "Facts and fantasies about commodity futures." Yale ICF Working Paper No.04-20.

15. Source: Black, Keith, and Satya Kumar, 2008. "The role of commodities in an institutional portfolio." QFINANCE. Available at: www.qfinance.com/asset-management-best-practice/ the-role-of-commodities-in-an-institutional-portfolio.

16. During this same period (i.e., January 1970 to September 2008), CPI averaged 4.7 percent annually and approximated the GSCI Spot Return (i.e., 4.8 percent).

17. The commodity index spot return is expected to keep pace with inflation as measured by CPI.

18. The roll return is forecasted to be zero. While historically greater than zero, we believe that a positive roll return is not inherent to commodity futures investing.

19. While the December 31, 2010, three-month T-bill yield was 0.12 percent, the 10-year holding period T-bill return forecast is expected to match the inflation forecast (i.e., 2.3 percent).

20. Represents the 10-year TIPS forecast return.

21. While our 10-year return forecast is expressed as if hedge fund returns were normally distributed, the Frontier Engineer model treats the return forecast as a median (rather than mean return), and fattens the left tail, increasing the magnitude of lower probability events.

22. MLPs pay out virtually all of their distributable cash flow and rely on the issuance of new equity to grow real distributable cash flow (DCF). Therefore, the expected long-term RPR is assumed to be constrained to growth in U.S. Energy Demand (~1.25 percent over the last 20 years). While we believe there is a strong case for accretive acquisition growth (unlike most other asset classes) over the next decade as C-Corps continue to divest energy infrastructure assets, we will conservatively assume no real price return (excluding yield expansion/compression) from accretive growth.

23. Assumes median scenario is zero yield compression.

24. Many midstream MLPs have inflation adjustors (i.e., PPI + 1.3 percent). Between 2012 and 2016, the Federal Energy Regulatory Commission (FERC) temporarily increased this inflation adjustor to PPI + 2.65 percent. Because many MLP investment vehicles have a tax drag, we will assume this PPI adjustor will equal the tax drag and net to zero. Therefore, we estimate nominal fee growth (or price growth) will equal to our 10-year inflation assumption of 2.3 percent with the PPI adjustors (i.e., 2.65 percent for 2012 to 2016 and 1.3 percent historical) being offset by MLP investment vehicle tax drag.

25. Commodity Futures assumed to be collateralized by TIPS.

26. Hedge Funds skewness and kurtosis adjusted for survivorship bias.

27. For modeling purposes, allocations to some esoteric asset classes will be treated as a carve-out from the modeled allocation. The allocations will be determined by qualitative factors including liquidity needs, time horizon, risk tolerance, overall portfolio objective, and tactical considerations. If an asset class is constrained, the model will be free to allocate the excess in various proportions to the most appropriate alternative asset class(es).

About the Authors

Matthew R. Rice, CFA, CAIA® is Chief Investment Officer and a Principal at DiMeo Schneider and Associates, L.L.C., a Chicago-based investment consulting firm that oversees more than $35 billion in institutional and high-net-worth investment assets. Matt directs the firm's capital markets research, asset allocation strategy, and alternative investments research. He also advises a number of the firm's nonprofit and corporate clients. In 2005, he co-authored *The Practical Guide to Managing Nonprofit Assets* (John Wiley & Sons). Matt received a B.A. in Economics from Northwestern University, is a CFA charterholder, a CAIA (Chartered Alternative Investment Analyst), and is a member of the CFA Society of Chicago.

Robert A. DiMeo, CIMA®, **CFP**® is co-founder and Managing Director at DiMeo Schneider & Associates, L.L.C., a Chicago-based investment consulting firm that oversees more than $35 billion in institutional and high-net-worth investment assets. Prior to co-founding the firm in 1995, Bob served as Vice President for Kidder, Peabody's Institutional Consulting Group, where he chaired the 401(k) consulting effort. He co-authored *Asset Management for Endowments & Foundations* (McGraw Hill), *The Practical Guide to Managing Nonprofit Assets* (John Wiley & Sons), and *Designing a 401(k) Plan* (Probus). Bob served on the Board of Directors for the Investment Management Consultants Association (IMCA), is an Advisory Board and Finance Committee member for Catholic Charities of Chicago, and served on the Governance Board for Notre Dame High School. Bob obtained the CIMA® designation from the Investment Management Consultants Association (IMCA) accreditation program at the Wharton School of Business, and he is also a Certified Financial Planner (CFP®). Bob obtained his bachelor's degree from Bradley University.

Matthew P. Porter, CIMA® is Director of Research Analytics and a Principal at DiMeo Schneider & Associates, L.L.C., a Chicago-based investment consulting firm that oversees more than $35 billion in institutional and high-net-worth investment assets. In his role as Director of Research Analytics, Matt is the Chair of the Investment Committee, which sets investment policy for the firm, establishes the framework for asset allocation, and approves investment managers. Matt also advises a number of nonprofit and corporate clients. In 2005, he co-authored *The Practical Guide to Managing Nonprofit Assets* (John Wiley & Sons). He obtained the CIMA® designation from the IMCA accreditation program at the Wharton School of Business and is a member of the Economic Club of Chicago. Matt received a B.S. in Finance from the University of Illinois in Urbana-Champaign.

About the Contributing Authors

Craig Adkins, CFA, CPA. As a Senior Alternative Investment Research Analyst at DiMeo Schneider & Associates, L.L.C., Craig sources and performs operational and investment due diligence on hedge funds managers. Craig holds an MBA from the University of Illinois and received his B.S. in Finance from Illinois State University. Craig is a Certified Public Accountant and is a CFA charterholder.

Bryce Anderson, CFA. As an Alternative Investment Research Analyst at DiMeo Schneider & Associates, L.L.C., Bryce sources and performs operational and investment due diligence on hedge fund managers. Bryce also serves on the firm's capital markets research team. Bryce graduated from The Ohio State University with a B.A. in Finance and is a CFA charterholder.

Douglas Balsam, CIMA®. As a Principal and Director of Institutional Consulting at DiMeo Schneider & Associates, L.L.C., Doug is responsible for oversight of the firm's institutional consultants and setting strategic direction for the firm's institutional consulting business. He also serves as a member of the firm's Investment Committee. In 2005, Doug co-authored *The Practical Guide to Managing Nonprofit Assets* (John Wiley & Sons). Doug earned his B.S. in Finance at Miami University and his M.B.A., with honors, from Loyola University in Chicago. He obtained the CIMA® designation from the Investment Management Consultants Association (IMCA) accreditation program at the Wharton School of Business and the Accredited Investment Fiduciary Auditor (AIFA) designation from the Center for Fiduciary Studies at the Joseph M. Katz Graduate School of Business at the University of Pittsburgh. Doug was a member of the Profit Sharing Council of America's Annual Plan Survey Committee and has been a featured speaker at their national conference. Doug is a committee member for the Greater Chicago Food Depository, a nonprofit food distribution and training center striving to end hunger in the local region.

Brian Carlson, CFA. As a Senior Consultant at DiMeo Schneider & Associates, L.L.C., Brian provides broad investment consulting services to the firm's institutional clients. Brian also serves on the firm's investment committee and is a member of the capital markets and real assets research teams. Brian graduated from Northern Illinois University with his B.S. in Finance and is a CFA charterholder.

Steven Dufault, CIMA®. As a Senior Consultant at DiMeo Schneider & Associates, L.L.C., Steve provides broad investment consulting services to the firm's institutional clients. Steve received a B.B.A. in Finance from the University of Iowa with an emphasis in Accounting. He obtained the CIMA® designation from IMCA's accreditation program at the Wharton School of Business and he is a member of the Investment Management Consultants Association, International Foundation of Employee Benefit Plans, and Defined Contribution Institutional Investment Association.

Richard Gallagher. Richard Gallagher is the former chair of the Tax and Individual Planning Department of Foley & Lardner LLP and focuses his practice on tax-exempt organizations and estate and trust planning for individuals involved in family-held businesses and/or who have a philanthropic focus. He has been chair of the Exempt Organizations Committee and of the Charitable Institutions Committee of the American Bar Association Sections of Taxation and Real Property Probate and Trust Law. He is a graduate of the Northwestern University Business School and the Harvard Law School and is a Fellow of the American College of Tax Counsel, the American College of Trust and Estate Counsel, and the American Law Institute.

James Jensen, CIMA®. As a Senior Consultant at DiMeo Schneider & Associates, L.L.C., Jim provides broad investment consulting services to the firm's institutional clients. He obtained the CIMA® designation from IMCA's accreditation program at the Wharton School of Business and he is a member of the IMCA. Jim received a B.B.A. in Finance from the University of Iowa.

Todd Leedy, CAIA. As a Senior Alternative Investment Research Analyst at DiMeo Schneider & Associates, L.L.C., Todd's responsibilities include researching and performing operational due diligence on fund of hedge funds, direct hedge funds, private equity, and real assets managers. He also leads the firm's extensive fund of hedge funds due diligence efforts. As the only firm analyst to serve on all three alternative investment research teams (Hedge Funds, Private Equity, and Real Assets), Todd also serves as the liaison between teams. Todd received his B.S. from the University of Richmond, Virginia in Business Administration and Finance. He earned the CAIA designation sponsored by the Chartered Alternative Investment Analyst Association.

James Modelski, CFS. As a Principal and Senior Consultant at DiMeo Schneider and Associates, L.L.C., Jim provides broad investment consulting services to the firm's institutional clients. Jim also serves on the firm's investment committee. Jim received a B.A. from Columbia College and an M.B.A., Finance and Economics from Loyola University. He is a Member of the Investment Analysts Society of Chicago, the CFA Institute, The Chicago Council on Global Affairs, The Profit Sharing Council of America's (PSCA) Research Committee, and The Union League Club.

Jacqueline Rondini, CFP, CMFC. As a Senior Investment Research Analyst at DiMeo Schneider & Associates, L.L.C., Jackie performs both qualitative and quantitative research on investment managers. In 2005, she co-authored *The Practical Guide to Managing Nonprofit Assets* (John Wiley & Sons). She received a B.B.A. from Iowa State University, the designation of Certified Financial Planner (CFP) from the College for Financial Planning, and is a Chartered Mutual Fund Counselor (CMFC).

Jackie is a member of the Board of Trustees for The Chicago Academy for the Arts, an independent college preparatory school dedicated to the performing arts.

William Schneider. Bill co-founded DiMeo Schneider & Associates L.L.C. in 1995 after holding a variety of leadership roles including Senior Vice President with Kidder, Peabody's Prime Asset Consulting Group. Bill is an acknowledged authority in nonprofit asset management having written and lectured extensively on the topic. Bill has also co-authored three books *Asset Management for Endowments and Foundations* (McGraw Hill), *The Practical Guide to Managing Nonprofit Assets* (John Wiley & Sons), and *Designing A 401(k) Plan* (Probus Publishing). He obtained the CIMA® designation from the IMCA accreditation Program at the Wharton School of Business. Bill graduated from the University of Illinois in 1967. On a personal note, Bill is an accomplished artist with gallery representation in the Midwest, Southwest, and West Coast.

Stephen Spencer, CIMA®. As a Senior Consultant at DiMeo Schneider & Associates, L.L.C., Steve provides broad investment consulting services to the firm's institutional clients. Steve also serves on the firm's investment committee. In 2005, he co-authored *The Practical Guide to Managing Nonprofit Assets* (John Wiley & Sons). Steve received a B.A. in Economics from the University of New Hampshire. He obtained the CIMA® designation from IMCA's accreditation program at the Wharton School of Business and he is a member of the IMCA. Steve is also a past member of the Board of Directors for Heartland Alliance.

Geoffrey Strotman, CFA. As Manager of Traditional Asset Research at DiMeo Schneider and Associates, L.L.C., Geoff heads the traditional investment manager research efforts for the firm. Geoff also serves on the firm's investment committee. Geoff received a B.A. in Accounting from the University of Notre Dame, an M.B.A. in Finance, Economics, and International Business from the University of Chicago, and is a CFA charterholder.

INDEX

2010 NACUBO Commonfund Study of Endowments, 95, 105

A

absolute returns, 73
active management, passive versus, 68–70
active trading strategies, 76
activist managers, 76
administrator, 93, 156–157
agricultural partnership, 110
allocation
  integrated, 28–29
  strategic, 27
  tactical, 27–28
alpha, 66, 126
alpha thesis, 98
alpha-beta framework, 85–86
alternatives–real estate strategies, 78
American Society of Farm Managers and Rural Appraisers (ASFMRA), 110
analysis, manager selection, 66
anchors, 172
arbitrary rebalancing, 34
ASFMRA. *See* American Society of Farm Managers and Rural Appraisers
asset allocation, 161
asset allocation steering mechanisms, 27–29
asset classes, fixed income, 39
asset segregation, 171

asset-based retainer, 167
assets under management (AUM), 65
attribution analysis, 128
auditors, 93
AUM. *See* assets under management

B

backfilling bias, 88
backwardation, 107
basket of securities, 120
batting average, 65, 126
Bauer, Rob, 151
benchmarks, 120
  hedge fund, 87–88
  private equity, 102–103
benefits, outsourcing, 139
beta, 86, 126
biased expectations, 170
blind pool risk, 100
board of directors, duties and responsibilities, 14
board-created endowments, 178
bonds, U.S. investment grade, 42–47
Bretton Woods Agreement, 115
broker/dealer, 153, 157–158
Buffett, Warren, 169
buyout funds, 96

C

California Public Employees Retirement System (CALPERS), 110

CALPERS. *See* California Public
    Employees Retirement System
Cambridge Associates, 103
Capital Asset Pricing Model
    (CAPM), 85
capital market assumptions, 20
    developing, 189–207
CAPM. *See* Capital Asset
    Pricing Model
carried interest, 100
cash, 40
cash rent, 110
catch-up provision, 100
CIO. *See* chief investment officer
clawback provision, 100
cognitive dissonance, 171–172
collateral return, 107
commingled funds, 67–68
commodities, 106–108
common stocks, 55
communication assets, 113
community development, 148
Community Foundation of Bedford
    Falls, 6–8, 10–11, 12–13
concentration, 91
conflict-free advice, 140
consistency, 63
consistent outperformance, 63
constraints, 10–11
consultant, effective use of, 135, 168
Consumer Price Index for All Urban
    Consumers (CPI-U), 40–41
contract, outsourcing firm, 142
contractual value, 105
corporate bonds, 44–47
corporate debt, 48–49
corporate dialogue, 147
correlation
    diversification and, 20
    expected, 18
counterparty risk, 33–34
coupon, 40
CPI-U. *See* Consumer Price Index
    for All Urban Consumers
credit arbitrage managers, 76
credit unions, 148
currency strategies, 77

custodians, 153–156
    duties and responsibilities, 15
custom farming, 110

D
deep-dive research, manager selection,
    66–67
desired return, risk versus, 2–3
developed markets equity, non-U.S.,
    56–58
DiMeo Schneider and Associates,
    LLC, 25
direct investment, fund of hedge funds
    versus, 89–90
direct private equity, private equity fund
    of funds versus, 101–102
discretionary investment consultant, 135
discretionary management, 137–138
discretionary thematic strategies, 77
dispersion risk, 100–101
distressed managers, 76
distressed strategy, 97
diversification, correlation and, 20
dollar-weighted basis, 119–120
donor-created
    endowments, 178
    funds, 179
    restricted gifts, 179
Dow Jones, 88
Dow Jones Credit Suisse Hedge
    Fund Indices, 88
Dow Jones-UBS Commodity
    Index, 108
due diligence, hedge fund investment,
    90–92
duties
    board of directors, 14
    custodian, 15
    investment committee, 14
    investment consultant, 14–15
    investment managers, 15

E
efficient frontier, 18–19
emerging market bonds, 47–50
emerging markets equity, 58–59
endowment funds, donor-created, 178

endowments
    created by the board, 178
    investing, 179
    nature of, 177–178
environmental, social, and corporate
    governance-focused (ESG)
    investing, 10–11, 145–146
    alternative investments, 150–151
    commingled funds, 149–150
    exchange-traded funds, 150
    incorporating into investment policy,
        151–152
    investment selection, 149
    mutual funds, 149
    performance impact of, 151
    separate accounts, 149
    strategy, 148
equity hedge fund strategies, 74, 76
equity
    emerging markets, 58–59
    non-U.S., 56 58
    U.S., 55–56
ETF. *See* exchange-traded fund
European Union, 57
event-driven hedge fund strategies, 76
exchange-traded funds (ETF), 116
expense, 161
experience, 140
expertise, 140
external debt, 48–49

F
factor exposures, 91
fallen angels, 51
familiarity, 173
Fannie Mae, 44
farmland, 109–110
FASB. *See* Financial Accounting
    Standards Board
fat left tails, 22, 25, 91
fear of regret, 172
Federal Energy Regulatory Commission
    (FERC), 112
fees, 85–86
    outsourcing firm, 142
FERC. *See* Federal Energy Regulatory
    Commission

fiduciary management, 137–138
fiduciary stewardship, 161
finalists
    interviewing, 141–142
    manager selection, 67
Financial Accounting Standards Board
    (FASB), 8
fixed percentage band rebalancing, 34
fixed retainer, 167
fixed-income asset classes, 39–55
fixed-income index, 121
fixed-income sovereign strategies, 77
fixed-income-asset backed
    strategies, 77
fixed-income-convertible arbitrage
    strategies, 77
fixed-income-corporate strategies, 77
forecasted correlation among asset
    classes, 18
forecasting, modern portfolio theory
    (MPT) and, 26–27
foreign bonds, 47–51
forward contracts, 106
Freddie Mac, 44
The Frontier Engineer™, 24–25
fund of funds, 99
fund of hedge funds, direct investment
    versus, 89–90
fund of private equity funds, 101
fundamental growth and value
    managers, 76
funds, donor-created, 179
futures contracts, 106

G
gambler, investor as, 170
General Hospital Reserves Fund III, 6, 8,
    10–11, 14
general partners (GP), 95, 99, 111
generally accepted accounting principles
    (GAAP) treatment, 179
global equities, 39
global equity asset classes, 55–59
global macro, 74
global private infrastructure, 112
gold, 115–116
government agency bonds, 44

government sponsored entities (GSEs),
  44
Great State University Endowment Fund,
  6–7, 10–12
Gross, Bill, 169
growth, 121
growth capital, 97
GSE. *See* government sponsored entities

H
hard commodities, 106
hedge fund benchmarks, 87–88
hedge fund indices, 87–88
hedge fund investment due diligence,
  90–92
hedge fund operational due diligence,
  92–93
Hedge Fund Research, Inc. (HFR), 88,
  150–151
hedge funds, 85–86
  after 2008, 93–94
  evolution of, 73–74
  indices, 87–88
  strategies, 74–78
  structures, 88–89
  terms, 88–89
  why choose, 78–84
hedging, tail risk, 21–33
herd mentality, 171
HFN Fund of Funds–Multi-Strategy
  Index, 79, 82
HFR. *See* Hedge Fund Research, Inc.
hierarchy of importance, 3
high water mark, 89
high-yield bond serial correlation, 23
high-yield bonds, 51–55, 68–69
holdings-based analysis, 62–63
HRFI Fund Weighted Composite
  Index, 88

I
ICCR. *See* Interfaith Center on Corporate
  Responsibility
idea generation, 91
illiquid assets, 8, 100
index benchmark, 119
index, selecting, 124

industry-specific index, 122
inflows, 1–2
infrastructure assets, 113
infrastructure investing, 112–113
initial screens, manager selection, 62–65
Institutional Shareholder Services (ISS),
  147
instruments, 91
integrated allocation, 28–29
Interfaith Center on Corporate Responsibility (ICCR), 147
intermediate bonds, 43
International Swaps and Derivatives
  Association (ISDA), 33
investible real assets, 116–117
investment committee
  duties and responsibilities, 14
  makeup, 133–134
  outside help, 134
  outsourcing firm and, 139
  procedures, 131–132
  size, 132–133
  structure, 132–133
  term limits, 133
investment consultant, 162
  duties and responsibilities, 14–15
  identifying, 162–167
investment consultant request for
  proposal, sample, 163
investment managers
  duties and responsibilities, 15
  evaluation, 15–16
  selection, 161
investment policy, 161
  incorporating environmental, social,
    and corporate governance-focused
    infesting , 151–152
investment policy statement (IPS), 1,
  5–6, 119
investment returns, management fees
  and, 120
investment review, 132
investment risk, need for, 4–5
investment strategy, 11–14
investment style, 121–122
investment vehicles, 67–68
investor personality types, 173

ISDA. *See* International Swaps and Derivatives Association
ISS. *See* Institutional Shareholder Services

J

Jones, Alfred Winslow, 73–74
junk bonds, 51–55

K

Kees, Koedijk, 151

L

large-capitalization stocks, 55
leverage, 91
leveraged buyout, 95–96
limited liability companies (LLC), 88
limited partnerships (LP), 88, 95, 99, 111
liquidation bias, 88
liquidity constraints, 8–10, 91
LLC. *See* limited liability companies
loan funds, 148
local currency debt, 48–49
long bonds, 43
Long Term Capital Management
long-short equity, 74
long-term hurdle returns, 4
long/short attribution, 91–92
low volatility tailwind, 29–31
LP. *See* limited partnerships
The LPX Group, 103

M

macro hedge fund strategies, 76–77
Madoff, Bernard L., 92
major market indices, 123–124
management fees, investment returns and, 120
manager selection, 61–67
manager, termination decision, 70–72, 129
margin requirement, 107
market bubbles, 174–175
market cap-weighted index, 120–121
market capitalization, 92
market index basics, 120–121
market timing, 28

market-neutral managers, 74
master limited partnerships (MLPs), 111–112
Measurerisk, 94
mental accounting, 171
merger arbitrage managers, 76
mezzanine capital, 97
mid-capitalization stocks, 55
MLP. *See* master limited partnerships
Modern Portfolio Theory (MPT), 17–18
    forecasting and, 26–27
    performance metrics, 126–127
    shortcomings, 20–24
Monte Carlo simulations, 27
moral anchors, 172
MPT. *See* Modern Portfolio Theory
multi-commodity managers, 77
multi-manager fund of hedge funds, 78
multi-strategy
    relative value strategies, 78
    equity hedged managers, 76
    event-driven managers, 76
    hedge fund strategies, 78
    macro managers, 77

N

NAFTA. *See* North American Free Trade Agreement
NAV. *See* net asset value
NCREIF Timberland Index, 114
negative screening, 146
net asset value (NAV), 89
netting agreement, 33–34
non-discretionary investment consultant, 135
non-parallel rising interest rate environments, 47
nonlinear beta, 23
normally distributed variability, 20
North American Free Trade Agreement (NAFTA), 57

O

Odean, Terrance, 169
offering memorandum, 99
offshore hedge funds, 88
onshore hedge funds, 88

operational due diligence, hedge funds, 92–93
operational failure, 92
Otten, Roger, 151
out-of-the-money options, 91
outflows, 1–2
outperformance, 63
outsourced chief investment officer (CIO) services, 137–138
outsourcing
    benefits, 139
    reasons for, 138–139
    services, 139
outsourcing firm
    characteristics, 140–141
    contract, 142
    fees, 142
    finding, 140
    interviewing finalists, 141–142
    investment committee and, 139
    reporting, 143
overconfidence, 170

P

P/E. *See* price/earnings ratio
parallel shifts, 47
passive management, active versus, 68–70
PB. *See* price-to-book ratio
peer group, 119
peer group universes, 124–125
percentage bands rebalancing, 34–35
percentage change rebalancing, 34–35
performance calculations, 119–120
performance monitoring, 119
performance reporting, 128–129
PIPE. *See* private investment in public equity
PME. *See* public market equivalent
Ponzi schemes, naturally occurring, 174–175
portfolio analysis, 128
portfolio construction, 91
    building blocks of, 20
portfolio duration, 44
The Portfolio Engineer™, 35–36, 37
portfolio optimization, 17–18

portfolio rebalancing, 34–38
positive screening, 146
price-to-book ratio (PB), 121
price/earnings ratio (P/E), 121
prime brokers, 93
priorities, 10–11
Private Edge Group, 103
private equity benchmarks, 102–103
private equity fund of funds, direct private equity versus, 101–102
private equity investment strategies, 95–97
private equity J-curve, 99
private equity managers, selecting, 102
private equity
    risks, 100–101
    structure, 99–100
    terms, 99–100
    why choose, 98–99
private foundation, rules, 184–185
private investment in public equity (PIPE), 97
private issue strategies, 76
private real estate, 108–109
probabilistic asset allocation models, 26
probabilistic optimization models, 24–25
process-oriented investor, 173
program-related investing (PRI), 148
project basis, 167
proprietary trading, 94
proxy voting, 147
prudent investor act, 180–181
prudent man rule, 180
public market equivalent (PME), 103
publicly traded private equity firms, 97
publicly traded private equity funds, 97
pulpwood, 114

Q

qualitative review, manager selection, 65
quantitative anchors, 172
quantitative directional managers, 74
Quantitative Easing, 106
questionnaire, manager selection, 66

R

R-squared, 126

random walk pattern, 20
real estate investment trusts (REITs),
    108–109
real estate, private, 108–109
rebalancing, 35–38
    considerations, 35
    traditional, 34–35
record keeper, 153, 156–157
REITs. *See* real estate investment trusts
relative value hedge fund strategies,
    77–78
reporting, outsourcing firm, 143
representativeness, 172
request for proposal (RFP), 140, 154
required investment returns, 1–2
research capability, 140
responsibilities
    board of directors, 14
    custodian, 15
    investment committee, 14
    investment consultant, 14–15
    investment managers, 15
restricted funds, nature of, 177–178
restricted gifts, donor-created, 179
return attribution, 91
return forecast, 18
return-distribution profile, 49–50
return, expected, 18
returns-based analysis, 62–63
Revised FASB ASC 820, 8–9. *See also*
    SFAS-153
RFP. *See* request for proposal
risk management, 141
risk premiums, 86
risk-adjusted basis, 119
risk-adjusted performance, 78
risk-seeking behavior, 173–174
risk, desired return versus, 2–3
RiskMetrics, 94
roll return, 107
Russell Investments, 95

S
S&P GSCI, 108
saw timber trees, 114
secondary investments, 97
sector specialists, 76

sector-specific index, 122
security type, 92
seeking pride, 172
selection bias, 88
self-reporting bias, 88
separate accounts, 68
serial correlations, 25
SFAS-157, 8–9
    inputs, 9–10
share crop, 110
shareholder advocacy, 146–147
shareholder resolution, 147
Sharpe ratio, 126
Sharpe, William, 62–63, 126
Shefrin, Hersh, 169
short bonds, 42–43
short-based strategies, 76
single commodity managers, 76
small-capitalization stocks, 55
snake bitten investor, 170
socially responsible investing (SRI), 123,
    145–146
soft commodities, 106
Soros, George, 74
sovereign bonds, 47
special situation managers, 76
special situations strategy, 97
spot prices, 107
SRI. *See* socially responsible
    investing
standard deviation, 126
    expected, 18
    forecast, 18
    rebalancing, 35
statement of objectives, 6–8
statement of purpose, 6
strategic allocation, 27
strategic tail risk hedge, 32
structured investor, 173
structures, hedge fund, 88–89
style analysis, 127–128
style corners, 127
style map, 62–63
survivorship bias, 87
suspicious investor, 173
systematic diversified
    strategies, 77

T

tactical allocation, 27–28
tactical rebalancing, 34
tail risk hedging, 31–33
tail risk, defined, 31–32
term limits, investment committee, 133
terms, hedge funds, 88–89
Thaler, Richard, 169, 172
third-party administrator, 153
Thomson Venture Economics, 103
three levers, 1–5
timberland, 113–115
timberland investment management
    organizations (TIMOs), 115
time, 161
time value of money, 114
time-dependent rebalancing, 34–35
time-weighted basis, 119–120
TIMO. *See* timberland investment
    management organization
TIPS. *See* Treasury Inflation-Protected
    Securities
total outsourcing, 138
transition manager, 153, 158–160
transportation assets, 113
Treasury Inflation-Protected Securities
    (TIPS), 40–42
Treynor ratio, 126
Treynor, Jack, 126
trust companies, 153
trustee, 153

U

U.S. equity, 55–56
U.S. nominal bonds, investment-grade,
    42–47
U.S. Treasury bonds, 44
UBTI. *See* unrelated business taxable
    income

unfunded debt ratios, 105
Uniform Prudent Investor Act (UPIA),
    180
Uniform Prudent Management of
    Institutional Funds Act (UPMIFA),
    61, 181–184
unrelated business taxable income
    (UBTI), 88–89
unstable correlations, 25
unstructured investor, 173
up-market/down-market ratios, 126–127
UPIA. *See* Uniform Prudent Investor Act
UPMIFA. *See* Uniform Prudent Manage-
    ment of Institutional Funds Act
The Use of Money, 145

V

value, 121
vendors, 161
venture capital, 95–96
venture capital funds, 148
vintage year, 99
volatility strategies, 77
Volcker Rule, 94
vulture investing, 97

W

watch-listed manager, 129
Wesley, John, 145
WGBI. *See* World Government Bond
    Index
World Government Bond Index
    (WGBI), 47
World Trade Organization (WTO), 57
WTO. *See* World Trade Organization

Y

yield-alternative–energy infrastructure
    strategies, 77